TRUGANINI

Journey through the apocalypse

CASSANDRA PYBUS

ALLEN&UNWIN
SYDNEY • MELBOURNE • AUCKLAND • LONDON

First published in 2020

This manuscript won the University of Melbourne's 2018 Peter Blazey Fellowship and the research was assisted by the Neilma Sidney Literary Travel Fund, The Myer Foundation and Writers Victoria.

Allen & Unwin
83 Alexander Street
Crows Nest NSW 2065
Australia
Phone: (61 2) 8425 0100
Email: info@allenandunwin.com
Web: www.allenandunwin.com

NATIONAL LIBRARY OF AUSTRALIA
A catalogue record for this book is available from the National Library of Australia

ISBN 978 1 76052 922 2

Internal design by Philip Campbell
Maps by Guy Holt
Set in 11/16 pt Sabon by Midland Typesetters, Australia
Printed and bound in Australia by the Opus Group

25 24 23 22 21 20

FSC www.fsc.org MIX Paper | Supporting responsible forestry FSC® C001695

The paper in this book is FSC® certified. FSC® promotes environmentally responsible, socially beneficial and economically viable management of the world's forests.

TRUGANINI

CASSANDRA PYBUS is an award-winning author and a distinguished historian. She is the author of twelve books and has held research professorships at the University of Sydney, Georgetown University in Washington DC, the University of Texas and King's College London. She is descended from the colonist who received the largest free land grant on Truganini's traditional country of Bruny Island.

Other books by the author

Enterprising Women
Epic Journeys of Freedom
Black Founders
The Woman Who Walked to Russia
American Citizens, British Slaves
Raven Road
The Devil and James McAuley
Till Apples Grow on an Orange Tree
White Rajah: A dynastic intrigue
Gross Moral Turpitude
Community of Thieves

For Lyndall Ryan

Country
You see it
You are going to the country
Go away to it.

Song of the captive women in the Bass Strait islands, 1830,
transcribed by George Augustus Robinson

CONTENTS

Van Diemen's Land

Nation boundaries

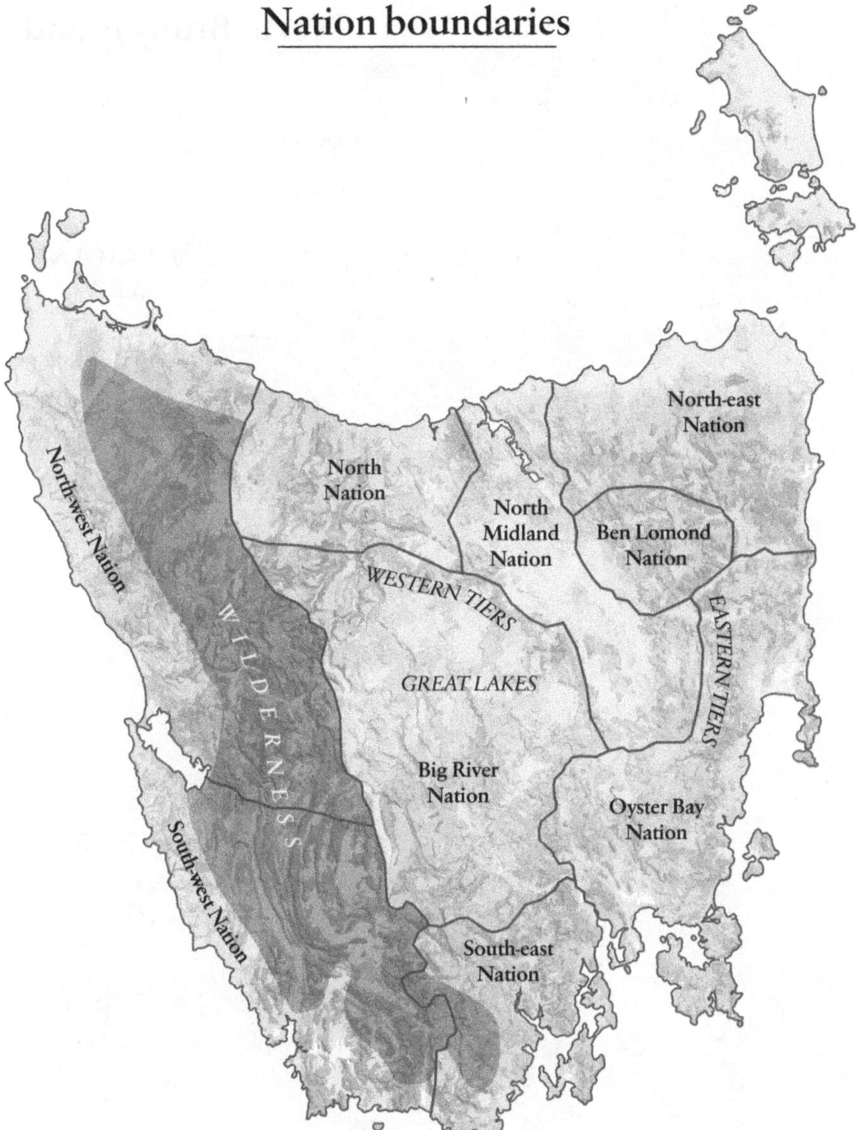

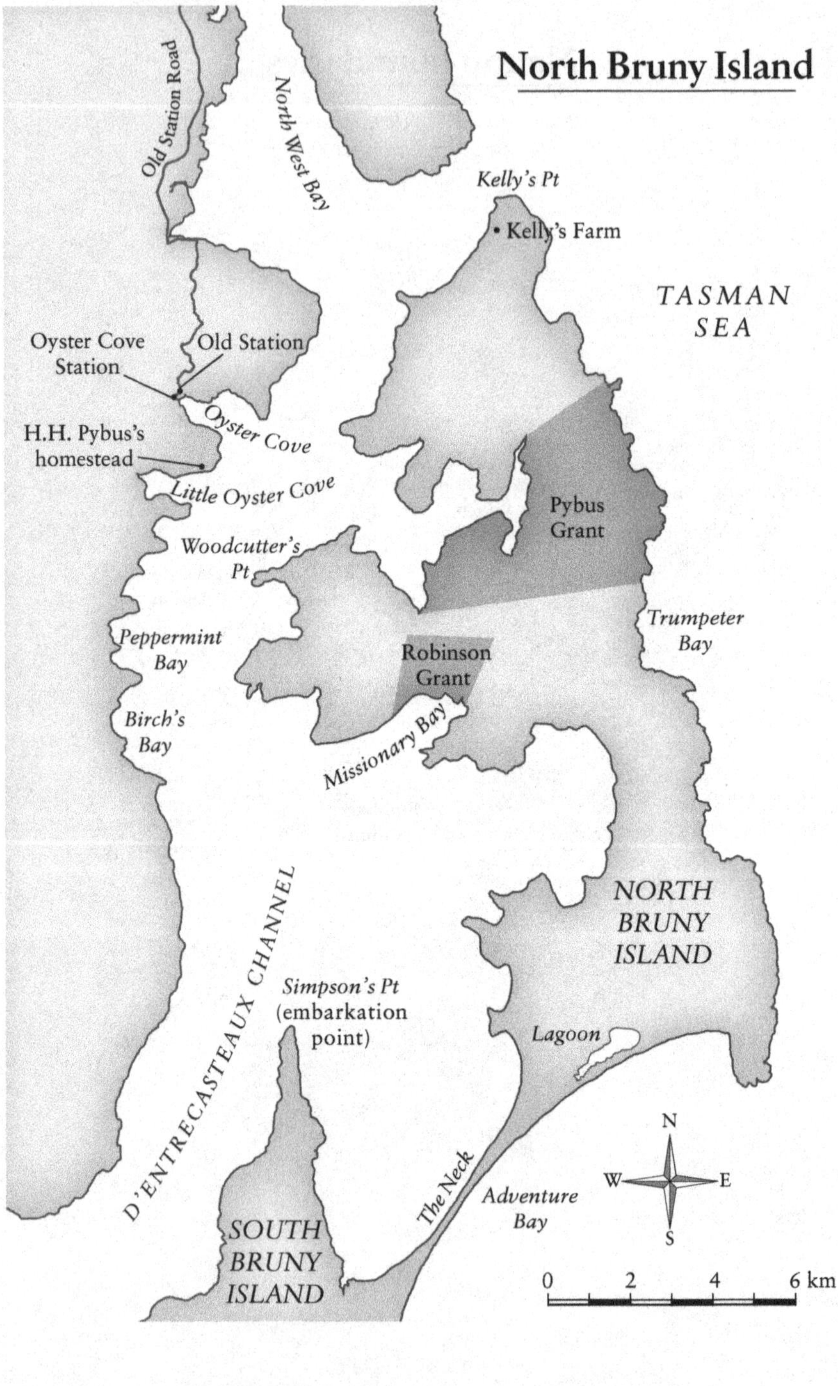

North Bruny Island
Old Station Road
North West Bay
Kelly's Pt
Kelly's Farm
TASMAN SEA
Oyster Cove Station
Old Station
Oyster Cove
H.H. Pybus's homestead
Little Oyster Cove
Pybus Grant
Woodcutter's Pt
Trumpeter Bay
Peppermint Bay
Robinson Grant
Birch's Bay
Missionary Bay
D'ENTRECASTEAUX CHANNEL
NORTH BRUNY ISLAND
Simpson's Pt (embarkation point)
Lagoon
N
W
E
S
The Neck
Adventure Bay
SOUTH BRUNY ISLAND
0 2 4 6 km

Bass Strait islands

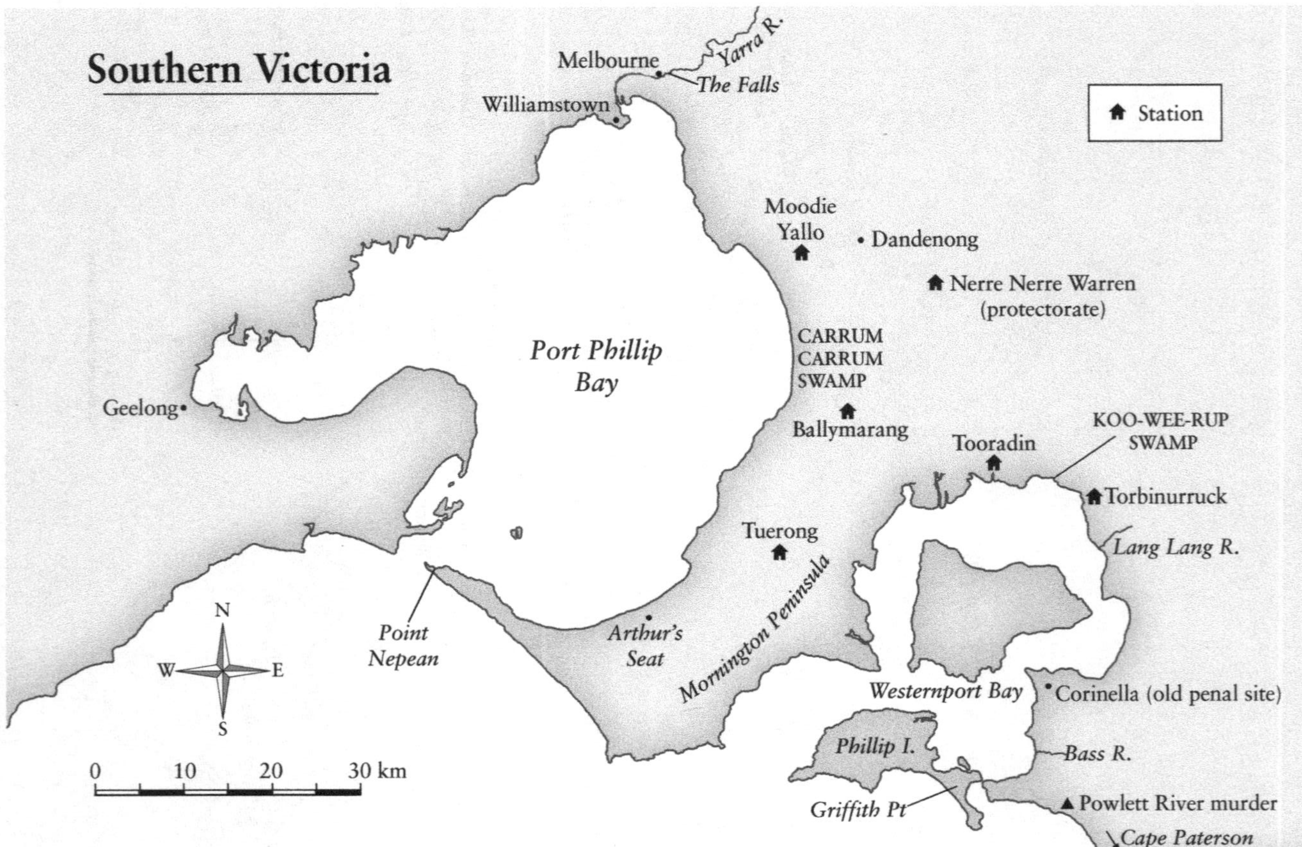
Southern Victoria
Station
Melbourne
Yarra R.
The Falls
Williamstown
Moodie Yallo
Dandenong
Nerre Nerre Warren (protectorate)
CARRUM CARRUM SWAMP
Ballymarang
Tooradin
KOO-WEE-RUP SWAMP
Torbinurruck
Lang Lang R.
Port Phillip Bay
Geelong
Tuerong
Mornington Peninsula
Arthur's Seat
Point Nepean
Westernport Bay
Corinella (old penal site)
Phillip I.
Bass R.
Griffith Pt
Powlett River murder
Cape Paterson
N
S
E
W
0
10
20
30 km

PREFACE

HALF BURIED IN the sand, uprooted stalks of kelp are like splashes of dark blood against the white quartzite, ground fine as talc. Tendrils of kelp flounce lazily in translucent shallows that gradually deepen to turquoise, turning Prussian blue at the horizon. Beyond the sand, matted tentacles of spongy pigface creep over the dunes to disguise rubbish middens of crayfish, oyster, abalone and scallop shells that have been tens of thousands of years in the making.

This beach reclines at the far end of an exquisite body of water in the far south-east corner of Tasmania known as Recherche Bay, so named by the French explorer Bruni D'Entrecasteaux, who rested his ships *Recherche* and *Espérance* in the bay during April and May 1792. Before the French arrived, this place was called Lyleatea. It was an important ritual site for the Nuenonne, who journeyed in bark canoes from the long offshore island to the north they knew as Lunawanna Alonnah to meet with clans who travelled overland from the west coast. For millennia they made this trip: the same seasonal migration, the same ritual feast. It was during one of these seasonal visits—some twenty years after D'Entrecasteaux named this place—that Truganini was born, the youngest daughter of Manganerer, senior man of the Nuenonne.

Today, the name of Truganini is vaguely familiar to most Australians for having achieved undesired celebrity as 'the last of her race', finding fame when she died in 1876. Sadly, a lot of what is said and written about her is myth and fabrication such as can be found on any Google search. Australians should know about how she lived, not simply that she died. Her life was much more than a regrettable tragedy. For nearly seven decades she lived through a psychological and cultural shift more extreme than most human imaginations could conjure; she is a hugely significant figure in Australian history.

Truganini compels my own attention and emotional engagement because her story is fundamental to my life story. My great-great-grandfather was the biggest beneficiary of the expropriation of Truganini's traditional country of Lunawanna Alonnah, renamed Bruny Island by colonial settlers. I owe Truganini and her kin my charmed existence in the temperate paradise where my family has lived for generations. The life of this woman, Truganini, frames the story of the dispossession and destruction of the original people of Tasmania. Their rapid dispossession, and its terrible aftermath, is the foundation narrative of my family.

Richard Pybus was fresh off the boat from England in April 1829, with his wife Hannah, son Henry Harrison and daughter Margaret, when he was handed a massive swathe of North Bruny Island, an unencumbered free land grant, even while Truganini and her family were still living there. Some time later he was rewarded with an equally huge land grant in the southern part of the island. For no payment whatsoever, he received well over 2000 hectares of Nuenonne hunting grounds while the original owners of the island, of whom Truganini was the last, were paid with anguish and exile.

Early in the twentieth century my great-grandfather William Pybus and his brothers regaled the British collector Ernest Westlake with stories their parents had told about the young Truganini when she was a regular visitor to the Pybus land, where they would give her gifts of tea and sugar, maybe potatoes or damper. The brothers had their own eyewitness accounts of Truganini as an older woman, living in exile yet still a common sight walking across their land in the 1850s and 1860s. By rights, of course, it was not their land but hers. They would never have seen it that way.

Growing up in Tasmania, I knew nothing of this. Like all Tasmanian schoolchildren, I heard the mawkish tale of the lonely old woman in the black dress and the shell necklace who was 'the last Tasmanian', but no one ever told me of my family connection to Truganini. I doubt anyone knew. Or cared. I left Tasmania when I was nine and never gave her any thought. A quarter of a century later, my friend Lyndall Ryan, who was in the process of rescuing the original people of Tasmania from historical amnesia, showed me references to my colonial ancestor in the journals of the self-styled missionary George Augustus Robinson, who had a smaller land grant adjacent to Richard Pybus's. The neighbours became friends, sharing evangelical commitment and a love of literature. Pybus's extensive library contained a copy of Thomas Macaulay's *Critical and Historical Essays*, with the inscription on its flyleaf: 'To Mr Pybus in token of Geo. Robinson's friendship and esteem.'

My ancestor's friend was a most problematic fellow. Tempting though it is for me to despise the man for his blinkered Christian intransigence, reading his journals turned my world around and set me to being a writer. His voluminous journals were the catalyst for my first book, written in 1988, the year of the bicentenary of European settlement of Australia. Thirty years later, I am still trying to liberate the stories of the original people trapped within his overweening self-regard. It is no less than a moral necessity—these are people whose lives were extinguished to make way for mine.

Robinson's daily devotion to writing in his journal has allowed me a precious glimpse into the lived experience of Truganini, who was his close companion for thirteen years. Thanks to him, Truganini is the most documented First Nations actor in colonial

Australia. Even so, recovering her life has proved to be a huge challenge. Other than Robinson, few colonial scribblers even noticed Truganini until she died, when the mythologising began. Invariably, she is seen through the prism of colonial imperative: a rueful backward glance at the last tragic victim of an inexorable historical process. No attention is paid to the experience of a living, breathing woman, but rather to a monumental tragedy without parallel in modern history, for which she has been made a symbol. She remains an international icon for extinction in the hands of the best-selling author Jared Diamond, and several others in America, Britain and Europe.

While one could never diminish the magnitude of the apocalyptic disaster that took place within the span of Truganini's life, nor moderate the poignancy of her experience as a final witness, to reduce a lively, intelligent, sensual woman to a helpless, tragic victim of relentless historical change is another thoughtless act of dispossession.

Robinson's documentation of day-to-day activities over the years she spent with him makes it possible for me to see her negotiating a path through a disintegrating world, always refusing to be a dupe or passive victim. Beyond that, there are no diaries or letters from her and next to no direct speech. There is no way I can truly know what she thought or how she felt. I cannot imagine what it was like to be her, or to feel what she experienced. It would be inappropriate to attempt it.

In writing this book, I have deliberately confined myself to first-person accounts from people who saw her and heard her with their own eyes and ears, then—ideally—made a contemporaneous record of it. Such sources are very few and they are all culturally loaded. Robinson's journals, however narcissistic and ideologically driven, are the best sources available, which bestows on this highly problematic man an outsized role in her story that he really doesn't merit.

Much of the time he was not paying attention, or saw only what he wanted to see, or was so preoccupied by the relentless demands of his own ego that he ignored her altogether. I can tell from the context of his daily entries that Truganini was part of the experience he was recording, but he wasn't interested in reporting her activities for weeks or even months at a time. Necessarily, telling her story means telling the stories of her husband and her other close male companions, also travelling with Robinson, who were often given more of his attention. So much of their experience was her experience, even if Robinson failed to include her name in his account.

There is no escaping the limitations placed on our understanding of the past by the callous indifference of colonial society to the people it usurped and replaced. Truganini and her companions are only available to us through the gaze of pompous, partisan, acquisitive, self-aggrandising men who controlled and directed the context of what they described. The challenge I have set myself is to somehow release these people from entrapment in a paternalistic and self-serving account of the colonial past.

I want to redirect the lens to find the woman behind the myth.

FRIENDLY MISSION

1829–1831

CHAPTER 1

Two craggy fists of land, joined by a long, thin neck of sand, made up the island of Lunawanna Alonnah, the country of the Nuenonne clan. An extensive coastline facing into the ocean provided nesting burrows for the inexhaustible supply of mutton birds that migrated every year from Siberia. Rocky outcrops were perfect nesting sites for equally numerous penguins that migrated from the sub-Antarctic. Undulating forests of bull kelp sprouting from rock ledges along the shore gave protection and nutrition to crayfish and abalone, while oysters and mussels grew in the myriad tidal rock pools. Further out to sea, tiny, barren islands were nurseries for the fur seals the Nuenonne would hunt in ocean-going canoes they constructed from rolled bark bound together with reeds.

On the western side, an extensive, deep channel separated the island from the much larger landmass Abel Tasman had named Van Diemen's Land. On the sandy coves of the western side, scallops, oysters and mussels were easily harvested, while sheltered lagoons and inlets were nesting sites for the black swans whose eggs were considered a great delicacy. Such abundant food sources supplied the varied Nuenonne diet. They did not bother to harvest scalefish, which they regarded with revulsion.

Over many millennia, using a regime of controlled burning, the Nuenonne created large areas of open grassland to support a plentiful population of wallaby. Continually moving from one end of the island to the other along a network of paths, family groups would camp for short periods at certain food-gathering sites. Here they constructed domed shelters made of pliable branches, bark and grass that could accommodate two or three adults with children.

The Nuenonne enjoyed reciprocal rights along the south-east coast of the large island, the territory of the Mellukerdee and Lyluequonny, as well as into the coastal country to the west that was the territory of the Needwondee and Ninine. All these clans were from the same language group, with interlocking kin relationships. Twice a year, the Nuenonne would voyage in canoes down the channel to gather food and engage in ceremony with these clans who had travelled overland from their country.

Since the beginning of time, it seemed, the Nuenonne had maintained this healthy, happy life, the continuity of people and place uninterrupted by invasion or traumatic upheaval. In the early nineteenth century, the senior man of the clan was Manganerer, whose wife was possibly a Ninine woman. In the second decade of the century, a third daughter was born to them: Truganini. She entered a dramatically changed world, one in which the timeless reassurances of Nuenonne life no longer held. Raegewarrah had been loosed upon the land.

In the cosmology of the Nuenonne, Raegewarrah was an intangible force of evil that could permeate all things. The full force of Raegewarrah was held in check by the creator spirit they knew as

Mouhernee, who lived as a star in the Milky Way. A perpetual struggle between these two forces had maintained the world in a precarious balance until two avatars fashioned by Raegewarrah floated in from the ocean and came to rest under a great fluted cape on the southern section of Lunawanna Alonnah.

From the cover of the trees, the Nuenonne watched the two floating islands pulled by clouds come to rest at the end of the sweep of bay. Two-legged creatures were disgorged into large canoes that brought them to the beach, where they walked along the sand to collect water from a small stream. Though they were not naked—their pale bodies were all but concealed by bright coverings—it was obvious to those who watched that these were men. They walked and made language like people, so they must be the dead returned, drained of all skin colour by the rigours of their journey. The Nuenonne could not have known that these ghost men had been following a map that named the country as Van Diemen's Land and the beach where they stepped ashore as Adventure Bay. All for the taking, so Captain James Cook believed.

Cook was agreeably surprised on 28 January 1777 when he landed on the beach at Adventure Bay in the HMS *Resolution*'s longboat to see eight naked men and a boy approaching with the greatest of confidence. Cook was unaware that these people believed they were meeting their own dead returning as pale shades of their former selves. Being treated as some kind of kin, rather than as trespassing aliens, Cook and his officers were not to witness the fierce territorial attachment of the Nuenonne to their country. The British mariners mistakenly supposed the inhabitants to be uninterested in the concept of property, and that they were, as the ship's surgeon wrote, a people with 'little to lose or care for'.

Cook had already taken possession of the whole east coast with no consideration of the property rights of the owners of the land. His maps told him that the place where he stood was still part of the east coast of the country he had claimed for his King. It was reassuring to believe these guileless people would not mind the expropriation of their territory; to imagine they might not even notice the loss of it.

On the third day of Cook's visit to Adventure Bay, a larger group of Nuenonne men came down to the beach, joined soon afterwards by a small party of naked women, who allowed their bodies to be examined without the slightest show of modesty. Bodily examination was one thing; penetration was quite another. Every inducement or entreaty for sex from the crew was rebuffed. After an hour of being prodded and stroked, the women retreated into the bush, leaving their men to fall asleep in the sun. Observing the men stretched out on the sand without any concern for their safety, the surgeon concluded that they were even more deficient in intelligence than 'the half-animated inhabitants of Tierra del Fuego'. They showed complete indifference to the food, the medals and the beads the English sailors gave them, and they lacked even the most basic technology: a maritime people without the wit to figure out how to fish with hooks was sure evidence of profound mental retardation, he reasoned.

Twenty-five years later, a group of French explorers under Nicolas Baudin came to investigate the southern coast of Van Diemen's Land and came ashore at various points on Lunawanna Alonnah. By then the Nuenonne were no longer 'without jealousy of strangers'; they no longer saw the ghost men as their kin. The tranquillity of Nuenonne life had been ruptured by violent incursions from the penal settlement established at Sydney Cove on the east coast of New Holland in 1788. Within ten years, a renegade coalition of time-served convicts and deserters were active in the coastal sealing grounds of the Southern Ocean. These brutal men answered to no authority and made sudden, murderous raids on the coastal clans of Van Diemen's Land to steal women to catch the seals and be their sexual slaves.

When Baudin and his well-meaning scientists arrived, they immediately noticed that the Nuenonne showed palpable terror at the sight of a musket, keeping a careful distance from the stick that spat fire. Although the French mariners enjoyed some happy interactions with the Nuenonne men—dancing and exchanging songs—no amount of singing and dancing could induce the women to come within arm's length. At the slightest movement towards them, the young women would leap to their feet and flee into the bush. Truganini's father Manganerer could well have been one of those men dancing and singing with the French sailors, and her mother among the young women making sure to keep out of the strangers' grasp.

Only a short sail from the northern tip of Lunawanna Alonnah was a wide river estuary where the Nuenonne would often hunt. The British called it Derwent River when they established a second penal settlement in 1804, named Hobart after the Secretary of State for War and the Colonies. Many convict and supply ships now sailed past Nuenonne country (which the English had renamed Bruny Island) to enter the Derwent. Crews often came ashore on the northern tip of the island to cut grass or get water. Pretty soon, escaped convicts and deserting seamen came to hide out in the extensive bush cover, bringing with them mayhem and disease. By the time of Truganini's birth, the Nuenonne clan was diminished and traumatised.

Manganerer was camped with his wife and three daughters on tiny Partridge Island off the southern end of Bruny Island, sometime around 1816, preparing for his seasonal visit to Recherche Bay. By cover of night, a group of sailors stealthily landed in a whaleboat and rushed at the family as they sat around their fire. Manganerer and the children dashed into the safety of the darkness as the sailors held fast to his wife. In the unsteady, feverish light of the fire, Truganini may have seen her mother resisting the sailors with their flailing fists and knives, before they vanished into the dark, leaving her ripped body leaking a pool of blood. The violent death of her mother was a profoundly traumatic experience indelibly etched into Truganini's memory.

In the years that followed, Truganini became only too familiar with the sight of male convicts deployed on the island, cutting timber, mining salt and burning shells for lime. In 1818, James Kelly secured a lease for a farm at the northern point, where he used convict workers to raise poultry and grow grain and vegetables to provision the passing ships. These convicts were alienated and brutalised men, without supervision, left to their own devices and supplied with muskets to hunt the ever-diminishing game—as well as any Nuenonne who might get in their way. Their rations of flour, tea and sugar were used to lure the Nuenonne women for sex.

In a matter of years, the seal colonies that had sustained the Nuenonne for millennia had been wiped out in the southern waters. Sealers remained active in the many islands that dotted the Bass Strait between Van Diemen's Land and the northern landmass of New Holland. These men would appear sporadically, on the hunt for women. John Baker was an African American sealer, commonly known as Black Baker, who brought his boat to Bruny Island sometime in 1826. Either with inducements or under the threat of a gun, Baker got Truganini's two sisters and a third woman into his boat and spirited them away to a life of slavery in the Bass Strait. Truganini never saw her sisters again.

The killing of seals was replaced by the killing of whales. The annual migration route of the southern right whale passed close by Bruny Island, and in 1824 James Kelly established a shore-based whaling station at the southern end of Adventure Bay, where he employed upwards of forty men in the busy months. By 1828, there were two whaling stations at Adventure Bay and another at Trumpeter Bay, employing over eighty men. A reciprocal relationship developed between the original people of the island and the men who worked at the whaling stations: in return for sex, whalers would give the Nuenonne flour for damper, plus tea and sugar for which they had developed an addiction. In this exchange, the motherless Truganini came to appreciate that sexual attraction was a key asset she possessed in the struggle for survival.

Given the desperate situation of the Nuenonne in 1828, it was remarkable that Truganini's father did not lead his clan to attack the intruders in retaliation for the abduction of their women, the increasing destruction of their food sources and the alienation of their land. The accommodating Nuenonne were a stark contrast to the remnant clans in the 'settled districts', who had taken to engaging in sporadic guerilla warfare against the waves of immigrants from Britain arriving to take advantage of free land grants. Up to 2560 acres was on offer to gentlemen with capital to make a start in the colony. In the Derwent River valley, on the east coast and in the midlands, these would-be farmers, fresh from England and Scotland, found fine expanses of grasslands, intricate networks of tracks through the bush, and a pleasing balance of open and timbered landscapes that offered the attractive prospect of making a fortune. That this land was so perfectly formed for productive use must show the hand of God: the idea that this superbly adapted landscape was the product of thousands of years of skilful land management was beyond them.

These new settlers could not understand why the original owners resented the dispersal of game from the grasslands, and believed that as freehold owners of the land it was their right to shoot dead anyone suspected of spearing their sheep or stealing their potatoes. Retaliatory spearing of farmers and stockkeepers drove the settlers into an angry frenzy. In every isolated farmhouse, settlers lived in fear of the unseen black enemy, imagining their own family as the target of an irrational attack that would not spare the women or children. In response to this hyper-anxiety, the governor authorised armed roving parties to scour the country for miles around the sheep runs and wheat farms, capturing or killing any people still trying to eke out an existence in their traditional country.

Driven to distraction by rising hysteria among the settlers, Governor George Arthur was forced to proclaim martial law in November 1828, expelling all the original people from the settled districts. He communicated the law through storyboards that were nailed to trees in the bush. Even if the people were able to decipher the narrative in the clumsy pictures, its absurdity was obvious. The original owners would not leave, the colonial secretary complained, because they were 'possessed with the idea . . . [of] their own rights over the country in comparison with the colonists'. Unwittingly, the governor had given every enraged settler a licence to shoot any original people should they appear in their own traditional hunting grounds.

Nuenonne country was exempt from this martial law. Though there were some leaseholders on Bruny Island, no settlers had yet been granted freehold title. The Nuenonne were regarded as role models for what was expected of the original people of the colony: they were unobtrusive, friendly and helpful. Captains of ships that called into Bruny Island or Recherche Bay reported that the Nuenonne were always useful to them, enthusiastically joining the crews in hunting and diving for shellfish. In May 1828, the overseer at the saltworks on Bruny Island travelled to Hobart with a man he called Bruny Jack and his wife Nelson. The couple were handed over to be guides for a roving party operating in the midlands. The *Hobart Town Courier* approvingly reported the recruitment of these tractable natives, observing that they 'displayed great quickness of understanding and force of mind'.

The editor had been equally impressed when Manganerer and other senior Nuenonne men persuaded a ship's captain to take them to Hobart to express to the governor their grievances over the abduction of women and the decimation of game that was their primary food source. Governor Arthur listened respectfully to the Nuenonne elders, impressed by their intelligence and adaptability. He was something of a rarity in colonial administration in that he was genuinely concerned at the gross injustice being done to the original people of the colony. The great pity was that his humanitarian concerns did not produce humanitarian responses.

This well-intentioned governor had his eye on Bruny Island as a potential incubator for a policy of conciliation and civilisation. The man he appointed to be the agent of this policy was George Augustus Robinson, an ambitious tradesman of limited education who had emigrated to the colony in 1824 in the hope of securing a more comfortable social niche for himself and his large family of five children. Remarkably, Robinson gave up his successful trade as a builder to become the butt of derisive jokes as custodian of 'the blacks'. He claimed to be solely motivated by a desire 'to do them good, to ameliorate their wretched conditions and raise them in the scale of civilisation'. Nevertheless, he was canny enough to negotiate with the governor to double the salary on offer and secure a land grant that would not have been available to him as a mere tradesman.

What conciliation and civilisation might mean for the Nuenonne could be gleaned from Nelson when she reappeared on Bruny Island in a dazed state in January 1829. After being taken as a guide, Nelson had been forcibly separated from her husband and kept at the camp to be raped by the soldiers, while Bruny Jack was taken into the bush where he was repeatedly beaten. While attempting to escape, he had been shot by a soldier, 'not knowing he was tame', as the *Hobart Town Courier* explained. Wounded, he ran to the river and plunged under the water, but he was unable to swim. Each time he surfaced to breathe, the soldier fired, until eventually he didn't come up again. Returned to Bruny Island, Nelson died a few months later.

Truganini was George Augustus Robinson's first point of contact with the Nuenonne. He found her, in April 1829, living with a gang of convict woodcutters just across the channel from Bruny Island at Birch's Bay. She was a lovely young woman, diminutive and fine-boned, with her hair cut close to her scalp, which emphasised lively dark eyes and a generous mouth. He thought she was about sixteen or seventeen. Impressed with this young woman's obvious intelligence and grasp of English, Robinson took it upon himself to take her back to her father on Bruny Island.

Robinson was profoundly disturbed by the prevalent carnal exchange between convict workers and local women in the colony, and he obsessively documented stories of abductions and violence, yet nowhere did he record that Truganini had been forcibly abducted. Though he was under no illusions about the brutal nature of the sexual transaction, it was not apparent to him that she was with the woodcutters under duress. It was two years later that she told him how one of the woodcutters had beaten her while others held her down.

Robinson's land grant on Bruny Island was 500 acres, fronting onto an inlet immediately across the channel from Birch's Bay on the western side of Bruny Island. His land abutted a much larger grant of 2560 acres that had been awarded to Richard Pybus, recently arrived with his family from England. Robinson named the waterfrontage of his grant Missionary Bay and here he intended to create a thriving Christian community for the Nuenonne.

He understood it was important to make the senior man, Manganerer, his ally if he were to succeed in this venture, and by returning Truganini to her country he hoped to win her father to his cause. He did his best to coax Truganini into being a chaste Christian woman, encouraging her to wear a shapeless smock made from blankets to cover her nakedness. She preferred to be unencumbered by clothing and generally went naked, rather to Robinson's discomfort.

Just as he'd hoped, Truganini's presence at Missionary Bay encouraged Manganerer to move there with his second wife and young son. A dozen or so demoralised and sick people followed him to receive the daily allowance of half a pound of biscuit and a pound of potatoes that Robinson provided.

Within the limitations of his own evangelical understanding, Robinson tried to make sense of the narrative of calamity they presented to him. It came as no surprise to him that the evil force of Raegewarrah was omnipresent in the worldview of these people, whom he judged to be sunk in darkness and savagery. Recognising the Miltonian parallel in the competing forces of good and evil that ruled their lives, he appropriated the name Raegewarrah to stand in for the Devil, determined to show them that the malevolent force that had delivered the apocalypse would be defeated by his God.

Robinson saw the original people as very low in the hierarchy of creation, yet not irredeemable. His self-appointed mission was to lift them from their state of savage ignorance. They must put their trust in God, he told them, and, by extension, in him, George Augustus Robinson: the good father sent to save them from obliteration.

Instruction in the Christian faith was central to Robinson's scheme, as was instruction in the principles of European civilisation, such as wearing clothes, living in houses and growing potatoes. Most especially, he wanted to instruct the Nuenonne in the principle of labour. To this end, he had persuaded the governor to provide him with extra daily rations of a pound of meat and discretionary allowances of tea and sugar for those who could be made to work. This strategy was entirely unsuccessful. The people were disinclined to labour, and the tea and sugar they craved could always be found elsewhere.

Essential to Robinson's scheme was that he must be the sole source of food and authority for the distressed Nuenonne. He was enraged by threats to his authority from men of the lower orders who had frequented the island for years. In his daily journal he railed against this debauched riffraff who gave generous gifts of flour, tea and sugar to the women in order to make them 'subservient to [the men's] carnal appetites'. He issued a steady stream of haughty directives, ordering these men to immediately cease their vile inducements and bring the women living with them to his mission, failing to grasp that this mutually exploitative association was well established. His moral outrage had no effect on either party: the women ignored his pious lectures, and the recipients of his letters simply laughed at him.

The contrast between the airs Robinson gave himself and his disreputable calling as the custodian of dispossessed Nuenonne made him the object of open derision, on Bruny Island no less than in Hobart. Even the assigned convicts jeered at his lowly social status. The more he was ridiculed for living in a hut among the Nuenonne, the more he sought to use them to transcend the class barriers that rendered him so vulnerable. His ambitious plan to put an end to the jeers was to create a model Christian community at Missionary Bay, complete with church, schoolroom, houses and a farm. Under his benign tutelage, the Nuenonne would shuck off their heathen beliefs and savage ways and be incorporated into settler society as a simple peasantry.

As much as the exploitative carnality of convicts and whalers outraged Robinson, his major concern was that their alternative source of food would reduce the Nuenonne's dependence on him and prove 'an insurmountable barrier' to his civilising mission. There was little he could do about it. Most of the women continued to visit the whaling stations, or Kelly's farm, a practice the men seemed to accept with the same equanimity with which they rebuffed Robinson's invitation to build huts to live in. Instead the men spent endless hours painting their bodies with red ochre and charcoal and dressing their long ringlets with a pomade of animal fat and ochre.

Robinson hung around making notes about their habits and picking up a few words. After a couple of weeks he had learnt enough words to offer a sermon of sorts. As death was their current preoccupation, his aim was to correct their belief about what happened when they died. Using their own language, he preached that there was the one God up in the sky, who was good, and the Devil in the fire below, who was bad. The good people who accepted his God would travel up to the sky when they died, whereas the bad ones would go into the fire. He liked to think his few listeners were attentive to the message of salvation he was offering, but instead they were puzzled. The sky was the realm of the creator spirits, they told him, and after death the Nuenonne went far away across the sea, possibly to England. There were plenty of the Nuenonne dead in England, they insisted; their grandfathers had seen some of them.

The two or three women who stayed around Missionary Bay spent their days diving for shellfish or collecting wild fruits and ferns, grinding ochre, and treating the wallaby skins to make cloaks and small pouches to carry relics of the dead. Truganini liked to collect tiny luminous shells from the beaches, clean them till they shone and then string them into exquisite necklaces. She gathered bundles of iris leaves, dried them over slow fires, and twisted the leaves into threads that she plaited and wove into globular baskets. In May, a month after he'd arrived, Robinson took several of her baskets to Hobart as gifts for the important people of the town. The editor of the *Hobart Town Courier* was impressed with the handiwork, declaring that the baskets 'would not disgrace as a reticule the hand of a London lady'. Robinson fancied that in Truganini's pursuits he had found the makings of a cottage industry.

Returning from Hobart, Robinson was delighted to see that Truganini had found a companion, a young woman named Dray from the Lowreenne clan on the remote west coast. Dray had walked overland to Recherche Bay with her husband and others from his Ninine clan, most of whom had stayed at Recherche Bay. She was part of the smaller group, including her husband and one child, who had voyaged in canoes for the annual visit to their Nuenonne kin on Bruny Island. It was never obvious to Robinson what kin Dray was to Truganini, but the two young women behaved like sisters.

Another new face at Missionary Bay on Robinson's return was Wooredy, an important Nuenonne elder in his forties who had left his semi-permanent camp on the southern part of the island to come to visit Manganerer. A renowned warrior, Wooredy was also a cleverman, so knowledgeable in ritual and healing that the convicts and leaseholders on his island called him Doctor. Like Manganerer, he went naked and wore his hair in the traditional fashion: long greased ringlets coloured with red ochre that fell over his eyes like a mop. Born more than a decade before settlement, Wooredy was witness to the arrival of some of the first colonists in 1804, just as his father and grandfather had watched Captain Cook land at Adventure Bay in 1777. Stubbornly attached to his customs, Wooredy was determined to induct Robinson into the Nuenonne way of life.

As the two senior men, Wooredy and Manganerer took Robinson hunting on the narrow neck leading to the south island, where the wallabies were more abundant. Although the hunters carried long spears, their weapon of choice was the shorter waddy, made of hard sheoak wood, that they threw with great dexterity, never failing to stun a bounding animal. Returning to Missionary Bay, Robinson sought to impress them with his own food-gathering skills. He threw a hooked line into the channel to catch some rock cod that he grilled over a fire. Unwittingly testing the limits of his companions' agreeableness, he tried to persuade the men to eat the fish. Reluctantly, they took a bite, but they would not swallow it. It took some time to make him understand that it was only shellfish that was a critical part of the Nuenonne diet; they never ate scalefish and harvesting shellfish was exclusively women's work. Men never learnt to swim and would rarely, if ever, enter the water.

Girls were taught by their mothers to be expert swimmers, which made them invaluable food gatherers. As game food of wallaby and possum became scarce, the Nuenonne were more dependent than ever on large fleshy abalone, as well as crayfish, scallops, oysters and mussels. A man might starve without a woman to harvest shellfish.

Truganini was a superb swimmer; she was constantly in and out of the water. Watching her exuberant swimming and diving for shellfish, Robinson could see yet again how critical she would be to his strategy. He inserted himself into her routine, using his dinghy to take Truganini and her friend Dray to places that would otherwise be difficult to reach. The young women would leap from the boat with woven bags around their necks and small sticks, sharpened at one end, clenched between their teeth. They'd dive into the water and use their toes to lever the large abalone shells off the rocks, securing them in their bags. They could stay under for a considerable time before surfacing to take a breath, diving again and again until their bags were full.

Robinson used these outings to interrogate Dray about her clan and the long journey she had made from the south-west coast. He was able to glean that there was a well-used track from Port Davey to Recherche Bay. Truganini told him how she had also walked this track with her father for reciprocal visits. One day, sitting alone in the boat while the women dived below, he decided he would take them to Port Davey to establish contact with the still-numerous Ninine and the other coastal clans further north. No sooner had he returned to Missionary Bay with the abalone harvest than he was off to Hobart to put this plan to the governor.

In July, a group of three Ninine families suddenly appeared at Missionary Bay. Their arrival occasioned great joy, such were the bonds of affection between the two clans. Robinson was no less delighted to see them. He had high hopes that this group would convey him to the west coast on their return journey, providing him with both food and protection. He was severely put out two days later when the group announced they were returning home and made no offer to take him. Robinson's only hope was that they would give their clan a favourable report of his good intentions. Further complicating his plans, Manganerer took his wife and son to South Bruny, where Wooredy was camped. From there they and the Ninine would travel to Recherche Bay together.

Dray elected to stay behind with her friend Truganini. Robinson judged these two young women to be the most intelligent and tractable of the dozen people left at his mission and that they would benefit from interaction with respectable women. Having dressed them in smocks, he took them to visit a ship that had run aground on the other side of the channel. The bored English ladies on the stricken ship were thrilled to meet Truganini and Dray, with their short-cropped hair, whom they first took to be two beautiful boys. Assured that they were in fact female, the women took the two into their cabin, where they rummaged through their travelling wardrobes to find gorgeous dresses of silk and satin to replace the shapeless smocks. Truganini and Dray emerged from this entertainment utterly transformed. Robinson was shocked to see that rather than being dressed simply as would befit a maid, each was dressed as if she were a belle in a drawing room in London's wealthy West End.

Truganini and Dray were much pleased with their transformation, but on their return to Missionary Bay the fancy gowns were quickly swapped for the shapeless smocks, which were in turn soon discarded. However, the lovely dresses were donned again when Robinson took Truganini and Dray to Hobart to display them to the colonial elite. The two young women were presented to the governor, who was duly impressed with their metamorphosis under Robinson's tutelage.

It was a terrible blow to Robinson's pride that as soon as Truganini and Dray returned to Missionary Bay they cast off their European finery and ran off to Adventure Bay. The migrating whales had returned and the whalers were back at the station. More haughty letters were sent to the whalers, to be met with more scornful resistance. In early August, Robinson attempted to retrieve Truganini and Dray from the whalers, only to be insulted to his face. He was doubly humiliated when the young women ran away from him and hid.

On his journey back from Adventure Bay, Robinson found Wooredy's camp, near the narrow neck between the north and south of the island. Wooredy and his sons were away hunting, and his pregnant wife, evidently very ill and weak, was able to indicate in words and signs that the people from Port Davey had not yet left the island. Some of them had fallen ill, just as she had. She also let him know that Manganerer was nearby with his wife and son, readying to travel to Recherche Bay. While they were conversing, Wooredy returned and greeted Robinson with evident pleasure, proudly introducing his three sons. He was very solicitous of his wife and promised to bring his family to Missionary Bay in the near future, once she was well again.

When Wooredy did come to Missionary Bay, a month later, it was in very changed circumstances. He arrived in mid September with his two older sons, carrying one in his arms, even though he was so ill he could barely walk himself. He told Robinson that his pregnant wife and youngest son were *loggerner nene*, meaning 'dead in the fire', as were all the people from Port Davey.

A few days later, Manganerer also struggled into Missionary Bay in a shocking state.

Disaster had struck Manganerer for a second time on his trip to Recherche Bay. Instead of the Ninine people he had been expecting to meet at the bay, he had encountered the convict mutineers who had seized the government brig *Cyprus*. These men abducted his wife and sailed away with her to New Zealand, then on to Japan and China. Hastily constructing a sturdy ocean-going canoe, Manganerer had attempted to follow them but had been blown far out into the Southern Ocean. His son had died and he himself was half dead from dehydration when he was found by a whaling ship.

The tragedy was almost too much for this proud man to bear. He had endured the murder of his first wife and the abduction of his two older daughters by the intruders, and now they had taken his second wife. His only son was dead and his remaining daughter had abandoned him for the whaling station. His distress was compounded when he discovered that in his absence almost all of his clan had succumbed to disease, as had all but one of the people visiting from Port Davey, who were under his protection.

It would not be the whalers' carnal appetites that proved the insurmountable barrier to Robinson's plans for his civilising mission with the Nuenonne: it was the influenza virus. Instead of dispensing the fruits of civilisation, Robinson was reduced to an impotent bystander in an apocalyptic nightmare. 'Death hath visited with dire havoc,' Robinson confided to his journal on 23 September, ruefully noting that only fourteen Nuenonne remained to receive the benefit of his proselytising. These traumatised survivors were slashing their faces and bodies in grief, in no state to heed his Christian platitudes.

His evangelical commitment was sorely tested by the daily burial rites, in which he was expected to participate. Traditionally, the Nuenonne burnt their dead, and then collected the ashes and a bone relic to wear as a ritual keepsake. With so few able-bodied survivors, the cremation rituals were reduced to a brutal minimum. Missionary Bay became littered with charred remains, some only partly consumed by the cremation fire and subject to the ravages of the many abandoned dogs.

By October, only a handful of people survived at Missionary Bay. Manganerer was barely clinging to life, a broken man. Within a few months he, too, would be dead, from venereal disease. The only male capable of decisive action was Wooredy. The Doctor had not been able to save his wife or most of his clan, but miraculously he and his two sons were restored to full health. In this very able fellow, Robinson recognised an indispensable ally. Wooredy was bound to Robinson by ties of obligation, and not just for the food he provided.

Wooredy needed a new wife and had set his sights on Manganerer's adolescent daughter. He made it clear that his support was contingent on Robinson's exercising authority over the whalers to secure Truganini. That she plainly preferred the attention of the whalers, Wooredy pragmatically acknowledged; his wife had been a regular visitor to the whaling station before she became ill.

Woorendy was not alone in his desire for Truganini; many men found her desirable. Robinson himself had undoubtedly been very taken with Truganini from the first moment he set eyes on her. Whatever desire he felt for her was powerfully tempered by his visceral horror of the venereal disease she had contracted. He expressed righteous resentment at the sexual liberties taken by other men, but his journals provide no suggestion that Truganini ever became his sexual partner. The role he cast for himself was even more intimate and binding than that of a lover: he was the good father who would protect and save her.

Robinson understood that it was much to his advantage for Truganini to be partnered with Wooredy. More letters were delivered to the whaling station, demanding her return, but even when the whalers left at the end of the season she did not come to Missionary Bay. With Dray and another friend, the recently widowed Pagerly, Truganini travelled north, crossing Richard Pybus's grant to reach Kelly's farm. It was reported to Robinson that all three women were so debilitated with venereal disease that they could hardly walk. Eventually, it fell to Manganerer to shoulder the humiliation of recovering his reluctant daughter; she would not hide from her father.

As well as retrieving Truganini and Dray, Manganerer was also able to remove Pagerly, whom he took down to his camp on the Neck to be his new wife. Neither Truganini nor Dray was well enough to travel much beyond Kelly's farm. They reappeared at Missionary Bay in late October, apparently cured of the 'loathsome disease', most likely syphilis. Rather than the women being cured, the disease had entered the latent phase when the symptoms were no longer evident and the women no longer contagious.

Truganini returned to Missionary Bay very reluctantly. Robinson found it a disturbing puzzle that she should continue to invite sexual exploitation by brutal and depraved men when a decent man such as himself could provide her with shelter, warm clothing, food and all the tea and sugar she might want. He would never understand that her predilection for sex with convicts and whalers, no matter how violent they might be, could be a psychological adaptation to the trauma of her short life—what modern psychiatry would describe as Stockholm syndrome.

Wooredy was ecstatic with gratitude, attributing Truganini's return to the awesome power of Robinson's magic paper. Notwithstanding Robinson's and her father's encouragement, Truganini was not interested in her Nuenonne suitor. She scornfully declared Wooredy to be Raegewarrah personified and rejected his overtures with tears of rage. In no way discouraged, Wooredy maintained his attentions until she resentfully submitted in October 1829, in 'dread apprehension', so Robinson recorded, of violating the cultural norms that required her to accept a suitor who had chosen her.

Confident that he had now secured Wooredy's fidelity, Robinson sailed to Hobart to finalise plans to leave the charnel ground that Missionary Bay had become. He had hatched a much grander scheme to lead a civilising mission overland to Port Davey and then up the remote west coast, contacting all the clans in the west and north-west and bringing them under his protection. He called this audacious project his 'friendly mission'. Dray, who was pining to be reunited with her people, would be essential to this mission, while Truganini and Wooredy had kinship connections and spoke the language. These three would be his intermediaries in his process of 'conciliation'.

He returned to Missionary Bay on the sloop *Swallow* on 29 January 1830, having garnered the governor's generous support for his plan. He had secured a supply vessel, a team of five convicts to provide logistical backup, and the promise of assistance from the penal settlement in Macquarie Harbour. In addition, the governor released into Robinson's custody several men from various clans who had been captured by roving parties and were languishing in jail. Months earlier, Robinson had rejected a request to take these men to Missionary Bay, protesting that it would be 'impossible to keep hold of any number of natives within a certain space . . . unless proper means of confinement were put into effect'. This principle of 'proper means of confinement' would guide his modus operandi for the next five years.

He had sailed back to Missionary Bay primarily to collect Dray, Wooredy and Truganini, and when they could not be found he sent the party of convicts to the Neck to convey these people to a nearby embarkation point. The next day, four adults and two children were taken aboard the *Swallow*, willingly enough. Among them was Pagerly. Manganerer had died days before, and his widow could see more possibilities for her future life with the men in Robinson's expedition than her precarious existence with the whalers. Dray was keen to make the journey, desperately wanting to be reunited with her brother. Wooredy was looking to Robinson to secure his own survival and that of his two sons, Myunge and Droyerloine. His recalcitrant young wife was unwavering. She had fixed on Robinson with a fierce determination: he was her father now and he would be the agent of her survival. Wherever Robinson went, Truganini would go.

Heaven only knows what sort of excursion Truganini thought she had embarked upon. Many times she had gone to Recherche Bay with her father in his bark canoe. Nomadic treks through the south-west to Port Davey were part of the timeless, seasonal pattern of her life. The purpose of a journey was the journey itself, a ritual interaction with the land over which they moved, recorded and recreated in stories and songs. A journey encompassed return, a completion, in accordance with the natural cycles of the environment. To journey for the purpose of reaching a destination was an entirely new concept. Not to return was unthinkable.

CHAPTER 2

On the afternoon of 31 January 1830, Robinson's mission party landed on a crescent of stark white sand at the far southern end of Recherche Bay. It was as Truganini had always known it, except for a few abandoned huts left by the *Cyprus* mutineers. For all the pain of the recent loss of her father, and the death of the baby half-brother she had often carried on her shoulders, Truganini was delighted to be returned to the place of her birth. She sprinted up the beach to gather armfuls of the fleshy pigface. While frolicking in the creek she caught a shy platypus. With Dray and Pagerly, she swam around the rocky outcrop at the far end of the beach to dive for shellfish, retrieving several bags of mussels and oysters. Everyone was in high spirits at the evening feast, except for Wooredy. He felt the presence of Raegewarrah everywhere.

For his entire life, some forty years, Wooredy had made trips to and from this place. As a small boy he had hidden in the bush with his family to observe the arrival of Bruni D'Entrecasteaux. Even then, he had known the pale strangers had been conjured from the sea by Raegewarrah. The malevolent spirit was still present, he knew, embodied in the tree the strangers had carved. Wooredy's concerns were amplified while hunting the next day when he stumbled upon the decayed body of a woman; the corpse showed no sign of violence nor any attempt at cremation. Raegewarrah had caught her, he was sure of it.

Viewing the body, Dray identified the woman as one of the people who had come with her from the west coast months earlier. She must have shown signs of the fatal illness and been left to die alone, Dray explained, strangely unmoved by this apparent callousness. Robinson was dismayed to observe another display of the belief 'that no human means can avert the doom to which they are consigned'. This stubborn fatalism about the irresistible force of Raegewarrah deeply rankled with him, even though Wooredy had given him a potent lesson in Raegewarrah's awesome power on the voyage from Bruny.

As they had sailed down the channel, Wooredy had identified the land they passed as the country of three interconnected clans—the Mellukerdee from the Huon Valley, the Lyluequonny from Southport and the Needwondee from Cox's Bight—all gone within the span of Wooredy's adult life. This land was empty now, Wooredy told him. Nobody in that country was left alive.

The survivors of that same holocaust were the five men and a youth who now accompanied the expedition, at the governor's pleasure. Kickerterpoller, in his early twenties, was from the Pardarereme clan from the east coast. He had been stolen from his people when he was about nine and given to a settler as a farmhand. In his youth, he had run away to join the remnants of his clan waging a guerilla war, until he was captured in 1824. Another man raised by settlers was Robert, who was 'found' in a remote area of the midlands when he was a baby and did not even know his clan or real name. Umarrah was the senior man of the Tyerrerontepanner clan from the northern midlands. A famous guerilla fighter, he had been captured by a roving party on 7 November 1828, along with his countryman Parewareter. Trepanner was from the north coast and also had a strong allegiance to Umarrah. Maulboyheener was a youth of about fourteen, from the Pyemairenerpairnener clan from the north-east, who had been captured with his mother by John Batman's roving party and had been living at Robinson's house.

Robinson was most impressed with the 'respectful and compliant' Kickerterpoller, whose command of English and knowledge of European customs made him an ideal negotiator. Robert, while a very good shot, was timid and not at home in the bush, getting lost on more than one occasion, and was largely consigned to work with the convicts. Umarrah was the most important because he commanded the loyalty of the other men. These men would all have preferred to linger at Recherche Bay, where the hunting was good and the shellfish plentiful. They were aliens in this country, did not know the language or customs and had no wish to meet the local clans.

Dray, however, was most anxious to start for the west coast and so too was Truganini, who had kin among the Ninine. Wooredy was not at all enthusiastic. He was inherently hostile towards the *toogee*—his collective name for people from the west coast—despite his strong cultural ties, and was reluctant to travel into their territory. Wooredy's superb tracking and hunting skills made this steady fellow the lynchpin of Robinson's mission, and he judged that Wooredy's determined attachment to Truganini would overcome his reluctance to move.

Wooredy's misgivings were shared by Umarrah and Kickerterpoller. Both men had previously been co-opted as trackers for roving parties sent out to capture people still trying to survive in the districts under martial law. They were very familiar with this kind of expedition and knew all too well the violent, coercive ways of settlers, which made them suspicious of Robinson's true intentions. Even though Robinson's expedition was not a paramilitary organisation like the roving parties, and no one was openly armed, the convicts all carried guns in their knapsacks, and the brace of pistols hidden in Robinson's knapsack told them this mission was not going to be as friendly as Robinson claimed. Yet they had reason to cleave to Robinson, at least in the short term: no longer confined in some disgusting lockup, they were at large in unoccupied country where they could hunt freely. And no one was shooting at them.

Kickerterpoller had another reason to stick with the expedition. He wanted to be around Truganini and was angling to take her from her ageing husband. It did not take him long to realise that despite his age Wooredy was a consummate warrior and jealously protective of his status. Kickerterpoller adroitly transferred his amorous attentions to Pagerly, although he was never satisfied with just one woman.

Another man with his eye on Truganini was the foreman of the convict support team, Alexander McKay. Technically still a convict himself, McKay was an experienced bushman who had assisted in survey explorations throughout the north-west of Van Diemen's Land, where he had had many interactions with local clans. Robinson instinctively saw him as a rival. Even as he was forced to rely on McKay's exemplary bush skills, Robinson despised and distrusted the man, never finding a good word to say about him or any of his assigned convicts. The antagonism was mutual. The convicts were openly contemptuous of Robinson, furious that he should make them walk to the west coast rather than travel by boat.

An enduring perception had taken hold among colonists that the south-west was a terrible place, a geographical extension of the inhuman horrors of the penal settlement at Sarah Island in Macquarie Harbour. Everyone knew the stories of convicts, driven beyond endurance by the cruelties of the penal system, who had escaped into the hinterland never to be seen again. One convict bolter who survived his encounter with this terrible land was sustained throughout his ordeal by systematically murdering and eating his companions. If the rigours of this hellish environment could drive a man to cannibal depravity, why would any Christian willingly set foot on it?

George Augustus Robinson was an odd kind of Christian. The new colony at the end of the world presented him with a Janus face: both a place where he could climb the hierarchy of civilised society and at the same time a place where the modifying impact of man was barely evident. He reasoned to himself that his object in plunging into the wild was to shine the light of God into the darkness, yet his wholehearted embrace of untamed nature revealed a passion for elemental experience much at odds with his evangelical posturing. He hankered to venture into the heart of darkness and immerse himself in the vast wilderness of this new world, even as his every step was driven by a voracious ambition to be feted and admired by the settler elite who had showered derision upon his enterprise. He was determined to return to their small world as a conquering hero.

Mid morning on 3 February 1830, the mission party began to walk overland from Recherche Bay to the west coast. The sun was shining and Robinson had high hopes. Estimating the distance to Port Davey to be about sixty miles, he figured it would take them three days to cover the ground. He knew nothing of the territory before him; no settler had ever attempted this trek. Striding out with confidence, he had no idea what he was getting into. His expectation was that the men would hunt game to supplement their meagre rations and Dray's desire to be reunited with her brother would get the party to the destination.

Walking in single file, with the convicts bringing up the rear, the party followed the creek westwards for a mile or so until they reached a flat plain that stretched for many miles, promising easy walking. To Robinson's dismay, they almost immediately sank into tepid water that rose to their calves. The pretty olive- and rust-coloured grasses that stretched as far as the eye could see grew in a porous layer of peat above a hard quartzite base, which trapped the heavy rainfall in a watery bog. For hours the party pulled their legs through marshland that at times sucked them down to their knees. Reaching higher ground, they were only slightly less dismayed to find an almost impenetrable belt of thick eucalypt scrub. It was almost dark when a viable campsite was located beside a freshwater creek. By then the party were exhausted. They had only covered eight miles.

Just after dawn the next day, Dray found the track on which her people travelled across the tricky terrain. It had not been used for many months, and in places it was swallowed by rainforest, which meant clambering over fallen trees slippery with moss, then a steep descent down a cliff face with almost every step causing a cascade of small boulders. After much slipping and stumbling they finally reached the southern coastline. As they made camp, heavy rain began to fall that persisted throughout the night.

At sunrise, disheartened and drenched to the bone, the expedition set off once more, climbing up and over rugged country covered with dense forest, punctuated by huge outcrops of barren rock with jagged edges, some sharp as knives. By the time they reached the southern coast again they were sweating profusely in the baking sunshine. They walked for several hours along a wide arc of squeaky, shifting sand pounded by heavy surf. A mile or two behind, the burdened convicts stumbled and cursed.

That night, camped at the bottom of a deep coastal ravine, Robinson was very apprehensive. The party had covered no more than twenty miles, and supplies were running dangerously low. The cracking pace had allowed no time for hunting, and there were no local people to render assistance. They had passed many bark huts of the Needwondee, completely deserted. Wooredy said all these people had been snatched away by Raegewarrah.

The fourth day involved negotiating a passage across a daunting mountain range that consisted of a series of polished quartz summits. Much of the time they crawled on hands and knees, clinging onto the wiry tufts of grass or the pitiful, wind-stunted trees. Even in these dire circumstances, Robinson was reaching for the sublime. Painfully hauling himself up to a bare summit, he turned back to watch the line of convicts cautiously winding single file around the mountain opposite, and was swept with regret that he did not have drawing materials on hand to capture such a romantic scene.

His companions were not so uplifted. After persevering all day in this unforgiving terrain without any food, they were at the point of total exhaustion. Truganini was smaller than anyone else in the group, and she could barely walk because her legs were badly swollen, a common complication of second-stage syphilis. Kickerterpoller was no longer compliant, and boldly remonstrated that this was not the way to travel. Even a roving party moving through cleared country on level ground did not go at such a pace, he protested. The indefatigable Wooredy was the only one not prone with exhaustion. Scanning the ragged, precipitous coastline, his sharp eyes located a schooner lying offshore, in a bay about six miles ahead. It was the support ship, the *Swallow*, which by sheer luck was not yet at Macquarie Harbour, the intended rendezvous, having been driven back by strong winds. The random meeting was lifesaving.

The colonists called the place where the *Swallow* was anchored Louisa Bay, but Wooredy knew it to be where the creator spirit fell from the sky into the sea. For many millennia it had been a ritual meeting place for all the clans of the south-east, and it was home to extensive shell middens and hidden rock paintings. Here his father and grandfather had built the sturdy canoes they took to distant Maatsuyker Island to hunt for seals. There were no more seals to hunt on Maatsuyker—they had all been killed by the sealers, who had stolen so many Nuenonne women.

Re-energised by the prospect of food, Robinson and his guides followed Wooredy in a headlong scramble down the mountainside, reaching Louisa Bay by late afternoon. Two hours later the shattered convicts arrived.

Watching Truganini gleefully diving for crayfish, Robinson ruefully acknowledged how close they had come to starvation. He was convinced that in the future he would have to defer to his guides and their way of doing things. Without their food supplies and local knowledge of the bush he would not survive the trip to Port Davey. 'My greatest confidence was in the natives,' he confided to his journal. 'They were well acquainted with the resources of the country and would not allow me to want.'

For the next six weeks, Robinson kept to the meandering, leisurely pace of his guides, for whom travel was subordinate to the requirements of hunting and food gathering. Truganini and Dray knew how to find their kin, but neither was in any hurry to do so. Slyly deflecting Robinson's pursuit, the two women spent their time diving for crayfish, oyster and abalone, or collecting small wild plums, sweet red berries and edible roots. The men went hunting for wallaby, wild duck, and an elusive animal somewhat bigger than a dog, with distinctive stripes on its back. Although there were many semicircular grass-covered huts, no people were ever sighted.

As the food became more plentiful, the terrain became more difficult. Moving from the coast further west towards Bathurst Harbour meant pushing into mountainous country covered with a tangle of trees that grew almost horizontal. Beset by mizzling rain that never let up, they were forced to crawl along precipices or wade for miles through thigh-high water. Impervious to the brutal terrain and the perpetual rain, Robinson found the experience thrilling. He stuck close to the guides, sleeping beside their fires and sharing their provisions of abalone, crayfish and wallaby meat.

The scornful convicts made camp a considerable distance away, spurning the freshly caught food in favour of their Christian supplies of damper and salted meat. Nor did they want any part of the heathen singing and dancing that went on every night.

Robinson was a fascinated participant in the nightly ceremonies, listening attentively as Wooredy told of the exploits of the creator spirit who made man from the kangaroo. The stories were sung with a repeated, chanted chorus, and Robinson inserted himself into these rituals by playing his flute, to his companions' delight. After years of terror and loss, they were all having a fine time in the bush, reviving their traditional way of life that revolved around hunting and ritual. And Robinson was there to make sure the surly men with guns were kept at a safe distance.

So began a system of mutual support and protection that for Truganini and Wooredy lasted thirteen years. They might not have properly comprehended Robinson's intentions, but they understood that their relationship with him had undergone a profound change. In contrast to his earlier behaviour, where his efforts had been bent on making them like himself, in the wilderness it seemed as if he was in the process of becoming one of them. True, he did not strip off his clothes and go hunting naked as they did, but he shared the food they caught and was at pains to make himself part of their rituals and daily activity. He watched and listened—writing up copious notes in his journal.

In the middle of March, the party reached the vast waterway of Bathurst Harbour. They had been walking for six weeks without any contact with the inhabitants of the south-west, who proved no more accommodating than the primordial landscape. The Ninine were 'fleeing before my approach as the clouds flee before a tempest', Robinson wrote in exasperation. At Bathurst Harbour, he was able to make contact with the *Swallow* again, and get a whaleboat to take them across the wide expanse of water to make camp at the head of the harbour at a spot known as Kelly's Basin. As they crossed the water, Robinson experienced a surge of expectation when Wooredy spotted something fluttering on the shore. It was revealed to be no more than a pathetic flag planted by three convicts who had escaped from the penitentiary at Sarah Island, many miles to the north. Their bleached skeletons, still in tattered government-issue clothing, were an unsettling reminder of how inhospitable this place could be for intruders.

While squatting on the ground to register this grim find, Wooredy suddenly pointed to smoke rising in the distant hills. Robinson's heart began to race all over again. At last the Ninine were in sight. Truganini and Dray set off in pursuit. In the following days the two women caught up with the Ninine time and time again, but the people would simply melt away into the bush. Only two young women could be persuaded to come with them to meet 'Mister Robinson'. He entertained them with baubles and they were utterly beguiled by the sound of his flute. Still, it took days to persuade them to take Dray to their hiding place. Robinson and Wooredy accompanied them, but Truganini declined to go, pleading exhaustion, although she may have had other reasons for staying behind at the camp without her husband.

Robinson followed Dray and the two Ninine women, pushing a long way through tough scrub. Reaching a hidden clearing, Dray gave several loud hoots, and ten naked women emerged, with six children in tow. After some cautious discussion with Dray, they hooted in turn and an equal number of men appeared, all of them standing more than six feet tall, naked and carrying spears, with dead wallabies thrown around their shoulders. Wooredy told the men he had walked all day to meet with them and how Robinson had constantly called out '*gozee*', meaning 'make haste', which caused great mirth. They kept repeating '*gozee*', then collapsing into gleeful laughter. Cautiously, they sniffed at the biscuit Robinson offered, before handing it back, and then they amused themselves by stroking and prodding his pale skin and meticulously examining the blue coat he was wearing.

A white man was an object of wonder to them, Robinson thought, but it was not so. The Ninine knew plenty about the pale-skinned men they called *num*, and what they knew made them very wary. Dray described Mister Robinson to her people as '*nyrae*', by which she meant 'good', and it may have been her description that caused their wonder. The pale-skinned men they knew about would certainly not be described as *nyrae num*.

These ten families made an impressive group, everyone in excellent health and good spirits. The jocular band agreed to accompany

Dray back to Robinson's camp, laughing and shouting all the way, until they breasted the hill above Kelly's Basin. Suddenly, they stopped in their tracks and fell silent. Coming towards them were a group of *num* in a boat. Robinson was livid with anger that the curious convicts had disobeyed his order to stay out of sight. He could not induce the Ninine to take another step. Leaving Wooredy and Dray to spend the night with them, he went alone to his camp.

Climbing the same hill with Truganini the next day, he was distressed to find that the Ninine had slipped away as his guides slept. Truganini and Wooredy followed their tracks for the next two weeks—a game of hide-and-seek in which the Ninine sporadically made contact only to disappear on a whim.

Frustrated by his failure to effect 'conciliation' with the local population, Robinson was equally perplexed by the attitude of his guides. He was alarmed when they told him they could round up the Ninine if he gave them his pistols. Alternatively, his convict retainers advised that alcohol would be the most effective weapon, explaining 'it would only be necessary to make them drunk and you could take them anywhere'. Robinson had expected this kind of crude suggestion from convicts, which is why he had kept them from any possible contact. And he was alert to potential antagonism from men from other language groups. But it was beyond his comprehension that Wooredy should want to capture people to whom he was closely related. Robinson began to suspect that his loyal and trusted companion could be causing the extreme wariness of the Ninine, especially when he heard Truganini warn them that her husband 'did not like *toogee*'.

Robinson was genuinely shocked to realise that his entire mission team—guides and convicts alike—believed that the purpose of their travails in this wet and wind-ravaged landscape was to capture the inhabitants. No one appeared to understand him when he reiterated that his friendly mission was to gain the confidence of the west coast clans. Taking captives had never been his intention, he told them. Then what was their task, his bemused companions may well have wondered, if not capture and removal? What other motivation could there be for making this insane expedition through barely penetrable wilderness?

Setting off up the coast in pursuit of his elusive quarry, Robinson left the convicts at his base camp, as well as Wooredy's two sons and Maulboyheener, who had been unable to cope physically with the rigours of the difficult terrain. Robinson, with Truganini, Dray, Wooredy, Pagerly, Kickerterpoller, Parewareter, Trepanner and Umarrah, proceeded northwards leaving Robert and the three boys behind with the convicts. They were pinned to the coast: on one side was impenetrable forest, and on the other side an ocean that stretched across the world from Africa to smash onto the land with frightening vehemence. Roiling waves broke onto the shore, creating huge hummocks of dun-coloured foam.

On 25 March, they encountered two Ninine men hunting beside the mouth of a wide river. Seemingly oblivious to Robinson, the men asked Dray whether there were *num* in her party. Reassured there were none, the hunters led the party a short way inland to a clearing with a fire pit. Some thirty people emerged out of the bush to extend a generous welcome. It seemed as if these people had never actually seen *num*, although Robinson could see they certainly knew of their existence, as they had many dogs, and had somehow acquired an axe.

The two groups held an exuberant corroboree well into the night, causing the dense forest to reverberate with their pounding feet and chanting. The tall, stately Ninine men were superb dancers, Robinson wrote admiringly, bounding from one position to another as they chanted, every part of the body in motion at the same time, even their eyes. Then Wooredy, Kickerterpoller and Umarrah danced in reciprocation. Robinson did not attempt to dance, but he was persuaded to play his flute.

Not only was Robinson obliged to perform, he was also obliged to share his accommodation. As the temperature plummeted and heavy rain saturated the ground, several men and their dogs crawled into his tent and under his blanket. They were packed in so tightly he could barely move. He knew that if he wanted their trust he could not protest against this intrusion and so lay awake, longing for daylight. Sunrise revealed his blanket and clothes to be covered with lice. Disgusted, he stepped out of his tent to find a young woman standing guard in the driving rain. She had been there all night, Dray later explained, to sound the alarm should he reach for the pistols in his knapsack. He was not pleased to hear that the Ninine knew about his guns. Truganini had probably told them. Silently wishing the firearms gone, he determined to never again take his guns with him on a search party.

When the wild weather cleared, the Ninine indicated they would swim across the river to move further up the coast. Against stern opposition from Wooredy, Robinson insisted his party must cross the river after them. None of the men, Robinson included, could swim. Wooredy constructed a narrow reed canoe that Truganini, Pagerly and Dray pushed across the river. Kicking their strong legs through the water, they returned time and time again, to ferry Robinson, his knapsack, his tent, and all the provisions. Begrudgingly, Wooredy agreed that the women could push him over on the canoe, and he was followed by Kickerterpoller. The last to cross was Umarrah, who had a terror of deep water.

Over the next four days they stuck close to the Ninine. All the men went hunting together, while the women dived off the rocks for abalone, or foraged for mushrooms and wild figs. When they were not hunting, the men meticulously decorated their bodies with feathers and ochre. Every night was spent in energetic corroboree. Robinson always played his flute, and while he did not join in the dances he did submit to having his face painted with ochre. The two groups formed an amicable fellowship, except for Wooredy, who grumbled to Robinson that these savage people would spear them all, or run away and leave them stranded. He pleaded with Robinson to take them captive and send them to Hobart. With evident scorn, Truganini interrupted, telling Robinson that her husband made 'too much talk' because he 'no like *toogee*'.

After the corroboree concluded on the fourth night, Robinson had no visitors in his tent and slept well. Waking at first light, he became painfully aware that the Ninine were stealthily moving away. Seeking an explanation from Dray, he learnt they feared Wooredy, who had stolen some of their spears. Also, Truganini had told them that Kickerterpoller and Umarrah had worked with roving parties capturing people in the east. Despite Dray's assurances to the contrary, her people had decided no one in the party was to be trusted. With his rations almost exhausted, Robinson knew there was no way to induce the people to stay. It was best to let them go, he decided, to 'shew them that my motives was pure and free of chicanery'. There would be another time.

Wooredy was having none of this high-minded talk about taking no captives. He was humiliated by Robinson's weakness in not asserting control over the Ninine. His vehemence puzzled Robinson, even though Kickerterpoller and Umarrah were just as resentful. As always, Robinson was oblivious to the implicit message he was giving these three men who considered themselves already to be captives. Captivity was the new order in which they lived. It was apparent to them that the convicts he left back at Kelly's Basin were also Robinson's captives. Why then would he not capture the Ninine?

From that point onwards, Robinson's daily journal entries detail a steady deterioration in his relationship with his male guides. He worried that his trusted companion Wooredy was about to abscond, while Kickerterpoller was no longer seen as compliant, instead described as 'innately wicked' for acting independently and walking off to hunt whenever it suited. Umarrah continued to appear a model of attentiveness until, a few weeks later, he coolly gathered his dogs and his companions, Parewareter and Trepanner, and disappeared into the forest, leaving Robinson almost apoplectic.

The disgruntled Wooredy was dispatched back to base camp at Bathurst Harbour to tell Alexander McKay to bring up Robert and the convicts as well as all the rations. He also carried instructions to the skipper of the *Swallow* to sail to Hobart with Maulboyheener and Wooredy's two young sons. When Wooredy returned with McKay, Robinson thought he was 'displeased', failing to gauge the emotional impact of his decision to separate the father from his children, and send them to a fate Wooredy could not possibly know. Seeing truculence rather than grief, Robinson directed Wooredy to go with McKay to fetch rations from the penal settlement on Sarah Island as well as medicine for the virulent skin infection he had caught from a Ninine man who shared his blanket. Truganini was also sent with McKay. Had Robinson been aware that McKay was having sex with Truganini, he would have kept her at his camp.

As long as Dray was with him, Robinson could nurture a hope of making a successful conciliation with her people. Leaving Kickerterpoller and Pagerly to wait with the convicts at the camp, he set off with Dray to walk up the coast. Soon they fell in with another group, all well known to Dray, and spent a night with them. Once again several men came to lie under Robinson's blankets, but on this occasion he slept soundly. He woke at dawn to find that everyone had disappeared, he was entirely alone. Dray was gone too. Thoroughly scared, he reflected that he had depended too much on her, 'for which the Lord was humbling me'.

Humbled indeed he was, as he struggled alone for days with his heavy pack, stumbling over sharp rocks and wading through chest-high streams, fearing being swept to a watery death at any moment. Should an escaped convict have come upon Robinson at this time he would have had difficulty making out what kind of man this was. He was half-starved, shoeless, wearing a tattered shirt and two hessian bags bound around his legs with bark. His skin was blackened with a mixture of gunpowder and urine he had applied to his horrible rash. The infection had glued his eyes till he was almost blind. It was fortunate that Truganini and Wooredy came across him as they were returning from Sarah Island.

Despite his pitiful condition, and his desertion by Dray, Robinson remained determined to continue up the coast. Kickerterpoller would be no help to him, as he did not know these people, and Wooredy was now resentful and belligerent. More than ever before, Robinson was dependent on Truganini. She made an effort to entice people she saw in the distance, but the suspicion that she herself had sown among them meant they kept well out of reach. It was Wooredy who managed to locate one small band by the mouth of a river. They had fled before Robinson and Truganini caught up, except for a lone man who remained on the hill above. He was anxiously watching his daughter, who had leapt into the sea in terror. She was being buffeted by huge waves smashing against the rocky outcrop to which she clung.

Over the din of the violent waves, Truganini implored the girl to come back to the *nyrae num*, but the girl was more afraid of Robinson than the rough sea. Plunging into the breakers, Truganini swam out and pulled her back to shore, where she stood quivering in such evident terror that Truganini could only retreat. The next day Truganini located the family again, and once again the daughter leapt into the sea to be dashed against the rocks, cutting open her breast. Truganini swam out again but this time could not induce the girl to return to shore.

Resigned to failure, Robinson continued up to the north-west corner, traversing a treeless coast indented with numerous sandy coves. Wooredy knew they were under surveillance but he only caught fleeting glimpses of any watchers. Nearing the mouth of the Arthur River, they had to walk through waist-high foam thrown up by the rush of fresh water into the sea. They could not see where to put their feet and kept tripping on driftwood logs that had been deposited by the river surge. These logs were ideal for constructing a raft, and on 10 June the party was able to cross the tannin-stained water, although the strong current made swimming the multiple crossings very arduous for Truganini and Pagerly.

Walking some short way inland on the north side of the river they saw the country was newly burnt and found substantial bark huts belonging to the Tarkiner people. On 12 June, Wooredy located fresh tracks that led him back to the shore, where he found an infant girl wrapped in a kangaroo skin and a boy aged about six with a skin over his shoulders. The boy was sobbing in distress, and was even more terrified by Robinson's attempts to amuse him with a lacquered box. From a hill above, Truganini observed a group of adults swimming out to a rocky island to hide. She ran down to the shore and dived into the ocean and swam out to persuade them to return to their children. A tall warrior came out of hiding to hurl large rocks at her until she withdrew. The best Robinson could do was wrap each of the children in a blanket and drape them with ribbons and baubles, to show the parents that his intentions were friendly. He hoped they would be more receptive the next time he came by.

By June they had entered the massive sheep runs of the Van Diemen's Land Company, which had been founded by a group of London merchants who had been granted a royal charter to more than 200,000 acres of hunting country to graze their sheep. Climbing to the top of Mount Cameron, Robinson could see the attraction of this remote corner. A broad plain of tussock grass had been created by burning, interspersed with small belts of tea-tree forest, which made it perfect for kangaroo—and for sheep. This country was not dissimilar to Bruny Island, although wilder and with a more exposed aspect. The extensive plateau stretched across to Cape Grim, where a majestic cliff rose abruptly from a sea dotted with an archipelago of grassy islands. This coastline, once home to tens of thousands of fur seals, was now almost denuded by the sealers, although the island still provided nesting sites for huge flocks of albatross that coated the cliffs with silver guano.

On reaching Cape Grim on 14 June, the mission party enjoyed the hospitality of Joseph Fossey, superintendent of the Van Diemen's Land Company establishment at Cape Grim. Fossey was most unusual among the colonists in that he had a high regard for the original people and was full of admiration for Robinson's project. These 'discordant qualities' put Fossey at odds with other company employees, most pointedly the company manager, Edward Curr, a callous pragmatist who believed that the continued existence of the original people on, or near, the Van Diemen's Land Company land was incompatible with the company's primary purpose of grazing sheep. He considered Robinson to be on a fool's errand and that the sooner the people were gone the better.

While the mission party was at Cape Grim, they heard terrible stories about the wanton killing of the local clans. One of the company shepherds blandly informed Robinson that two years earlier he and three others had shot an unarmed group of about thirty Pennemukeer and Pairelehoinner, who had gathered at Cape Grim to collect mutton birds. Their bodies had been thrown off the cliffs onto the rocks in retaliation for the killing of a large flock of the company's sheep. What was to be done, the shepherd plaintively enquired of Robinson, when the blacks kept spearing them and killing their sheep?

This massacre was not a singular act. The company employees openly boasted of their murderous intent towards the local people. Another shepherd told the wife of a sea captain, who visited the area in 1828, that they wished 'to extirpate them entirely'.

Confirmation of the Cape Grim massacre and other killings came from a Pairelehoinner youth Robinson met in the sealers' camp on nearby Robbins Island on 19 June. Peevay (also known as Tunnerminerwait) was aged about fifteen and well acquainted with the treachery and brutality of the *num*. As children, he and his three brothers had survived an ambush by sealers in 1820 in which all the adult men had been killed and seven women abducted, possibly including his mother. His father was probably a victim of either internecine warfare with other clans or the routine violence of Van Diemen's Land Company employees, which together decimated the clans of the north-west coast. Peevay had been driven into a dependency on the Van Diemen's Land Company, and was fraught with apprehension. He had learnt to speak English while working as a shepherd. For the past ten days he had been working with the sealers, who called him Jack. He suspected they intended to kill him.

Also at the camp were six women, all wearing cumbersome dresses made of kangaroo skins, with red caps pulled down to their eyebrows. One woman was from a local clan and the other five had been abducted from various clans from the east coast. These five threw themselves on Truganini in sheer joy at finding someone they could talk to. They were kept in such cruel conditions that Robinson determined to take them away. The sealers would not surrender the women, although they did allow Peevay to go, to his undisguised pleasure.

Robinson was very impressed with this industrious and capable young man and gave him special attention, spending hours learning his language and personal history. Recognising that a dependency on Robinson was a more promising prospect than the Van Diemen's Land Company, Peevay demonstrated his loyalty by informing Robinson that his brother Pendowtewer and a Peerapper youth named Nicermenic were still living on Robbins Island. Robinson was very keen to get them, rationalising to himself that it would be 'the greatest act of humanity to take them out of the hands of their enemies'.

Peevay was sent back to Robbins Island by boat to locate Pendowtewer and Nicermenic, as well as two others, to assure them of Robinson's goodness and persuade them to join the mission. Actually, Robinson had no intention of keeping these people with him as they were superfluous to his needs and would have to be supplied with rations. They were worth money. Thanks to the bounty the governor had just introduced for any people captured alive, he would be paid five pounds a head. All he had to do was keep them with him till they reached the port at Emu Bay. This, too, he regarded as a great act of kindness.

Before leaving Cape Grim on 25 June, Robinson gave a special dinner in his tent in appreciation of Fossey's generous hospitality. The storekeeper and other company employees were invited, as were the two couples: Wooredy and Truganini, and Kickerterpoller and Pagerly. For the occasion, Truganini and Pagerly wore shapeless smocks made from blankets, whereas Wooredy and Kickerterpoller 'looked remarkably well' in the smart red jackets and cream trousers that had been gifts from the commandant of the penal station at Sarah Island. Dinner consisted of roast duck and mutton, accompanied by giblet pie, potatoes, vegetables and plum pudding, with rum and port wine to follow. It was a far cry from the privations of the previous six months.

After a round of spirits, Truganini and her friends sang for Fossey, who was greatly impressed and much taken with the flirtatious Truganini. 'I often think of her singular expression respecting me,' he wrote to Robinson a few days later. 'Could I meet with one as faithful as she is to you—black or white—it might work a great change in me: an evening companion would be exceedingly agreeable . . .' Fossey's use of the phrase 'an evening companion' was highly ambiguous. Robinson would certainly have been affronted at any suggestion that his relationship with Truganini was anything more than paternal.

The headquarters of the Van Diemen's Land Company was on the north coast at Circular Head. From here Edward Curr commanded a sweeping view dominated by the stump of an old volcano eroded over millennia to produce bold, steep-sided bluffs that rose five hundred feet out of the sea. Curr was icily polite to Robinson, offering him a room at his house, which Robinson declined, preferring to pitch his tent among the bark huts his guides erected near the jetty. He did accept invitations to dine with Curr. On these occasions his fellow diners did not include any of his 'sable companions'.

It was at Circular Head that Wooredy received the first news of his sons since they had been sent away four months earlier. Letters received from Mrs Robinson, written in April and early May, reported that Maulboyheener and Wooredy's sons had arrived safely from Bathurst Harbour and were living in the annex of her house in Hobart. The two older boys, Maulboyheener and Myunge (she called them Jemmy and Davey), were to be admitted to the Orphan School.

She also reported that Maulboyheener's mother had left her house by the time her son arrived, having been released from detention by order of the governor. Together with Umarrah's wife and four other women living in the annex, she had left Hobart on 18 March by bullock cart, guarded by two constables. The six women had been taken to Launceston jail, and kept there for ten days—on the advice of John Batman who had originally captured several of the women—before being released into the bush. The hope was that they would find any clan members who still remained and persuade them to surrender. This came as unwelcome news to Robinson, yet by some mysterious process his guides had already learnt this some two months earlier, precipitating Umarrah's abrupt departure from the west coast in mid May. By now, Umarrah had found his way over the Western Tiers, taking the migratory routes from the west coast to the ochre mines of the Surrey Hills, into his own country, where he was reunited with his wife.

On reaching the port at Emu Bay at the beginning of August, Pendowtewer and Nicermenic were put aboard the Van Diemen's Land Company ship bound for Launceston, to be forwarded to the governor in Hobart. Peevay was distraught as he watched the ship weigh anchor and the wind fill its sails. 'With them had fled his hopes,' Robinson observed as the tears streamed down Peevay's anguished face. Robinson himself could not help but be moved by this heart-wrenching scene, noting that 'the affection of these people is very striking'. He was quick to find a self-justifying rationale: the Peerapper and Pairelehoinner people were now so few in number that to leave these two youths in their country would expose them to the dangers of being shot by a shepherd or speared by hostile clans on the west coast. Sending them into the care of the governor was the most humane thing to do.

Robinson was therefore greatly annoyed to discover the men never made it to Hobart. After languishing in the horrid Launceston jail, Pendowtewer was released back into his country by order of the governor, and it was years before he was caught again. Nicermenic was stolen from the jail by John Helger Wedge, the assistant surveyor. The previous year, he had kidnapped Nicermenic's younger brother from the west coast and kept him as a kind of household pet, known to the settlers as 'Wedge's boy'. When the boy died in August 1830, Wedge came to the Launceston jail and simply took Nicermenic away, together with two brothers, Lacklay and Merape. Within weeks, the three had escaped and were raiding around Port Sorrell, including robbing a sealer's boat.

Lacklay and Merape were recaptured and sent to Robinson on 21 September, while Nicermenic remained at large for another year. Lacklay and Merape were closely connected to Peevay's clan and spoke the same language. Their arrival at Robinson's camp at Port Sorrell comforted Peevay, who was still bitterly grieving the loss of his brother and friend. The very next day he ran away with them, only to be captured by a roving party four days later. It was a hard lesson for Peevay, one he learnt well. In the Launceston jail he refused to escape with the other two, hoping that Robinson would free him and extend his protection once more. Robinson did just that when his exhausted party limped into Launceston in early October.

CHAPTER 3

SIX HUNDRED MILES of trekking through rugged country had taken a huge physical toll on Truganini. Her legs were now so swollen that she could barely walk. As they approached the town of Launceston, Wooredy had to carry her heavy bundle as well as his own. Their epic trek was a remarkable achievement, but no one in Launceston was about to hand out any accolades; the town bristled with hostility.

The whole colony was now under martial law and the burghers of Launceston were gearing up to rid the island of whoever remained of the original owners. They were not of a mind to make any exceptions for Truganini and her companions, who were all on the point of being thrown into jail to join the despondent Peevay when George Whitcomb, the clerk of customs, came to their rescue. Whitcomb was shocked to see Robinson's emaciated state and very concerned for his vulnerable guides. He took them all to live at his house, out of harm's way.

In the first days of October 1830, the town was beginning to resemble an armed camp. The governor had decreed that every able-bodied male—settler and convict—was required to muster into a militia. Reinforced by three military regiments, they would form a human chain and march south, converging with another human chain moving eastwards from Hobart Town. This pincer movement—known as the Black Line—would push all the original people of the colony onto the narrow Tasman Peninsula, where they would be captured and removed from the colony. The word on many lips was extirpation, an antiquated term from the Middle Ages that meant to pull something up by the roots; it had come to mean 'destroy totally', or exterminate, and was usually applied to unwanted animals, such as wolves or vermin.

The colonial bureaucracy was totally absorbed with minute preparations for this preposterous manoeuvre and almost every settler had caught the scent of adventure. In such excitement, Robinson's epic mission of conciliation was almost completely ignored. No matter where he turned, all he heard was talk of 'the extirpation of the original inhabitants', he complained in a letter to his wife. He thought the Black Line was morally indefensible, logistically absurd, and that it would never work. No one paid him the slightest heed. Only the sardonic editor of the *Colonial Times* thought the venture was ludicrous, reminding readers that 'the colony was even more mountainous than the highlands of Scotland'—given such terrain, he opined, 'the folly of the undertaking must be apparent'. It was not.

Robinson did manage a hasty meeting with the distracted governor to secure a second mission to the north-east corner of the island, to locate any remnant clans in that region. Sightings between Pipers River and Cape Portland had fed fanciful rumours among the hypervigilant settlers that as many as seven hundred people might still be at large in that region.

As the Black Line began a cumbersome sweep southwards, Robinson set off in the opposite direction. Privately, he discounted the large number of claimed sightings—he doubted there were more than fifty original people in the whole eastern half of the island. No matter how many there were, he wanted to get to them before they were caught up in the Black Line.

Now that the governor's priorities had changed from conciliating the original people to removing them from the colony, Robinson's mission was no longer a friendly meet-and-greet. His instructions were to make contact with the remaining people and get them to accompany him to the coast. He was then to signal to John Batman, who would be waiting with an armed party and boats at Spring Bay, to come and take them away. That was never going to happen; Robinson loathed John Batman and deeply resented the fact that the governor had given this ruffian equal authority to Robinson.

For the past two years, Batman had been in charge of roving parties tracking the Plangermairener clan of Ben Lomond and the Pyemairenerpairnener clan from the Pipers River region, who were implicated in occasional attacks on stockkeepers. His method was to launch surprise night attacks on their camps, killing as many men and youths as he could. Women and young children were the only captives his roving parties turned over to the authorities, although some of the boy children he kept for himself. Like his friend John Helder Wedge, Batman liked to have boys living with him. Terrible stories about Batman's unbridled violence had reached Robinson in December 1829 when he rescued Batman's women captives and their children from brutal conditions in jail.

No way was Robinson going to allow a murderous lout like Batman into his operation. He had formed an alternative plan, which was to create a temporary holding station on Swan Island, just off the north-east tip of Van Diemen's Land, where he would contain all the people he could find. He kept this plan for capture and confinement close to his chest, telling nobody.

The mission party consisted of Truganini and Wooredy, a chastened Peevay, finally sprung from jail, as well as Truganini's friend Pagerly and her husband Kickerterpoller. Truganini and Wooredy were Robinson's closest associates, yet even they had no idea of his true reason for tramping around the north-east. All they knew was that being with Robinson kept them safe and allowed them to continue their nomadic life.

Robinson took the view that the authority granted him by the governor extended to the sealers' captives on the Bass Strait islands. To facilitate the removal of these women—known to the clans of the north-east as Tyreelore—he co-opted James Parish, a former sealer, to be the boatswain for one of the whaleboats attached to his mission. Parish was sent to Preservation Island, where he found his one-time compatriots defiant. They would never relinquish their captives, they told him; they had just as much right to the women as the governor did. In any case, most of the women were hidden in the bush on nearby Cape Barren Island, where Parish would never find them.

John Brown was one sealer who did agree to surrender one of the three Tyreelore he held: Tanleboneyer, a woman in her mid twenties who had been taken from Oyster Bay. And James Munro relinquished one of his four slaves: Bullyer, aged about nineteen, whom he had stolen from Cape Portland when she was a small child. Parish also secured the release of an old woman named Ghonyennener, who ran away as soon as they reached her country at Pipers River. Tanleboneyer and Bullyer became part of Robinson's mission. Having been with the sealers for a decade or more, they could provide a wealth of information about this renegade community.

The stories they told were grim, describing a life marked by extreme brutality and privation. In addition to their continual sexual violation, and being traded between the men for sealskins, they were forced into the dangerous and exhausting work of hunting seals and skinning them, as well as catching and plucking albatross and mutton birds. Bullyer stretched out her arms to show how the sealers tied women to trees to 'flog them very much, plenty much blood, plenty cry'. More than a dozen lashes of a rawhide whip was a common punishment for taking the hardtack biscuits or sugar, she explained. Any woman who failed to club enough seals or catch enough birds could be cruelly mutilated, or even killed. Life was so dreadful that pregnant women often aborted the child by beating on their belly, as Bullyer herself had done. Others took their infants into the bush to kill them when the men were not around. Sometimes it was the men who did the grisly deed.

For almost as long as Bullyer could remember, this had been her life. She retained a distant memory of being with her clan on the beach at Cape Portland when a group of men rushed their fire, shooting and grabbing. Motherless, and too small to run quickly into the bush, she had been caught by James Munro and had been with him ever since. Six women were taken in that one attack, just as her mother and other kinswomen had been stolen a few years earlier. How many were still alive, Bullyer could not say, but she knew her mother was living with one of the sealers on Kangaroo Island. Bullyer sang the mournful song of the Tyreelore in their island captivity. She explained the meaning of the words so Robinson could copy it down in a rough translation.

Country
You see it
You are going to the country
Go away to it.

Bullyer and Tanleboneyer also performed what Robinson called 'the devil dance', which was much the same as the dance he had seen women perform in the sealers' camps on Robbins Island in the north-west. Here was evidence that women from different language groups were being traded between these far-flung groups of men. Curious about the devil for whom they danced, Robinson asked what they had been taught of Christian belief. The women pointed to the heavens, telling him that the Christian God stopped up in the sky, and his enemy stopped below, at which they pointed to the blue flame flickering in the fire. They were very precise that they danced for a black man who 'stopped in the bush and was very strong'. They danced to keep him distracted, to deflect his dangerous desires. Truganini recognised that they danced for Raegewarrah, even though Tanleboneyer spoke the name in a language she did not understand.

Tanleboneyer and Bullyer had news for Truganini about her sisters, Lowhenune and Magerleede, who had been stolen from Bruny Island by the sealer known as Black Baker. Her sisters were alive, they told her, although the third woman Baker had stolen had been killed. More disheartening was the news that Baker had traded her sisters to a sealer on distant Kangaroo Island, well out of reach of the colonial authorities.

For several leisurely days the mission party travelled through the grassy plains of the north-east coast. This region had attracted no settlement and Robinson recognised it was country 'well suited to the natives'. Evidence of their management of the landscape was there for Robinson to see every day, as he traversed large tracts of recently burnt country, some trees still smouldering. Surveying the immense grassy plain and occasional borders of forest through his European lens, he did not see a landscape carefully constructed by thousands of years of controlled burning; he saw a countryside ready-made for cattle to graze and perfect for horseriding. Wooredy's expert eye recognised a landscape that had been purposely made for kangaroo, and he relished the opportunity to hunt the big boomer kangaroos that were everywhere in abundance in this region.

Compared to her arduous trek to the south-west and up the west coast, Truganini had an easy time in the north-east corner. The simple canoes that Wooredy made from long strips of bark bound together with vines were relatively easy for her to push across the numerous rivers they crossed. The ground they walked was mostly level. Game was plentiful, the late spring sunshine was pleasantly warm. The coastal heath was in full bloom and the people decorated their hair with flowers, adding bird feathers and red ochre for the nightly dances. Sitting around the fire, Kickerterpoller and Peevay vied good-naturedly with Wooredy to recount the pugnacious exploits of their respective clans. Robinson watched and listened, taking notes by the flickering light. Even the tormenting swarm of mosquitoes feasting on his fair skin failed to diminish his pleasure in this bucolic adventure.

There was great excitement early one morning when a feral dog was seen running past their bark shelters carrying a small marsupial in its jaws. The people all agreed that the dog was taking food for her pups and were anxious to find her den, but Robinson insisted they move on. Crunching over the spiky, scorched ground, they sighted two more wild dogs. This time Kickerterpoller sprinted after them, shouting to his companions to help catch the animals. Robinson angrily called them back, remonstrating that 'it was blacks I wanted, not dogs'.

They reached the east coast at Cape Naturaliste, a little south of Cape Portland, on 19 October. There was no sign of the people, although wide patches of scorched vegetation provided evidence of their recent presence. From the highest point in the landscape they could see spirals of smoke from several cooking fires at

Cape Portland. Bullyer urged the party to press on, insisting that once her people had eaten they would move on again. She alone felt the urgency—everyone else wanted to stop to enjoy the bounty that Truganini and Pagerly brought up from the ocean floor.

After feasting on cooked crayfish and abalone, the party walked north along the beach a short way to reach the inlet of the Musselroe River. On this exquisite piece of coast, the river formed an elongated lagoon behind the beach that was home to huge flocks of ducks and pelicans. In the middle, the water was almost covered with floating swans' nests. Truganini and the other three women swam out to them, taking about a hundred eggs. Somewhat doubtful at first, Robinson tried one and pronounced it very good. Still it was not his intention to camp at that place, despite the vast food resources on offer.

Later that day, they reached Little Musselroe Bay, where a river inlet had formed a smaller separate lagoon behind, also well stocked with ducks' and swans' nests. Here they would make base camp, Robinson announced. The place was gorgeous. Between the lagoon and the sea, a curve of dazzling sand was contained by jagged pink and grey granite boulders. A short distance across the clear turquoise water was the low outline of tiny Swan Island and, beyond, the high peaks of distant Flinders Island were faintly visible rising above the dark blue horizon.

The choice to make camp in such close proximity to Swan Island was of no particular significance to Truganini. What she could see was a sheltered place with an abundant supply of delectable things. The ocean offered up abalone, oysters and crayfish for easy taking. Exceptionally large mussels could be plucked from the river inlet, while dozens of floating nests cradled swan eggs. Beyond the lagoon, new shoots pushing through the burnt ground fed many kangaroos that bounded away in every direction.

She and her companions had this veritable paradise all to themselves; there were no settlers for many miles around. Visible shell middens several feet deep indicated this had been a feasting site for clans of the north-east for thousands of years, yet there was no sign of people anywhere in the vicinity.

Bullyer was correct to warn that her kinfolk would move on quickly. She looked in vain for more smoke. On the second day, Robinson took Kickerterpoller to walk across Cape Portland to Ringarooma Bay in order to make contact with the coxswains of the two whaleboats, James Parish and Alexander McKay, so he could increase the range of the search. As they walked, Kickerterpoller found fresh tracks in the burnt ground he said belonged to one small group of maybe five or six people, but no one was seen and there was no smoke.

A glorious sunny day presented them with a grand vista of headland and sea that Robinson thought was 'altogether the finest country I have ever seen'. There was not a cloud in the sky, yet suddenly the view before them darkened, as if a storm were approaching. Overhead the sun was blocked by a vast mass of migratory mutton birds returning from the Bering Strait between Siberia and Alaska to their burrows in the Bass Strait islands. For almost two hours they watched this continuous stream and still the birds had not passed. Robinson had never seen anything like it.

After locating McKay and Parish, Robinson instructed them to sail around the coast to look for smoke from fires. Eight days later their boats pulled into Little Musselroe Bay with no sightings to report. McKay was told to sail to Hobart to take reports to the governor, and Parish was left in charge of the base camp, while Robinson and his guides walked south to the Bay of Fires. The reluctant Truganini was only persuaded to go on with the promise that Parish would bring his whaleboat to take them back.

For three days, they travelled over the soft sand and rocky points of the scalloped coastline till they reached the mouth of the George River. Scorched shell middens were everywhere, evidence of generations of occupation, with no indication that anyone had been on the coast in recent years. The adjoining bush had not been burnt for several seasons and there were no tracks. Robinson believed the fear of predatory sealers was keeping the people away. Then, to Truganini's dismay, he announced they would have to walk inland to find them. Having been induced to accompany him on the promise they would return by boat, she was exceedingly put out and complained bitterly that her legs were too painful to walk any further. This familiar complaint did her no good. No boat was coming and they would all have to walk.

As small compensation, Robinson allowed Truganini to dive for crayfish. Suddenly catching sight of smoke in the distance, he refused to let the people stay to cook her catch. With only damper in their bellies, and each carrying a heavy knapsack, they walked along the eastern edge of a high range known to the settlers as the Blue Tier. Tramping up and down gullies, they pushed through dense pockets of slippery rainforest of giant moss-covered myrtle trees and towering tree ferns, every step precarious. Then it began to pour with rain.

Crossing into drier, open bushland, they found that even in the rain, grass fires were still burning, which had the double benefit of reassuring them they were on the right track as well as keeping them warm. The exhausted party finally made camp for the night and cooked the crayfish, hoping the smoke of the smouldering bush would camouflage their cooking fire.

Pushing north-west at daylight on the first day of November, they noticed that all the big trees had recently been stripped of bark and footprints were visible in the wet ground. Tanleboneyer had developed a hacking cough, so Robinson made her drop well behind the party lest she give their position away. The others were commanded to strip off any clothing and drop onto their bellies to crawl forwards. Wisps of smoke were issuing from a long bark hut, which was surrounded by many large, fierce-looking dogs.

Detecting movement, the people inside the hut fled into the bush while the dogs remained on guard, perfectly quiet, apparently reassured by the dark naked bodies of the approaching people. Inside the hut they found spears, waddies and red ochre scattered about. A kangaroo was cooking on the fire, a sure sign, they told Robinson when he joined them, that the occupants would not have gone far.

Bullyer and Kickerterpoller were from the same language group and they walked into the bush calling out in reassuring tones. Quite soon they got an answer: a naked man appeared before them. He was strong and muscular but no longer young, with much scarification on his ochre-stained body and an impressive mop of ochre-coloured hair. Watching from the entrance to the hut, Robinson did not fully appreciate the significance of what he was seeing. Bullyer and Kickerterpoller were speaking with the most powerful man on the east coast: Mannalargenna, the legendary leader of the Trawlwoolway clan.

An awesome warrior and cleverman, Mannalargenna was gifted with special ways of knowing. After victories in rolling wars with clans from the midlands and central plateau, he was believed to be physically invincible. He had been skilfully evading Robinson ever since the mission party arrived at Pipers River. He knew about Robinson because he had recently travelled with two of the women sent from Robinson's house in Hobart the year before. They had told him this man represented his best chance in country that was crawling with armed settlers of murderous intent. Now it was time to parley.

Robinson approached to present the stranger with the usual baubles, and was clasped in a powerful, aromatic embrace. Mannalargenna then called his four companions, presenting Robinson with two young warriors and his close ally, Trowlebunner, leader of the Plangermairener clan from Ben Lomond. The old woman Ghonyennener, who had run away at Pipers River, was there as well.

Anxious to remove these five people, Robinson told Bullyer to explain that he had come to save them from the imminent danger of hundreds of soldiers and that they should go with him. To illustrate the threat, Robinson traced a line in the ground to indicate the Black Line, and impress upon them that they could not afford to linger in that place a moment longer. Mannalargenna and Trowlebunner did not need the visual aids. After years of debilitating conflict with the interlopers, they understood the determination of the settlers to wipe them out. And they were already well aware of the Black Line.

A few weeks before, these people had been part of a much larger group from the midland and north-east clans, travelling across country to the central plateau to do battle with their traditional enemies, the Lairmairermener, known to settlers as the Big River people. Returning, battle-scarred from the fight, they had encountered a detachment of soldiers travelling northwards to join the Black Line. The soldiers had shot three of them dead. Retribution had followed swiftly: two soldiers were speared to death as they sat by the campfire. Further eastwards, the war party witnessed the Black Line in progress. The sight of this armed phalanx caused great alarm. In order to penetrate the line more easily, the people agreed to separate into several smaller groups. Mannalargenna's party had slipped through the line on two separate occasions. He had been watching Robinson for weeks, and in a desperate gamble had finally allowed Robinson to make contact. He wasn't just looking for protection, he wanted to make a deal. Using Bullyer to interpret, he outlined his grievances against the sealers.

Mannalargenna had a long and turbulent history with the sealers. When these strange men first arrived, he had seen the potential of incorporating the interlopers into his tribal power base. Trading sealskins for flour, tea, sugar and dogs, he had established a good relationship with them, and allowed women to go with the sealers for a season to harvest seals on the many islands in the Bass Strait. Seeking to bind the sealers to him, Mannalargenna had encouraged reciprocal obligations and involved them in tribal life. In 1810, he arranged for his eldest daughter, Woretemoeteyenner, to marry the dominant sealer, George Briggs, seeing this as a way of cementing the obligations. Briggs and his compatriots were not interested in reciprocity, and by 1816 Briggs had reneged. The sealers took to stealing rather than trading. What had been a seasonal relationship became a lifetime of slavery for most of the women of the north-east. Sealers now held his four daughters and his sister, who was Trowlebunner's wife.

Humiliated and betrayed, Mannalargenna sought revenge on the sealers and he wanted his daughters returned. He agreed to go with Robinson only if his conditions could be met. Robinson led him to understand that if the group came with him right away, he would take Mannalargenna to negotiate with the governor. Furthermore, he promised he would personally go to all the islands in the Bass Strait to recover the captive women and return them to their country. Having extracted these promises, Mannalargenna and Trowlebunner agreed to leave then and there, even though one other man and a woman were still hidden in the bush, and another group that included Trowlebunner's sister and her husband were away at the coast.

Setting off with the five new people and their twenty-three dogs, Robinson was mightily pleased with himself. Writing up the episode in his journal, he was awash with self-congratulation: 'no guns; no tying of hands; no shooting of men; and to think that I was the means of saving the lives of these unprotected natives'. The newcomers sang, laughed and chatted, one of them unerringly leading the way north-east as Robinson checked his direction on the compass. Although the party was moving at a rapid pace, the men would not be deterred from going after the big kangaroos. They hunted as if they were starving. Soon everyone in the party was walking with a dead kangaroo draped over a shoulder and still the men hunted, leaving the dead animals displayed on fallen trees for their absent companions to find.

Truganini was delighted to be accompanying these strapping male warriors, unlike the truculent Wooredy, who never liked men from other clans around his young wife. He was extremely apprehensive about them and complained to Robinson that the strangers were permitted to carry their spears. Robinson dismissed his concern. He was less afraid of being speared by Mannalargenna and his group than of their disappearing, taking Bullyer, Tanleboneyer and possibly Truganini with them.

By the time they reached Ansons River, Truganini was exhausted and protesting she could not take another step. Several fires were kindled to cook the weighty kangaroos they had been carrying. While they cooked, Mannalargenna's people painted their bodies with a mixture of red ochre and grease. That night, they performed a series of narrative dances that told of their amorous exploits and the recent military excursion against the Lairmairermener people. Most impressive was the story of Trowlebunner outrunning a settler with a whip who was chasing him on horseback. One of the male dancers bent down on all fours while another leant against his back, and together they pranced around the fire in a mock gallop, while a third man used a branch to make them go faster. Beside them, another man ran on all fours, stopping, then starting again, and shaking his head. The dancers' exquisite mimicry—recreating the horse, the whip-wielding driver and even the yapping dog—caused great hilarity.

At dawn the next day, the party was startled by a sharp crack in the distance. Although Robinson privately thought it was probably a tree limb breaking off, he was quick to announce it as musket fire. Feigning terror, he said the soldiers of the Black Line were approaching and if they did not get going they would all be shot. His performance was effective. Everyone took off at a rapid pace, with not one of the many dogs making the slightest noise. Robinson was astonished by the skilled control the people had over their fierce dogs, and he was equally astonished when a man and a woman stepped out of the bush to join them. They had been silently following, without being detected. Robinson could now see why he had been so unsuccessful in tracking this group, but stopped short of reaching the logical conclusion that Mannalargenna had deliberately enticed him into finding them.

Observing their skill in negotiating this unoccupied country, Robinson was moved to lament the 'unfortunate circumstances that prevented them from the peaceful enjoyment of this useless tract of land, so well suited to them'. Those unfortunate circumstances included the whaleboat he was pushing them towards, in which he intended to carry them away from this land that suited them so well.

A cone-shaped hill known as Mount Direction loomed out of the plain in front of them. At the sight of it, Truganini pleaded fatigue once again, asking that they stop to make camp for the night. Robinson dared not take the risk of Mannalargenna and his group slipping away at night, so he allowed Truganini and the others to take the less arduous route around the base, while he and Peevay climbed up and over. Scanning the landscape from the summit, Robinson was reassured to see that his camp was close by, with Parish's whaleboat waiting for them. He had had no intention of telling anyone about this boat, but Peevay couldn't wait to reveal what he had seen at the beach. As the party approached the coast, the newcomers grew uneasy and hung back in the bush. Kickerterpoller had to stay behind to persuade them they had nothing to fear, and eventually led them into the camp.

Rain and wind delayed the crossing to Swan Island and Robinson was in a lather of anxiety that Mannalargenna's people would leave. He pressed baubles and blankets on them to keep them close. His masterstroke was to issue them with clothing. 'Trousers is excellent things and confines their legs so they cannot run,' he wrote with satisfaction. The rain stopped and Truganini began to pull up the marram grasses she used to weave baskets, causing the strangers to shout abuse and gesticulate that she would make the rain come again. Indulgently dismissive of such foolish superstition, Robinson closed his eyes and sent up his own prayers for fine weather.

After a sleepless night of anxious watching lest his prize slip away, Robinson was much encouraged to have his prayers answered when the sun rose on a clear bright day with only a light breeze. Telling everyone to put on their trousers and follow him, he walked to the whaleboat and climbed in. Truganini and Wooredy dutifully followed, then the other guides took their seats in the boat, giving verbal encouragement to the five newcomers, who followed suit. Had Mannalargenna and Trowlebunner known Robinson was lying to them, and that his plan was for them to stay on the island, they would never have been so compliant. Having made a deal, they trusted him to keep it.

Once everyone was seated, Parish launched the boat for Swan Island. Flushed with success, Robinson cast himself as the antipodean Caesar: 'Here was no force, no violence, no tying of hands, no muskets, etc. I said come and they came, go and they went.' A second trip in the whaleboat two days later brought their new blankets, as well as their twenty-three dogs.

After landing his unwitting captives on Swan Island, Robinson was hugely relieved that he would no longer have to keep constant watch over them. There was nowhere they could disappear to. Swan Island was little more than an accretion of sandhills covered with bracken and coarse grass, providing a nesting habitat for seabirds and penguins. The island possessed the initial attraction of a deposit of high-grade red ochre that the people could use to decorate their bodies and hair, but little else.

Truganini and Wooredy were delighted by the profusion of penguins, and set about pulling the birds out of the burrows to snatch the eggs, only to discover that the whole island was infested with venomous tiger snakes that also hunted for eggs. Truganini was frightened almost out of her wits when she stepped on a snake. Then she dived for crayfish and was driven out of the water by a large shark. This was not an auspicious sign. Truganini knew that nothing happened without a purpose. She had seen a relative eaten by a shark off Recherche Bay and knew it was the work of Raegewarrah. She took an intense dislike to this new place, but even for such a strong swimmer, Musselroe Bay was a daunting distance away, with a treacherous current running through the channel between.

It was soon obvious to everyone that Swan Island was no place to stay, even for a limited time. The groundwater proved to be unhealthy, and for several days the powerful westerly winds known as the Roaring Forties buffeted the island, sending up clouds of sandy grit that caused nasty inflammation of the eyes. It was an ominous beginning for the new life Robinson envisaged for the original owners of the land across the water. 'The fresh natives seemed not disposed to mirth,' he noted in his journal during the first evening on Swan Island. All night long his sleep was disturbed by the sound of a woman wailing.

Five days later, the gale-force winds finally dropped and McKay arrived with the second whaleboat, allowing Robinson to get away. Leaving McKay in charge, he set off with Parish on 9 November to fulfil his promise to visit the sealers on various islands and recover their captives, taking Bullyer with him to act as intermediary.

When smoke was seen across the water at Musselroe Bay on 15 November, Trowlebunner identified it as a signal from his sister and her husband, who was leader of the Pyemairenerpairnener people from Pipers River. A fire was kindled to return the signal, and McKay was persuaded that personal contact must be made before the Pyemairenerpairnener would go away again. He agreed to let Wooredy, Peevay, Kickerterpoller and Pagerly take the boat back to Musselroe Bay. Truganini, he kept close to hand.

At the sight of the approaching boat, the people at Musselroe Bay fled into the adjoining bushland. Kickerterpoller stepped ashore and strode up the beach, calling out, and was surprised when a woman ran out to greet him as if he were her long-lost son. It was Luggenemeener, the mother of Maulboyheener, and in a way Kickerterpoller did represent the next best thing to her lost son. She and Maulboyheener had lived with Kickerterpoller at Robinson's house in Hobart and she had not seen her son since he left with Kickerterpoller on the mission to the west coast in January. She did not know whether he was alive or dead.

Kickerterpoller had little information to give her, only that Maulboyheener had been sent to Hobart in March and arrived at Robinson's house soon after his mother had been returned to her country. He had run away to find her and that was the last anyone had heard of him. Kickerterpoller explained that the boat belonged to Robinson, and that her brother Trowlebunner, as well as Mannalargenna, were with him on Swan Island. Reassured, Luggenemeener called her husband, Woreternaterlargner, who came out of hiding with their eldest son, a youth named Tillabunner, and three other young warriors.

Tillabunner had previously been captured by Batman and forced to act as a guide for roving parties who called him Mungo or Batman's Jack. He spoke good English and explained that they were the last of the Pyemairenerpairnener clan. They had recently lost another two men, shot by soldiers from the Black Line. Eager for the temporary protection that Kickerterpoller promised them, the five people clambered into the whaleboat with their seven dogs, landing on Swan Island just as Robinson returned in the second boat with Bullyer, who was also of their clan, and three Tyreelore he had emancipated from the sealers.

After a joyful reunion, Luggenemeener had the miserable task of telling Bullyer that the brothers with whom she was so keen to be reunited were both dead, one of them shot by soldiers only days before. With this awful news, a haunting, aching sorrow swept through the camp. Bullyer's anguish for her dead brothers became everyone's anguish for a dead brother, son, father, mother, sister or daughter, and the inconsolable pain of being the survivor. Everyone wept without restraint. Robinson was so moved by this spontaneous outpouring of awful grief that he wept too. He wept for the terrible cruelties visited upon this 'unbefriended and hapless people' and for what they had not yet fully comprehended: the irrevocable loss of their country.

One of the three women Robinson had rescued from the sealers was Toogernupertooner, Mannalargenna's sister, the wife of Trowlebunner. Her emancipation from the sealers was a significant sign that Robinson would deliver on his promises. Even though Robinson had not yet managed to rescue any of his daughters, Mannalargenna was gratified to see that Robinson's hatred of the sealers was as implacable as his own. He was insistent that Robinson must immediately go back to the outer island and get them.

Robinson had more pressing considerations. There was no longer enough food to be found on Swan Island for the twenty-three people and their thirty dogs, as well as the convict boat crews, two coxswains and Robinson himself. The penguins, the eggs and the small game had all been eaten, and while the mutton birds had arrived in great profusion there was a limit to how many of these greasy, malodorous birds the convicts would tolerate. On 16 November, Parish was sent to Launceston for much-needed supplies.

It was now starkly apparent to Robinson that Swan Island would not work as 'a proper means of confinement' and that the people he had enticed onto the island would rebel against it soon enough. For the moment they seemed content, eating mutton birds and spending their days painstakingly grinding ochre. They mixed the powder with smelly oil from the birds to make a carrot-coloured grease with which to groom their hair and paint their bodies for the nightly dances. After adding charcoal, they also rubbed the mixture into the incisions they cut in their chest and shoulders. Robinson doubted he could keep them so occupied for very much longer.

He permitted Wooredy, Kickerterpoller and Peevay to take some of the dogs over to Musselroe Bay to hunt kangaroo. They returned with a kangaroo apiece and news that they had seen smoke from fires to the south-west. Luggenemeener confirmed that this smoke was likely a signal from another group of the original war party, mainly Tyerrerontepanner people from the northern midlands. Robinson considered sending Luggenemeener to make contact, but she insisted her husband come too, which made Robinson suspicious. Fearing they would run away, he ruled that none of 'the fresh people' were to leave the island.

Ten days had passed since Parish had gone to Launceston and he had still not returned with supplies. The mutinous convicts were bilious from the monotonous diet of mutton birds and were ravenous for meat and flour. Peevay was so seriously ill that amulets taken from bodies of the dead were fastened to his slender body. It was with a huge sigh of relief that Robinson sighted Parish's boat on 27 November.

Better even than the food supplies and medicine, Parish brought intelligence that the military commandant in Launceston, who had so rudely dismissed Robinson's mission, was now praising him for having achieved what thousands on the Black Line had completely failed to do. Robinson was cock-a-hoop to receive a formal letter of congratulations, conveying news that the Black Line had been ignominiously disbanded. After seven weeks of scrambling through the bush in a disorganised fashion, 1650 settlers and convicts, together with 550 soldiers, had managed to capture just one old man and a boy, while Robinson and his guides had obtained custody of fifteen, mostly adult warriors.

Barely containing his glee, he penned self-congratulatory reports to the commandant and the colonial secretary. McKay was rowed to Musselroe Bay with instructions to walk to Launceston and personally deliver these missives. Robinson was pleased to have this excuse to get McKay away from the island, having finally discovered that the man was having sexual relations with Truganini. In the longer term, Robinson determined to get rid of this degenerate and insubordinate convict once and for all.

Robinson was careful not to let news of the end of the Black Line spill to his unwitting captives, for fear they would demand to be returned to their country. Within days of arriving on the island, Mannalargenna had made a very satisfactory match with Tanleboneyer but now he was increasingly restive at being confined to Swan Island with no news of his daughters. To placate the great man, Parish was dispatched to the Bass Strait islands to negotiate with the sealers once more.

Occasional sightings of smoke to the south-west continued to torment Robinson, who calculated it was fires made by a group of not fewer than twenty people. He desperately wanted them. Information from Luggenemeener made him suspect that these people were led by Umarrah, who had absconded from his first mission the year before. Umarrah and his Tyerrerontepanner clan had been part of the big war party that had gone into battle with the Big River people the previous year, when his wife and son had been killed. To get through the cordon of the Black Line, Umarrah had offered his services as a guide, then disappeared into the bush soon afterwards. He was now said to be at large somewhere in the north-east.

Robinson set off to find him, taking Umarrah's old companions Truganini, Wooredy, Pagerly and Kickerterpoller. For nine days they walked across mountainous country known as the Eastern Tiers, happily hunting the boomer kangaroos and telling stories, not managing to make any contact. Utterly frustrated, Robinson abandoned the search. The last of the Tyerrerontepanner were out there somewhere, of that he was sure, and he was eventually going to get them.

The smoke was seen again on 10 December and this time the old woman Ghonyennener was sent to seek out the group. Her job was to find Umarrah, explain that his compatriots were safe on

Swan Island, and persuade him to return with her. Ghonyennener was chosen as the envoy because she was too old to be stolen away and Robinson knew she would want to return to her kin on Swan Island. He arranged for Truganini, Wooredy, Kickerterpoller and Pagerly to stay at the base camp at Musselroe Bay and wait for Ghonyennener to return. Nothing could have suited them better.

For five days, Truganini and her three companions ranged up and down the fecund coastline, filling their bellies with mussels, abalone and crayfish. Although this tranquil stretch of coast was empty of people, they found haunting reminders of them everywhere. At places where sealers could land their boats, the beach was littered with human bones, Truganini later told Robinson. She knew the sealers were responsible for the gruesome bone scatter. She explained how they would entice people to the beach by pretending to trade, displaying flour and sugar, as well as the coveted dogs. As soon as people came close enough, they would open fire on the men, simultaneously grabbing as many females as they could. The women and girls would be rowed away while the dead and dying were left on the sand to rot in the sun. No one remained to perform rituals for the dead.

On 15 December, Ghonyennener returned to the base camp alone. She had found no one and discovered the smoke they had seen was from a fire started when wind ignited embers left smouldering during their previous search. With reluctance, Kickerterpoller signalled for the whaleboat to collect them. One of the convict boatmen picked up an intact human skull from the sand, taking it with him as a memento.

On 11 December, Parish had returned from the Bass Strait islands with six healthy young Tyreelore, all wearing shapeless dresses made of kangaroo skins. On the same day as Ghonyennener's return, he brought in another five. These stolen women, all from the north-east, included two of Mannalargenna's daughters, Wotecowidyer and Woretemoeteyenner, as well as Plorenernoopner, a sister of Woreternaterlargner. Women now outnumbered men.

The arrival of the Tyreelore caused a great outpouring of joy. Day and night there was singing and dancing, stamping feet filling the air with clouds of fine black dirt and sandgrit. Over and over again, the Tyreelore performed the 'devil dance', which caused Robinson to sourly observe that this heathen devil demanded a great deal of gratification—the women seemed to him 'excessive in their devotion'. He thought the version of the dance introduced by the Tyreelore was 'the most obscene that can be conceived', exhibiting gestures so overtly sexual they could only have been learnt in bondage to debauchery. The dance was wildly admired. All the women joined in, Truganini included. New partnerships were rapidly made and remade. The display of sexual abandon so shocked Robinson that he threatened to send the Tyreelore back to their depraved captors.

He was outraged to find his own guides participating enthusiastically in this sinful display. Kickerterpoller threw himself into the action with gusto, having sex with as many women as he could entice into his arms. As a baptised Christian, he should know better, Robinson scolded, and told him he must mend his bad ways or be sent to jail. Privately, Robinson admitted that he was in no position to control the behaviour of any of the people in his charge. Kickerterpoller was the sole professed Christian among them and if Robinson could not control *his* immoral behaviour, what hope was there for restraining the rest? He made a note to himself to ensure that in future he must have 'the proper means' to compel them to conduct their relationships with propriety.

CHAPTER 4

TRUGANINI SPENT THE first two weeks of 1831 walking down the east coast to the town of Hobart on the Derwent River, the place she knew as Niberloone. Eleven months before, she had been taken from her country and still she was painfully putting one foot in front of the other on a journey with no comprehensible motivation and no anticipated return. Robinson had his reasons, he just didn't tell his companions what they were.

After an absence of nearly a year, Robinson needed to see his wife. She was grieving the loss of their youngest son nine months earlier, and it was also time to reconnect with his five surviving children. The stronger pull was to make the most of having succeeded where the Black Line failed so dismally. Since the governor was not responding to his prolix reports, he was determined to have a face-to-face meeting. Rather than take the boat, he chose to walk the two hundred miles to Hobart. He took Truganini, Wooredy, Pagerly and Kickerterpoller, which served the dual purpose of curtailing Truganini's and Kickerterpoller's sexual adventures and ensuring a reliable food supply.

Long treks in the colonial wilderness lifted Robinson's cramped puritan spirit. He always thrilled to be roaming about in untamed country in the company of people who were completely at home in that environment. Fancying himself as an ethnographer, he paid close attention to his 'sable companions', fascinatedly observing their mental and physical adaptation to the natural world. Watching and recording, he was forming the idea that he could make his name by publishing a book about the original people of Van Diemen's Land, since they would soon be no more.

It was not lost on Truganini that Mannalargenna was not chosen to go to Hobart, despite having been promised a meeting with the governor. The great man remained on Swan Island, effectively a prisoner, reinforcing a sense of her own privileged status as a partner in Robinson's mission. Now that Robinson was riding high in the governor's favour, honour bestowed on him must surely be due to her and Wooredy as well.

That was not how Robinson saw their relationship. Robinson could acknowledge that his guides possessed great skill and intelligence, fundamental human feelings not dissimilar to his own, and the capacity for commitment and loyalty; however, to grant any one of them a relationship of equality would have destroyed the whole rationale for his mission. Truganini was closer to him than anyone outside his immediate family. In the past two years he had spent more intimate time with her than everyone in his family put together. The idea that she might regard herself as a partner in his enterprise would never have entered his head.

For ten days, the party walked steadily down the east coast, moving too rapidly for Truganini's comfort, even though they stopped periodically to hunt. On reaching Spring Bay, the party turned west towards Hobart, following a track cut through heavily wooded hills along the Prosser River. Littering the track were shoes with gaping soles and other detritus, evidence of the monumental foolishness of the Black Line. Emerging onto the Prosser Plain, they found the land stripped bare and deeply rutted by wagon wheels. The sight of a brush fence extending across the plain as a defensive barrier elicited hoots of derisive laughter, as did the hundreds of bark huts that had been hastily constructed beyond the fence: some basic humpies, others four-posted huts with a veranda, seats and table. Not so amusing was the impact these shenanigans had wrought on the surrounding forest. Many huge trees had been felled, while thousands more had been entirely stripped of bark, leaving great stands to wither and die. The magnitude of the devastation was stunning. 'Nature had been completely dismantled,' Robinson wrote in dismay.

Truganini arrived in Hobart just two weeks short of twelve months since she had been taken from her country, after completing a circumambulation of the entire island. She and her companions were lodged in the annex to Robinson's house. The next day Robinson went alone to meet with the governor.

In the usual run of events Governor Arthur regarded this pompous tradesman with distaste, finding him a tedious blowhard. On this occasion, he was full of praise, rewarding Robinson with an additional land grant of 2500 acres to be taken up anywhere he chose, a salary increase to £250 backdated to 1829, plus a bonus of £100. In presenting himself to the governor as a one-man operation, Robinson did not consciously intend to exclude Truganini and her companions from reward in the way he determinedly ousted rivals like John Batman—he just could not bring himself to acknowledge the enormity of his dependence on them. Belatedly, he suggested that some small recompense for his guides might be appropriate. In recognition of their 'unremitting exertion and uncommon fidelity', the governor awarded them clothing and the two couples were given

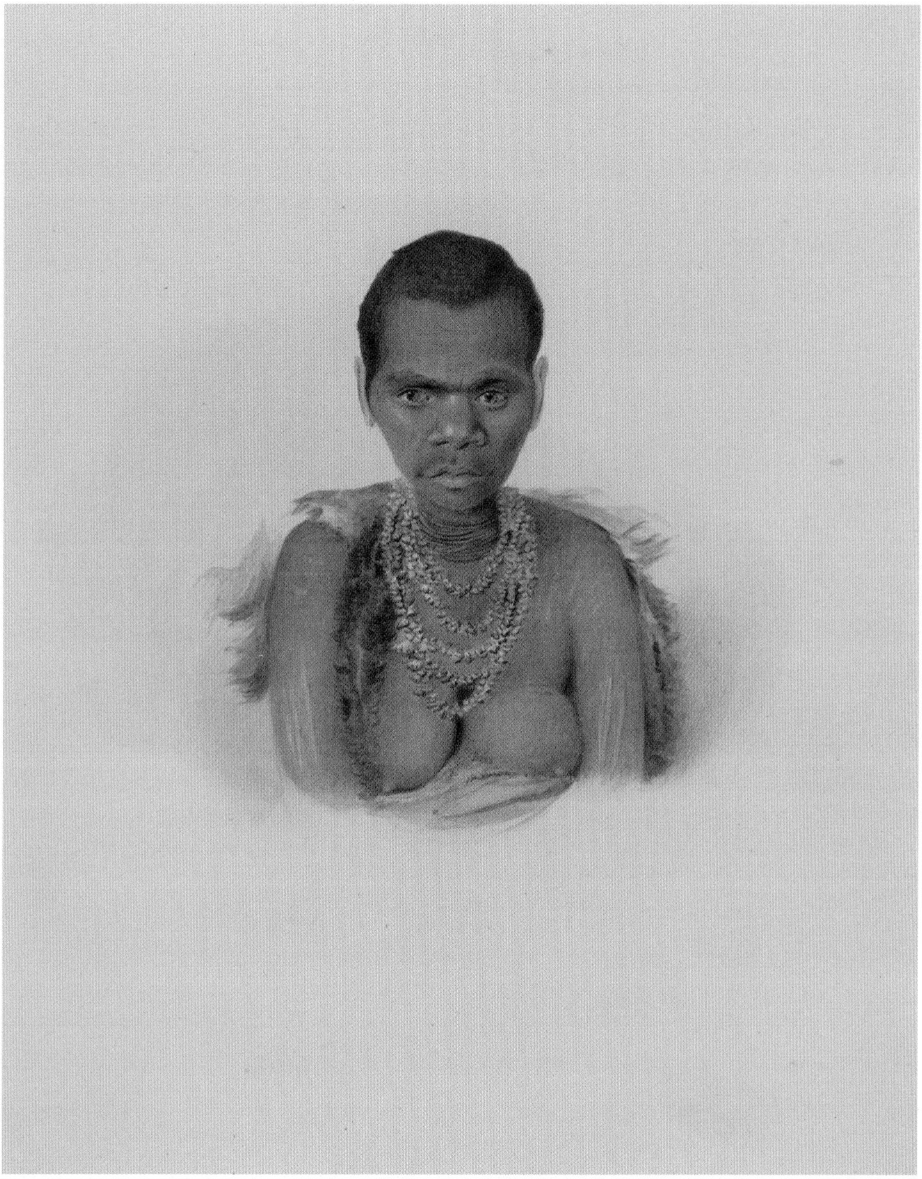

Truganini (mislabelled as Fanny), by Thomas Bock, 1835

Wooredy, by Thomas Bock, 1835

Peevay, by Thomas Bock, 1835

Maulboyheener, by Thomas Bock, 1835

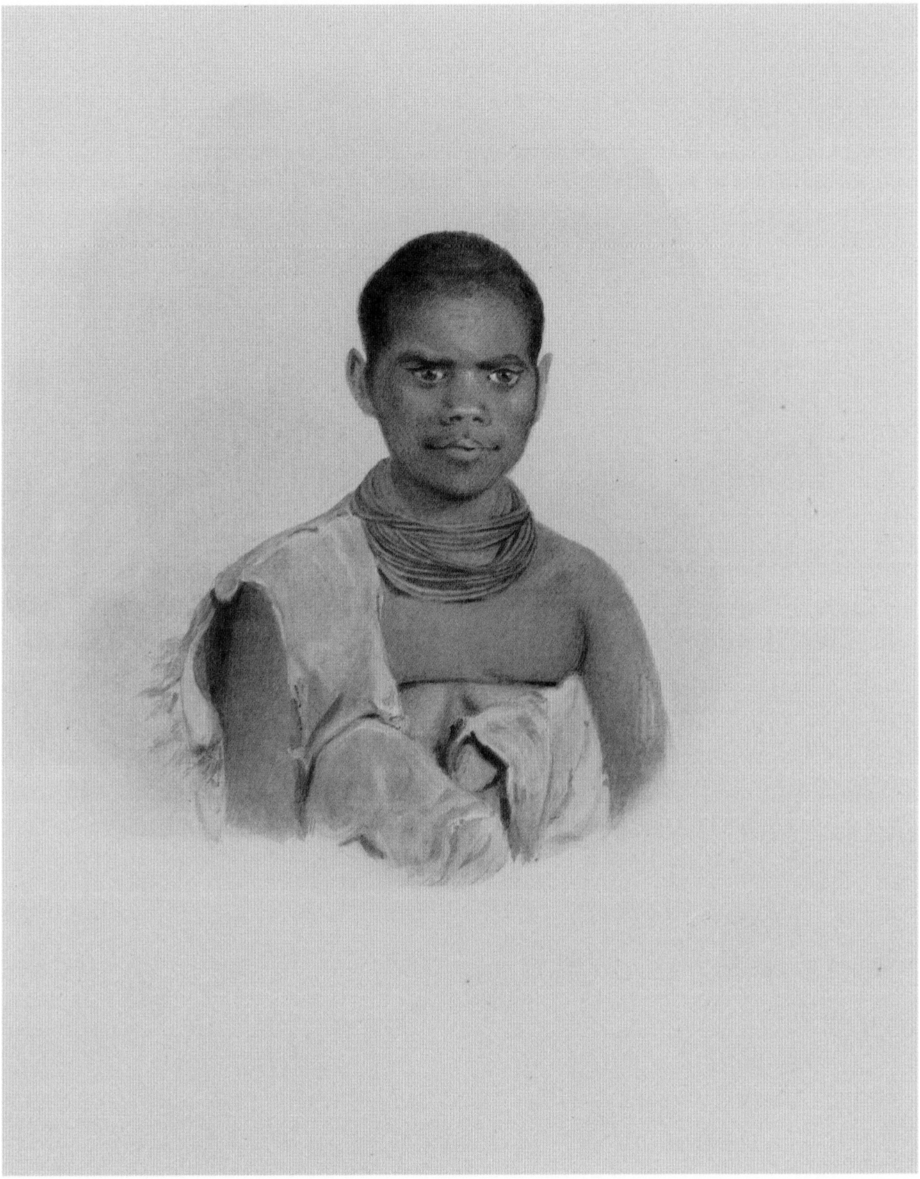

Plorenernoopner (mislabelled as Truganini), by Thomas Bock, 1835

Mannalargenna, by Thomas Bock, 1835

The River Nile, Van Diemen's Land, from Mr Glover's Farm, John Glover, 1837
COURTESY NATIONAL GALLERY OF VICTORIA

Patterdale, Van Diemen's Land, by John Glover, 1840
COURTESY W.L. CROWTHER LIBRARY, STATE LIBRARY OF TASMANIA

Tasmanian woman believed to be Truganini, attributed to Thomas Lempriere, 1834 (previously unpublished)

a boat. They never got to see the boat, since Robinson arranged for it to be hired out on the Derwent River with the money paid into a dedicated account that he controlled. They did get to wear the clothes.

Demure in their new printed-cotton dresses, Truganini and Pagerly promenaded daily through the streets of the town, accompanied by Wooredy and Kickerterpoller in trousers and blue coats of fine wool—'for all the world looking like gentlemen with no shoes on', mocked the editor of the *Colonial Times.* Eighteen months before, when Truganini had previously been in town, she'd been dressed in flouncing silks and the subject of curious admiration. Now, the public mood had hardened from well-intentioned curiosity into outright enmity. Only the protection of Robinson as chaperone—and, by extension, the overarching protection of the governor—kept the foursome from facing overt aggression. After nearly three months of daily perambulations, the promenading quartet became something of a fixture around the streets, no more incongruous than the clanking chain gangs of convicts going to and from the nearby Prisoners' Barracks.

During these tedious months in Hobart, Truganini and her companions were mostly confined to the annex of Robinson's house, while he made numerous trips into the country to find suitable land for his new grant. Also living in the annex were Wooredy's sons: Myunge, now aged thirteen, and Droyerloine, aged eleven. Wooredy had not seen or heard from these boys since Robinson had sent them and Maulboyheener away from the west coast nine months earlier. While Maulboyheener had run away to find his mother in May 1830, Wooredy's sons had stayed behind with Robinson's family, who gave them new names: Davey Bruny and Peter Bruny. These boys meant the world to Wooredy—they were the future of the Nuenonne.

Robinson still held land in Nuenonne country—only a short boat ride across the water, so close Truganini could almost smell it—but Robinson was never going to take her and her family back to their country. In January 1830, when Truganini, Wooredy and Pagerly were taken away from Bruny Island, Robinson had informed the colonial secretary that the Nuenonne were now 'extinct', as were all the clans of the south-east. Since then a great deal of Nuenonne territory had been distributed as large freehold land grants to newly arrived settlers, including a second grant to Richard Pybus of 2560 acres on South Bruny Island.

The colonial authorities made no substantive distinction between Robinson's guides and the other sorrowful, dispossessed people in custody in Hobart who had been forcibly removed from settled areas, never to return. No matter how tantalisingly close her country was, Truganini would not get to walk the beaches to gather the tiny shells for her necklaces, and Wooredy would not get to teach his sons about their country and clan obligations.

While basking in the governor's good graces, Robinson took the opportunity to entrench himself as the preeminent expert on the control and management of the original people. He met with the Aboriginal Committee the governor had established, and made the case that all the people captured in the settled districts, whether in jail or living with settlers, should be transferred into his charge. He then outlined his plan to create a permanent asylum on an island in the Bass Strait and identified Gun Carriage Island, a small landmass lying between Cape Barren and Flinders islands. This had the advantage of being sheltered from the full force of the Roaring Forties by the high peaks of those larger islands.

Although the governor and most of the members of the Aboriginal Committee were well disposed to his ideas, the influential chief justice was firmly opposed. He ventured the eccentric idea that it would be inhumane to remove the original people of the colony to a small offshore island. Deprived of their traditional country and nomadic lifestyle, the people would all pine away and die, he argued, which would be a terrible stain on the honour of the British Empire. His alternative proposal was for the governor to make a treaty with important clan leaders such as Mannalargenna, to restrict the remaining clans to a designated area on the mainland where no settlers would be permitted. In such protected areas, the people could continue to live a traditional life free from harassment, the kind of arrangement that had been put in place in the North American colonies.

Robinson had passed through just such a suitable area during his trek in the north-east. The finest country he had seen, he had thought at the time—extremely well suited to the original people yet quite useless for settlers. Only a few months later he strenuously rejected the chief justice's solution.

More than any other colonist, Robinson understood the intense bond between the original people and country. Having watched the people sing the land, he knew it was the wellspring of their spiritual life and their material culture. For them, land and life were indivisible. Until this bond was completely severed, he believed their souls would never be saved for God. He was not consciously relegating the people to extinction, as the chief justice feared—he had boundless faith in the power of the Christian word and in his own judgement. In this contest with the chief justice, it was Robinson's judgement that held sway.

The tedium of being confined in Hobart with only a daily walk for diversion was finally broken at the end of February 1831, when

Robinson announced he was ready to return to the north-east. Truganini was no doubt relieved that they would go by ship rather than walk all the way. On 1 March, she boarded the government cutter *Charlotte* along with her family and friends. They were joined by another seventeen people taken from the jail, the colonial hospital, and the households of various settlers. In addition to these twenty-three people, there were two convicts assigned to Robinson and a detachment of six soldiers for the new settlement on Gun Carriage Island.

Robinson's understanding was that the *Charlotte* would sail directly to the Bass Strait, conveying himself and these passengers, as well as a supply of rations and building materials. The haughty master of the *Charlotte* had other plans. He was not about to take orders from the likes of Robinson and arranged to stop over at the penal settlement at Port Arthur, where he would deliver a huge load of stores and four chained prisoners. Furious at this young man's impertinence, Robinson disembarked to complain to the governor, and the *Charlotte* sailed without him.

The ship was packed so tight that there was not enough room below decks for all the passengers. With no one to intervene on their behalf, all the twenty-three people Robinson had embarked were compelled to sleep on the main deck, wedged in between the longboats, the stacks of lumber, and the barrels of salted meat. Miserable, and dehydrated from seasickness, they were completely exposed to the elements, drenched in the salt water that splashed over the deck, saturating the rough smocks they were given to wear, which clung to their bodies in the biting wind. Without the protection of the animal fat with which they traditionally coated their skin, they were chilled to the bone. Two days later, when the prisoners and additional stores were offloaded at Port Arthur, they were permitted to sleep in the poorly ventilated hold, crammed together among the remaining stores of building materials and rations.

One woman had died and two more were very ill when the *Charlotte* called in at the penal station on Maria Island to collect Robinson, who had walked overland from Hobart with his eldest son. Still confined in the hold, the people lay in their own urine and excrement until the stench became so intolerable they were again forced onto the exposed deck to be buffeted by driving rain and gale-force winds. On 14 March, sick and disgruntled, they disembarked at Swan Island.

The *Charlotte*'s arrival at Swan Island coincided with that of a government cutter conveying four people released from jail in Launceston. One of these was Maulboyheener, who had been feared dead. He had kin relationships or close friendships with almost all the people on Swan Island, and his unexpected restoration brought a spark of life-affirming energy to the demoralised captives. Witnessing the emotional reunion with his mother Luggenemeener, his father Woreternaterlargner and his brother Tillabunner, Robinson had to turn away to hide his tears. No one else felt the need for such restraint. A spontaneous explosion of weeping and joyous celebration rocked the island for the rest of the day and well into the night.

Among those dancing for joy was Peevay, who had finally recovered from his long illness. He had more than one reason to celebrate: the cutter from Launceston had brought the orphaned youths Lacklay and his brother Merape, whom Peevay had last seen about six months earlier when they had run away together from Robinson's custody. Peevay immediately took charge of Lacklay and the two became inseparable.

All fifty-one people on Swan Island were embarked on the *Charlotte* the following day for a voyage further into the strait.

They were landed on the small Preservation Island off the western end of Cape Barren Island, where the mutton bird rookeries were well stocked with plump young birds. Robinson did not reveal that he intended to move them all to a permanent settlement on nearby Gun Carriage Island. Leaving the people eagerly pulling birds out of the rookeries, he continued on to Gun Carriage Island with Truganini, Wooredy and Kickerterpoller, as well as six soldiers and his convict clerk.

On the most sheltered side of Gun Carriage Island was a self-sufficient village where ten resident sealers had built cottages, made vegetable plots and bred plenty of fowls, pigs and goats. Robinson promised his guides that these productive small homesteads would soon be theirs. He wanted to give them a privileged preview of their new home, in the hope it would mollify their evident discontent, and he was pleased to believe they were entirely satisfied with this bargain. His clerk thought otherwise, noting that Truganini, Wooredy and Kickerterpoller complained vociferously that they did not want to live on this or any island. They wanted to go back to Musselroe Bay, or even Hobart.

All of Robinson's attention was focused on expelling the island's current residents. Summoning his considerable reserves of self-righteous pomposity, he directed the soldiers to round up the sealers. Reading aloud from a proclamation, he announced that he was the governor's appointed envoy and that they must immediately hand over their captive women and leave the island. Disingenuously, the sealers protested that they had no women. Robinson scoffed in disbelief; however, a search of the island revealed none—the sealers had already sent the Tyreelore into hiding on the heavily forested Cape Barren Island. Somewhat deflated, Robinson reiterated his demand that the sealers quit the island, and offered to purchase their many pigs, goats and fowls. The cottages and vegetable plots were simply appropriated.

One week later, all the people were transferred to Gun Carriage Island. As promised, one cottage was allocated to Truganini and Wooredy with his two sons, another to Kickerterpoller and Pagerly, and a third was given to Mannalargenna and Tanlebon-eyer. Robinson took a cottage for himself, although he did not stay there, leaving almost straightaway for the other islands to find the Tyreelore and expel any remaining sealers. It gave him great satisfaction to think that he could rid the strait of these miscreants and liberate their slaves. 'It is therefore no small honour,' he reflected, 'that I should be the individual appointed to ameliorate the conditions of this hapless race and to emancipate them from bondage.' He was getting way ahead of himself.

Robinson's sweep through the islands failed to entice even one woman out of hiding. The Tyreelore were tough and resourceful, maintaining a supportive culture among themselves with their own lingua franca and unique ceremonies. Far from being passive victims, humbly grateful to Robinson for his intervention, they provided an unexpected challenge to his emancipation project. They persistently defied his humanitarian intentions by choosing to stay with the men who had enslaved them.

The ageing householders living in the Bass Strait islands were hardly the depraved and debauched men Robinson obsessively complained about in his journal and official reports. The fur seal population of the straits had been wiped out in the 1820s, and by 1830 that transient life had given way to one of settled domesticity—the sealers had turned to subsistence farming and selling the feathers and oil of the mutton birds. In some households, the brutal intimacy they'd inflicted on the women stolen from Van Diemen's Land and New Holland had developed into a rough kind of mutual affection. Although infanticide had been practised, a number of children survived to bind these ageing renegades into family units.

The acknowledged leader of the Bass Strait sealing community was James Munro, known as Governor of the Straits. A decade earlier, Munro had established a small settlement on Preservation Island where at various times he kept four or five Tyreelore he had abducted from the coast of Van Diemen's Land and New Holland. This canny ex-convict had gained a degree of respectability, having been appointed constable of the Bass Strait by the superintendent of police at Launceston. His settlement on Preservation Island served as a trading and administrative centre for the ten sealers who lived on Gun Carriage Island, and the seven more living on Woody Island. Between them, these men ran a small fleet of boats with Munro acting as their agent. They proved more cunning and resourceful than Robinson had reckoned.

Munro was deputised to go to Hobart to petition the governor, taking with him one of his mixed-race children, a handsome boy who could say his prayers. Munro proved to be an excellent foil for Robinson. He was a literate and intelligent man able to persuasively argue that the sealers were victims of an unlawful seizure of their property. By forcibly removing their wives from home and family, Munro protested, it was Robinson who was engaged in deprivation of the women's liberty, not the sealers. The governor found him a convincing advocate, and agreed that Robinson's action constituted an unwarranted invasion of the sealers' domestic affairs. That news took some time to reach Robinson.

Robinson returned empty-handed to Gun Carriage Island on 30 April, when he was met by Truganini pleading with him to take her family away from the island. Far from being gratified by the gift of a cottage, she refused to enter it. Her family were sleeping outside at night, as was everyone else. Wooredy believed

Raegewarrah had infested the cottages; he saw evidence of this malevolent spirit everywhere. Many of the people were ill. The ticket-of-leave convict appointed as the medical superintendent was unable to alleviate their suffering. Raegewarrah had already caught two people, whose bodies had been burnt; more such cremations were likely to follow.

At least fifteen people were now dangerously ill, a calamity Robinson attributed to their sleeping outside at night instead of staying warm inside the huts the convicts were building for them. All the blame was heaped on the medical superintendent left in charge, who was denounced as a debauched drunkard. The convict clerk was no better, spending his time soliciting the women for sex. Adding further insult, Robinson discovered that the expelled sealers were returning to the island, and they paid no heed when he threatened to have them taken into custody. They had got wind of the news from Hobart and were no longer cowed by his piece of paper.

Everything was going wrong. Robinson had rid himself of his licentious convict boatswain Alexander McKay by recommending him for a pardon and sending him off to Hobart. Once there, McKay took it upon himself to meet with members of the legislative assembly and traduce Robinson's reputation. As a consequence, the generous payments made to Robinson were now in dispute. Robinson was furious that this disreputable ex-felon had somehow secured the governor's approval to set up a roving party in the north of the colony, in direct competition with him. And McKay wasn't the only one. Another of the men employed as a boatswain for the mission had done the same thing, again with the governor's backing. Then there was the problem of John Batman, who was still in the roving business, now operating with a group of trackers taken from various clans along the coast of New South Wales.

This array of unscrupulous competitors were all after the big reward on offer for capture of the Stoney Creek band, said to be responsible for several fatal attacks on settlers and stockkeepers around the Tamar River. Almost certainly these were the same people Robinson had been tracking months earlier, led by the wily Umarrah. If anyone was going to claim that reward, it should be him. There was nothing for it but to abandon the management of Gun Carriage Island to the drunken medical superintendent and organise another mission.

On 4 May, Truganini's wish to be removed from Gun Carriage Island was granted when Robinson gathered her family, together with her friends Pagerly, Kickerterpoller and Maulboyheener, onto the *Charlotte* and headed for the base camp at Musselroe Bay, where preparations were underway for a new mission. They landed on Swan Island in order to transfer to the mainland by whaleboat. A storm was brewing and the master of the *Charlotte* was determined to get away. In the confused landing, many of the stores were left on board. The full disaster only became apparent the next day.

Overnight the storm set in, which meant that no transfer to the mainland was possible until the weather cleared. Truganini and her friends were once again marooned on a clump of snake-infested sandhills with a gale blowing and next to nothing to eat. The supplies that had been offloaded were ravaged during the night by an army of rats, and by midday the salt pork was squirming with maggots. The small game on Swan Island had long since been hunted out, the mutton birds had flown away and the mating penguins had not yet laid any eggs. In desperation, Wooredy, Kickerterpoller and Maulboyheener risked disturbing the drowsy tiger snakes to catch the rats, which they roasted on sticks over a fire.

Being trapped on this miserable island with bountiful Musselroe Bay in sight across the water brought into sharp focus the advantages of owning a boat. Wooredy and Kickerterpoller pestered Robinson as to why the boat the governor had given them had not been brought from Hobart and when they would get it. He promised to write a letter, something that always impressed Wooredy, although he maintained nothing could be done till the weather cleared.

Ten days of persistent gale-force winds caused chest infections, and inflammation of the eyes became their common lot. Not even Robinson's sturdy constitution could withstand a steady diet of rats as sand was whipped into his face all day and night. The infestation of venomous snakes, the screeching penguins and the howling winds combined into nightmarish conditions that wore away his equanimity, making for 'painful and gloomy foreboding', he confessed on 15 May. His mood did not improve a week later when the weather finally cleared and boats began to arrive carrying letters and food stores. If anything, it grew even darker.

Robinson's first act as soon as he had access to a boat was to send Wooredy's young sons back to Gun Carriage Island. He chose to believe that conditions there were more conducive to their health, even though three more people had died. The despairing medical superintendent reported that the place simply did not agree with the people, and implored Robinson to ask the governor to find somewhere more congenial. Robinson disagreed, blaming the widespread malaise on exposure to the heavy dew that fell at night. The people must be made to sleep in the houses the convict workmen were building, he instructed.

Every letter Robinson received carried more bad news. The worst arrived on 24 May, when James Munro stepped ashore to hand-deliver instructions from the governor. Munro did not try to contain his glee as Robinson absorbed the impact of the order to relinquish the Tyreelore he had taken into his care. Only if a woman determinedly refused to go back could he reject a sealer's claim to her. Moreover, he was obliged to cease his campaign to expel the sealers from the islands. He saw it as a huge humiliation for the governor to side with brutal and immoral brigands against his high-minded project of emancipation. He took no comfort in being allowed to continue to occupy Gun Carriage Island, since the place was a disaster. He was further humiliated when most of the Tyreelore he had rescued requested to be returned to the sealers.

The only women who stayed were those the sealers did not bother to claim, or those like Tanleboneyer and Bullyer who had formed strong relationships with men on Swan Island. Mannalargenna's daughter Woretemoeteyenner was one who stayed, but another daughter, Wotecowidyer, returned at her own request to James Everitt and her four children on Woody Island. Mannalargenna saw the removal of the Tyreelore as a very bad omen. It was his first intimation that Robinson was like George Briggs—a man who would not honour his obligations.

Truganini and her companions were eventually transferred to the base camp at Musselroe Bay on 2 June. As soon as the whaleboat reached the beach, Wooredy, Kickerterpoller and Maulboyheener ran off to hunt boomer kangaroo while Truganini and Pagerly took their digging sticks and baskets to get tender fern roots in the bush. Being able to hunt and gather in the food-rich environment of Musselroe Bay, with its several inlets and large lagoons, once again brought to mind the usefulness of a boat. Under pressure, Robinson made a big show of writing a letter to the Aboriginal Committee in Hobart seeking information about the gifted boat.

He actually wrote to ask how much money was being paid into his account. Money accruing in an account was hardly going to satisfy Wooredy and Kickerterpoller, but the last thing Robinson wanted was for his guides to have the independence to put to sea.

With everyone returned to good health, the rituals of dancing and singing became an essential part of the daily routine at the base camp. Careful not to stay aloof from the people on whom he relied, Robinson again joined in with his flute. He even danced and sang, stamping his feet in the sand as he repeated the chanted choruses. He was intrigued to hear a song from Maulboyheener's country and asked for a translation of the words to copy into his journal. Maulboyheener was unwilling to tell him because he might show it to the settlers as a way of stealing his people's secrets. There was nothing to fear, Robinson assured them, because he 'was one with themselves'. Did he not eat kangaroo and dance with them every night?

Reluctantly, Maulboyheener gave him the gist of the song. It told how the people had watched settlers arrive in their country on a bullock cart loaded with wood and sacks of flour, then how they had robbed the settlers' huts to take the flour and firearms. They hid the heavy muskets in the bush and made damper with the flour. This was a song sung by all the clans of the north and east, Robinson was told. Months later, he detailed the contents of this song to the colonial secretary, citing it as evidence of the violent intentions of the people still at large.

By late June, Robinson was ready to begin his new mission to the interior to capture the Stoney Creek band. He had a support party of half a dozen convicts as well as his guides, including Bullyer and Tanganutura, both Tyreelore from the north-east corner who knew the country well. The party began walking south-east from the second base camp on the western side of Cape Portland at

Ringarooma Bay, with Kickerterpoller leading the way, followed by the rest of the guides in single file, holding the dogs tied to a rope so they would not bark and draw attention. Robinson and the convict servants brought up the rear.

For once it was not Truganini who was the straggler. The usually indefatigable Wooredy was literally dragging his feet. Around his orange locks and his neck he had wound garlands of aromatic leaves, which he inhaled as he walked to seek relief from a mystery ailment that was slowing his progress. They were making less than ten miles a day.

As they plunged into the rainforest of the Eastern Tiers, their pace slowed even more as they negotiated a passage through soggy, slippery gullies covered with furry thickets of huge tree ferns, on ground made treacherous by moss-covered rotting logs. Robinson completely trusted Kickerterpoller to find a path through the dank rainforest, and was gratified to see that he made notches in the tree ferns as they passed so that no one would lose the way. Moving cautiously through a subterranean tunnel of arching fern fronds, the snaking line of burdened walkers looked sublimely romantic, Robinson thought, even though he had to admit the journey was becoming 'irksome in the extreme'. Most irksome of all were the tenacious leeches that indiscriminately latched onto every body, naked or clothed. All of the party had blood running down their legs and even the more private parts. At night they found itchy sores developing where the vile creatures had been feeding.

On 6 July, Kickerterpoller suddenly confessed he had no idea where they were. Some of the guides said they should head in one direction, others argued for the opposite. Exasperated, Robinson pulled out his compass and found the way back to where they had camped the previous night. Unrepentant, the people immediately disappeared into the rainforest to hunt wombat and possums.

Kickerterpoller took a different route the next day, into less challenging country, finally emerging onto a freshly burnt plain. Without bothering to request permission, Kickerterpoller and Maulboyheener ran off with the dogs to hunt the boomer kangaroos. Robinson was infuriated to hear the dogs barking, which he knew would alert anyone around to their presence. Returning with several dead kangaroos, Kickerterpoller and Maulboyheener reported that people were close by. They had seen fresh tracks and found a large hut made with freshly cut bark that could shelter eight people or more. Robinson was sure that the resident clan of this region was extinguished, and elated to conclude it must be Umarrah's band that was within his grasp.

Knowing their old friend was close by, probably watching them, failed to spur his guides into action. Oblivious to Robinson's urgings, the men kept after the kangaroos and the women hunted possum. Truganini was an expert at catching possums. She deftly wove a rope from the long wiry grass and hooked it around the trunk of a tree to pull herself up, cutting notches in the bark for her feet as she ascended. Once in the canopy, she would grab at the possum to knock it to the ground, where Wooredy would smartly dispatch the winded animal with his waddy as Truganini inched her way back down. When not hunting possums, she and Pagerly wandered off to look for watercourses. It was egging season and there was no keeping them away from the swans' nests.

A niggling displeasure began to appear in Robinson's journal entries. He described the hunting and food gathering as if this activity was mere entertainment, inconsequential to his mission. Despite all the evidence of his eyes and ears, he persisted in regarding his guides as children, lost without the care and guidance that he, the good father, could provide. Schooling himself to be patient, he wrote 'the greatest forbearance is required with these natives when in the bush for they feel more independent and shew a disposition to be idle'. Forbearance was not Robinson's strong suit. His guides drove him crazy with their disobedience, dawdling and general lack of purpose.

Umarrah must have been highly amused to watch his old companions engaging in an elaborate game that only Robinson did not understand. Whether or not by tacit agreement with Umarrah, the guides continued to frustrate the mission to find the Stoney Creek band, quite deaf to Robinson's scolding at the folly of their conduct and how it was 'useless of me to have left my home, my wife, my children to go in quest of their countrymen and to save them from total annihilation unless they co-operated'.

Robinson had been living in the bush for the greater part of eighteen months. He had relied on his companions' bush skills, slept next to them, eaten their food, sung and danced with them. Without intending to be disingenuous, he had proclaimed that he was one of them. In all that time it had never occurred to him that they might regard this as a reciprocal relationship: that they were trying to induct him into their way of life.

Wooredy took the lead, holding the people spellbound every night with his animated stories of how sky spirits formed the world. He told how two stars came down from the Milky Way to touch the ground and shape the landscape by cutting out islands and making rivers. To inhabit that landscape, the creator spirits drew various species out of the ground. The first man had a tail like a kangaroo and no joints in his knees, which obliged him to sleep standing, so he cut off the tail and rubbed grease into the wound to create joints in order to be able to sit on the ground, which was much more comfortable. He then went up into the sky, where he could now be seen as the bright star in the southern sky known to colonists as Canopus.

Wooredy and Kickerterpoller revealed an intricate knowledge of the sky country, telling stories of the creator spirits who resided in the various constellations of the Milky Way. Truganini told how the Moon emerged from a far distant place over the sea and came to rest at Oyster Bay. As the Moon was roasting abalone over the fire, the Sun tried to seize her and she tumbled into the fire, then rolled into the sea to douse the flames. The Sun plucked her out of the water and swept her up into the sky to be his wife. The dark side of the Moon revealed where she had been burnt. Everyone participated in the nightly ritual narratives and re-enactments, asserting in song and movement the palpable reality of their world, at odds with Robinson's preachings about heaven and hell. Even Truganini, who was in every other respect so attentive to Robinson, remained stolidly resistant to his Christian message.

The only one to show any ambivalence was Kickerterpoller, who had been baptised as a child and grown up with stories from the Bible. He told Wooredy he believed what the settlers had told him, yet he was torn about his spiritual allegiance. He could not understand how the good spirits who lived in the sky, as described by Robinson, could exist without eating food. He accepted that the settlers had one devil and his people had another of their own. When Robinson protested that there was only one Devil, Kickerterpoller replied he did not know about that, as he hadn't seen the devil, although he had heard him whistle. Once he interrupted Wooredy's creation story to protest that the Christian story was the only true one, causing Truganini to lash out, 'Where did you come from, white woman?'

By 24 July, the mission party had walked in one long loop and was heading back to Cape Portland without a single sighting of Umarrah and his band. Once again they were in Mannalargenna's country and once again Robinson reflected that the land was perfectly suited to the traditional life of the people and would never be of any use to settlers. If only 'a proper arrangement' had been entered into earlier in the process of colonisation, he lamented, the people could have continued their life in this country. It was too late now. 'In a short time the ancient inhabitants will become annihilated,' he mused in another lachrymose reflection, 'a great sacrifice of human life by reason of our occupying this land.'

They arrived back at the base camp opposite Swan Island on 26 July, mightily pleased to be back in this coastal cornucopia. Truganini and her companions scattered in search of kangaroos, oysters and swans' eggs. By means of smoke signals, the coxswain from Gun Carriage Island was summoned, and he arrived with dispatches from the governor addressed to the Superintendent of the Aboriginal Establishment. Robinson was very pleased to be so addressed. The governor informed him that Gun Carriage Island was to be abandoned and that henceforth he would be Superintendent of the Aboriginal Establishment on the more distant Flinders Island, the high peaks of which could be seen on the horizon. This was thrilling news, but he knew it meant nothing if he failed to capture the Stoney Creek band.

Robinson had finally grasped that he was not going to capture Umarrah with his present group of recalcitrant guides. The coxswain was sent back with an order that Peevay and his friend Lacklay be brought to join his party. He was particularly anxious to secure the services of Umarrah's traditional rival, Mannalargenna, but this would be tricky. Mannalargenna was very angry at Robinson for failing to deal with the sealers and was chafing at the absence of his wife Tanleboneyer, who had been taken away as a guide for another roving party. However, he enthusiastically embraced the offer of escape from Gun Carriage Island, to the consternation of the despairing people he left behind.

Mannalargenna arrived at the base camp with Peevay and Lacklay on 5 August. Using Kickerterpoller as his go-between, Robinson made a formal request for assistance to capture Umarrah. In response, Mannalargenna launched into a litany of complaints, protesting that Robinson had not given him the promised audience with the governor, that he had let the sealers take the Tyreelore away, and that he had allowed Mannalargenna's wife to be removed from him. In return for any further assistance, he was looking to make a better deal. Robinson made him a firm promise that if there were no attacks on settlers, Mannalargenna and his people could stay in their country, protected by 'a good white man' who would live with them and go bush with them so they could hunt. He offered himself as an example of just such a person. The people would be protected from men with guns and supplied with flour, tea, sugar and blankets, he promised.

It was a measure of Robinson's intense anxiety that he would resort to such a deception. What he proposed to Mannalargenna was the exact same policy he had staunchly rejected, a policy he knew the governor would never countenance—and only days earlier Robinson had dismissed this policy as no longer viable. Foremost in his mind now was the reward for the Stoney Creek people. He must prove that he could do what nobody else could, or lose the governor's patronage. On Mannalargenna, he pinned his hopes for an illustrious future. What were a few lies in the balance?

Mannalargenna readily took the bait. After nine months confined on a barren offshore island, he was delighted to be back in his own country, although reluctant to move without his wife. Only after Robinson assured him that he had ordered Tanleboneyer be returned did the old man agree to accompany the mission. Even so, he was in no hurry to gratify Robinson's desires—hunting was the main thing on his mind. In this, he was fully supported by the other guides, who all deferred to him, even Wooredy. Most devoted was Kickerterpoller, who made himself Mannalargenna's factotum.

Robinson himself was swayed by the awe that Mannalargenna inspired and his legendary prowess as a warrior. He soaked up Mannalargenna's boastful stories of spearing Umarrah and making him beg for mercy, but Mannalargenna failed to tell him about the more recent alliance with Umarrah in the battle against the Big River people. Ignorant of that connection, Robinson was perfectly happy to cede his authority and follow the great man's lead. As days turned into weeks, Robinson became scornfully uneasy that he had entrusted his mission to satanic delusion.

Within Mannalargenna dwelt a powerful spirit that protected him and guided his actions, communicating through the twitching muscles of his left breast, rather like the tremors of palsy. Twitches of his shoulder one way or another would indicate the direction in which they were meant to go. After many days of Mannalargenna's leading the party hither and thither as his convulsions dictated, Robinson was beside himself with frustration. Over and over again, Wooredy and Kickerterpoller solemnly assured him that Mannalargenna's spirit guide was infallible, and that they would definitely find Umarrah, who was a very clever quarry.

For his part, Mannalargenna gave every indication of relishing the game they were playing as his spirit led them around in circles and the others casually lit fires to give warnings of their presence, or created diversions at critical moments, ensuring no direct contact with Umarrah was ever made. Despite escalating concern that he might be being played for a fool, Robinson persisted in describing this behaviour as stupidity and the devotion to Mannalargenna's spirit guide as the superstitious foolishness of innocents.

He was also increasingly anxious about Wooredy, who was limping so badly that Robinson had to carry his load. Such was Robinson's dependence on his 'old and faithful companion' that the possibility of losing him loomed as a calamity. How would they be able to get across the many rivers without Wooredy to construct his ingenious canoes? The mysterious aches and pains that had been slowing Wooredy down were probably caused by lymphoedema, a disturbance of the lymph system, possibly as a result of a tick bite, or it may have been the emergence of symptoms associated with the tertiary stage of syphilis.

Soon after leaving base camp, Wooredy had developed a painful swelling in his thigh, which he had tried to alleviate by making deep gashes in his flesh. By mid August, he could barely take a step without crying out in pain. He could proceed no further. Truganini stayed behind to care for her ailing husband while the rest of the party moved on. It was several days before the swelling in Wooredy's thigh reduced sufficiently to permit him to walk while leaning on Truganini. Slowly, they made their way to the coast.

Stopping to rest about a quarter of a mile inland from the mouth of the Boobyalla River, Truganini made an unsettling discovery. While gathering swans' eggs for Wooredy to eat, she became curious about a deep indentation in the ground, and after digging further into the hole she uncovered an old wooden chest that contained a jumble of human bones. Days later, at the mouth of the Tomahawk River, she saw two bleached male skeletons lying a few hundred yards apart that no one had tried to hide. Awful though it was, Truganini had seen similar sights before—the beaches and inlets of the north-east corner were repositories of many human bones, invariably male and often shattered by a musket ball.

Wooredy's condition gradually improved over the next three or four days as they rested at the coast. He was still unable to hunt, so the task of food gathering fell entirely to Truganini. She was well supplied with tea and sugar, as well as flour for damper, but it was swans' eggs they craved. She was annoyed to discover that sealers and Tyreelore had already come to the bay to raid the nests. Still, she found plenty of abalone to rebuild her husband's strength.

Isolated from the mission party, Truganini fretted about what would happen to Robinson and her friends if they were to encounter the fearsome Stoney Creek band. Wooredy was glumly convinced they would all be speared. As soon as he was well enough, they journeyed to the base camp at Waterhouse Point to seek news of their companions. On 31 August, they were astonished to see the mission party approaching, in high spirits, swelled by the addition of seven new people and fourteen dogs. Leading the party was their friend Umarrah, singing loudly and looking very pleased with himself.

Much had happened in their absence. Robinson had gained the essential services of two additional Tyreelore, who had been working as guides for other roving parties. One was Mannalargenna's daughter Woretemoeteyenner, whose presence was needed to remind the old man of what was at stake and motivate him to find the prize, and the other was Plorenernoopner, who had a husband and brother in the Stoney Creek band, making her a vital intermediary.

The addition of Mannalargenna's daughter did not work the magic Robinson hoped for. The party had spent another week wandering in circles. By 26 August, Robinson had reached breaking point with Mannalargenna. Convinced that the spirit guide was a feint, he accused the old man of 'dragging the people off their legs for no good purpose'. Sternly, he presented an ultimatum:

Mannalargenna would only be allowed to stay in his own country if he could capture the Stoney Creek people.

The next day, Mannalargenna consulted with the tremors in his breast, as he did every morning, and then set off into the bush with his trusty factotum Kickerterpoller, as well as Plorenernoopner. A day later, these three emerged from the bush with Umarrah and his band, all of them in a jolly mood. Unabashedly, Umarrah bounded forward to extend his arm to Robinson for a handshake. He had come to get the same deal as Mannalargenna: he wanted an assurance that he could stay, unmolested, in his own country.

The Stoney Creek band were surprisingly few: six men and one older woman surrendered to Robinson, and three more men remained somewhere in the bush. They were from several different clans, all with bitter grievances against settlers and sealers, chiefly the loss of their young women. Jovial as they appeared to be, Robinson was well aware that these were ruthless guerilla fighters, implicated in the murder of several settlers, with a big reward on their head. It was essential to persuade them to follow him back to the coast. To bind them to him, he glibly promised that 'if they would not spear white men, they might remain and hunt'.

Having got the Stoney Creek band to Waterhouse Point, Robinson feverishly concocted schemes to lure them to Gun Carriage Island even as he continued to reassure Umarrah that his people would be permitted to stay unmolested in their own country. He even promised that he could keep with them the four Tyreelore in the mission party as their wives. Kickerterpoller effectively scuttled Robinson's scheme to get the Stoney Creek band into a boat by continually goading them with the prospect of an island prison. In the end, his taunts were more effective than the offer of the Tyreelore. Four people, including Plorenernoopner's husband, disappeared back into the bush to join their compatriots still at large. Kickerterpoller was pleased to see them go; he wanted to keep the Tyreelore for himself. On extended hunting trips away from Robinson's watchful gaze, he had been having sex with both Tanganutura and Bullyer.

Robinson did not try to recover the four defectors, because he was confident that Umarrah would eventually lead him to them and the other people still in the bush. Still, Robinson kept a vigilant watch on Plorenernoopner, anxious that she would be induced to go after her husband. He was reassured to see that she wanted to remain with her brother at Waterhouse Point, fully expecting Robinson to deliver her husband back to her. That, he was unable to do. Her husband and three others were captured by a boat crew and sent to Flinders Island, where all four died while Plorenernoopner was on a mission with Robinson.

Umarrah found a less perilous way to avoid island captivity. He boldly declared that he could find the Big River people of the central plateau. Despite the traditional conflict between himself and Mannalargenna, he persuaded Robinson that the two seasoned warriors could subordinate their mutual enmity to capture their common enemy. Together, they had defeated the Big River people once before, and they could do it again. Robinson was very pleased with the prospect of Umarrah and Mannalargenna securing him the reward for the capture of the Big River people.

His displeasure with Kickerterpoller for scaring off most of his quarry boiled over when Kickerterpoller brazenly requested that Robinson 'put away' his marriage to Pagerly. Robinson had explained that money for hire was paid on the boat in Hobart and now Kickerterpoller offered Robinson this as an inducement, saying he did not need money; all he needed was tea, sugar and a different woman to sleep with. Thoroughly disgusted at such 'innate wickedness', Robinson told him never to speak of the matter again, privately noting that neither 'one nor twenty women would suffice him'.

Maybe there was one woman who would suffice. Emboldened by Wooredy's infirmity, Kickerterpoller had renewed his schemes to take Truganini for himself.

EXTIRPATION AND EXILE

1831–1838

CHAPTER 5

TRUGANINI AND THE other guides returned to Launceston in September 1831, finding it to be more congenial on this occasion. A local newspaper had smoothed their way with exultant reports of their success, possibly provided by Robinson himself, eliding the inconvenient facts that most of the Stoney Creek band were still at large and Umarrah was responsible for the death of at least one settler. In this telling, Umarrah had been transformed from murderous savage to potential saviour with his prediction that he could easily capture all of the Big River people. 'If all this is true (and we have every reason to believe it is),' the editor gushed, 'we rejoice.'

Seamlessly, Umarrah had resumed his role as one of Robinson's most trusted guides; he was promised a meeting with the governor to present his grievances and seek restitution. Robinson even secured a new wife for him—Polare, a Punnilerpanner woman from Port Sorrell.

Robinson had gone to the Launceston jail to interrogate Polare and another woman captive about the recent murder of two settlers at Port Sorrell. He took with him Lacklay, who instantly recognised Polare as a woman from his country taken into the Luggermairrernerpairrer clan of the Western Tiers, allies of the Lairmairermener. Polare was thrilled to meet one of her clansmen and proved to be a willing informant about the Big River people among whom she had lived. She appeared to Robinson to be a perfect guide and intermediary for his new mission. He arranged for her to be released into his custody, then married her to Umarrah.

As well as satisfying Umarrah's desire for a wife, Robinson was anxious to keep Polare out of the grasp of his nemesis, Alexander McKay, who had the effrontery to come to the jail when Robinson was there, brandishing a letter from the colonial secretary giving him permission to take female captives as guides. He was accompanied by a Tyerrerontepanner woman named Karnebucher, who became agitated as soon as she saw Robinson.

During 1829 and 1830, Karnebucher had lived at Robinson's house in Hobart with her young son Meelerleeter, and had been one of the women sent back to her own country in May 1830. She had subsequently been recaptured with her husband and sent to the Campbell Town jail, from where she was removed by McKay. Her husband was presumed dead and somehow her son had come into the possession of John Batman, who had baptised the boy Jack Allen. Karnebucher begged Robinson to take her to Umarrah, who was of her clan, and to get her son returned to her.

McKay protested that Karnebucher was his guide and belonged to him. Although Robinson was sure McKay had taken the woman for his own sexual gratification, there was nothing he could do except rail about it in his journal. When Umarrah heard about Karnebucher he insisted that she be taken away from McKay and included in the mission party. When Robinson proved unable to do so, Umarrah raised the matter directly with Governor Arthur.

The long-promised audience with the governor took place in Launceston on 6 October. Both Umarrah and Mannalargenna related the extensive history of abuse their people had suffered from settlers and sealers. They emphasised how much they wanted to remain in their own country, unmolested, as Robinson had promised them. Governor Arthur listened respectfully and then arranged a private meeting with Robinson later that night, at which John Batman was also present, much to Robinson's disgust.

Dispensing with any niceties, Robinson launched into a litany of complaints about the lack of consideration his mission had received and demanded that all the other roving parties must be under his direction. He singled out Alexander McKay as a brutal, disreputable fellow, unsuited to the object of conciliation, who took women with him to serve his own depraved purposes. He then turned his outrage on Batman, for having stolen away two young boys who must be returned to their parents. He further demanded that the seven men Batman had imported as trackers from New South Wales be attached to Robinson's mission. Finally, he delivered a scathing assessment of the governor's decision to allow the women he had rescued from enslavement to be returned to the sealers, who were nothing but a bunch of brutal outlaws.

The governor found all this voluble carping insolent and irritating, but he was buoyed by Robinson's boast that he could capture the Big River people. He delivered to Robinson a long-desired triumph, telling Batman to surrender the two stolen boys he called Jack Allen and Ben Lomond and to transfer his trackers. McKay was ordered to deliver Karnebucher to Robinson, and the master of the *Charlotte* was instructed to sail around the Bass Strait islands to collect Mannalargenna's daughters to be reunited with their father.

In return for getting his way, Robinson was straightaway to proceed to the midlands, where an area would be set aside 'constituting a kind of home' for his guides, with a hut to be built for Umarrah and another for Mannalargenna. In this way, the governor appeared to be fulfilling Robinson's promises. However, Arthur fully understood that the settlers would never countenance any part of the colonial mainland being set aside for the original people. No such area was ever set aside, and no huts were built. Indeed, none of the governor's instructions were carried out, except one: Batman's trackers were transferred to the police constable Anthony Cottrell, who was instructed to work under Robinson's direction.

The mission to capture the Big River people left Campbell Town on 15 October. Robinson was on horseback and everyone else walked: Wooredy and Truganini, Mannalargenna and Tanlebon-eyer, Umarrah and Polare, Kickerterpoller and Pagerly, in addition to the youths Maulboyheener, Peevay and Lacklay. A boy known as Richard, who had recently been recovered from a settler's farm near the South Esk River, was a last-minute addition. There was also a resupply team, with four assigned convicts and a packhorse.

To curtail Kickerterpoller's improper dalliances, Robinson left three Tyreelore behind, taking only Tanganutura, and she was probably the one who told Robinson that Kickerterpoller was planning to kill Wooredy and take Truganini for himself. Robinson recognised it as a vain boast. Truganini was hardly a devoted wife, but she showed no interest in the husband of her close friend Pagerly, while Wooredy had made a full recovery from his mystery ailment and was, as ever, the jealous warrior determined to see off any threats to his status.

As soon as they were away from Campbell Town, all the guides except Richard cast off their woollen trousers and smocks and smeared their bodies with ochre and oil. They wore only thick kangaroo-skin cloaks draped over their shoulders and carried knapsacks containing a blanket and food supplies. The men also carried a firestick and a squat waddy, while the women carried digging sticks, with a sharpened end like a chisel to dig for grubs and peel bark from trees to make huts. The women also carried small bone implements, glass to cut their hair, and the precious red ochre, along with a flat stone, to prepare hair paste for the men.

Umarrah, Mannalargenna and Wooredy made a formidable team. Robinson was gambling that their rivalry could be put aside for the cause of capturing their traditional enemy. As it happened, these powerful warriors displayed a remarkable unity of purpose: they were equally determined *not* to find the Big River people. Having been assured by the governor that they were under his protection, they went hunting, which was much more to their liking than confronting a dangerous foe. For nearly three months, they enjoyed a meandering trek through excellent kangaroo country without coming within cooee of their old enemy.

Mannalargenna's spirit guide told him the party needed to travel east towards the coast at Spring Bay, where the Big River people would meet with a remnant of Kickerterpoller's clan, the Pardarereme, known to settlers as the Oyster Bay people. Kickerterpoller was, as always, in lockstep with Mannalargenna, insisting that this was indeed so. Polare concurred, explaining that the Pardarereme people often collaborated with the Lairmairremener. When settlers talked of attacks by the Big River people, they were often unaware that it was clans from two separate nations working together.

Mannalargenna led them south-east in a zigzag procession along the edge of the Eastern Tiers, walking well ahead of the group while majestically holding up a smouldering firestick, regardless of wind or rain. This was rough country of dry peppermint gum forest and shrubby ground cover, where large sections had been burnt to stimulate native grasses for browsing kangaroos. It was still untouched by settlers and their sheep. As the ground was broken by lumps of granite and wombat burrows, Robinson had to lead his horse as often as he rode. 'Hills upon hills, and succeeding hills and interspersed with gullies,' he wrote in his journal on 22 October, 'and in the distance high mountains whose sombre appearance would seem to say this country is formed for the children of nature.'

The children of nature were certainly enjoying their time in this rough landscape, even if he was not. As a precaution against distraction from his pursuit, Robinson had provided his guides with four cakes of high-grade ochre, used by the colonists as a dye pigment, which he had purchased with money from the hire of the gifted boat. He had not reckoned on the considerable amount of time they would spend each day carefully painting their bodies and dressing their hair for ceremony. They danced every night and afterwards Umarrah would compete with Wooredy to sing long epic narratives, each verse with a repeated chorus, keeping the mesmerised group awake until the morning hours. Exhausted, Robinson likened the experience to being trapped in the *Arabian Nights*.

During the day, they dawdled in the pleasant spring sunshine. Truganini collected grasses and wove ropes to catch possums. Wooredy made spears and went hunting with the other men, killing kangaroos and wallabies in such numbers that they only bothered to bring back the hind legs and tail. The women dried the sinews of the kangaroo tails that they twisted into ornaments to wear looped around their necks. Exasperated, Robinson threatened to tell the governor that they were just hunting and not tracking their quarry. Mannalargenna coolly replied that he could tell the governor that Robinson was just basking in the sun. 'He is a shrewd man,' Robinson ruefully acknowledged. Not only was he shrewd, Robinson had to admit that Mannalargenna was the one truly in charge.

Robinson had expected that competition between Umarrah and Mannalargenna would speed the chase, so he was dismayed that Umarrah proved to be as much in thrall to the dictates of Mannalargenna's mercurial spirit guide as everyone else. Umarrah and his wife Polare were greatly familiar with this country, as was Kickerterpoller, yet they followed wherever Mannalargenna's tremors indicated without a murmur of dissent. Grudgingly, Robinson conceded that he had no choice but to indulge them, and with increasing anxiety sent up prayers that the mission would be a success. His future depended on it.

As they progressed across the hills, Polare excitedly pointed out the cold ashes of fires, and sites where people had been splitting flints to sharpen their spears. One time she took the party to the hollow of a dead tree, from which she retrieved bundles of spears tied with blankets, a shotgun and a musket, as well as several bags of shot, all concealed for future use.

Still they saw no people. As the days became weeks, Robinson grew very tetchy. He doubted that anyone was nearby, and even if people were lurking in the vicinity, he knew they would be aware of his presence and keep away. It was a source of constant frustration that the hunters refused to quiet the excited barking of the dogs that reverberated around the hills. He was at his wit's end one day to see Truganini and Pagerly making a large bonfire with the sheets of shed bark that littered the ground, sending billows of smoke into the air that would be visible for miles around.

After two weeks of meandering towards the coast, Robinson dropped his indulgence towards these diversionary tactics and gave Kickerterpoller and Polare an ultimatum: unless they could produce the people at once, the party must turn back and walk towards the territory of the Lairmairermener on the central plateau. Every one of the guides reacted with alarm, crying out that this was very cold country and they would all die if they went there. Undeterred, Robinson pointed out that the weather was mild and that summer was coming. Kickerterpoller continued to protest that this country was full of bad spirits who would kill any strange people, especially if they were carrying knapsacks. For his part, Mannalargenna looked pitiable and pleaded that he was an old man who would expire if he were made to walk that far. Rebutting all these objections, Robinson held firm to his order.

The people shouldered their overburdened knapsacks and walked westwards, keeping to the wooded hills well out of firing range of the extensive farms that spread for miles along the river plains. Robinson had been warned that the settlers and their convict workers all carried guns and would shoot his guides on sight. A settler from the area had told him that 'a great many natives had been killed in that part'. That was true. Some seventy people had been killed around the Clyde and Ouse rivers in the past few years.

The settler gave an account of an armed posse of stockmen killing seven people at their camp, in reprisal for the spearing of one of their companions. Days later the stockmen tracked the fleeing survivors to a lagoon, where they killed ten more. It was hard to imagine there could be many Lairmairermener left in their country.

In preparation for entering the country of their enemy, the men had paid particular attention to dressing their hair and bodies with red ochre. On 4 November, they crossed the Hobart-to-Launceston road into Lairmairermener country. They walked close enough to settlements to hear cocks crowing. Robinson knew it was essential to keep the people away from the farms, and it proved to be a daily trial. He was much relieved when the resupply team brought fresh supplies of the tea and sugar the people so craved. In vain, he tried to stop their dancing and singing at night, for fear it would invite a surprise attack on their camp.

Even when the party climbed into the heavily forested high country of the central plateau there were signs of settler intrusion. Massive stumps as big as wagon wheels were all that remained of tall eucalypts and giant stringybark trees felled by convict timber cutters using a two-handed crosscut saw. Here the game was plentiful and Mannalargenna hunted kangaroo as though his life depended on it, pursuing them along ridges and down precipitous gullies while his companions watched in awe.

Moving north-west, over many days, they found no more signs of settlers, but plenty of evidence of occupation by the Lairmairermener. The massive stringybark trees had prominent horizontal scars on the trunks where the dense fibrous bark had been peeled off to make huts. There were empty huts, large enough to house several families, marked with perfectly drawn circles. One day they came upon a village where each hut was decorated with drawings of humans and animals, as well as the ubiquitous circles. The meaning of this decoration eluded Robinson, and his guides knew better than to explain what they signified and endure his scornful lectures about their foolish superstition.

The first tangible evidence of the continuing presence of the original people came when smoke was seen in the distance, somewhere near Lake Echo to the north-west. Greatly encouraged, Robinson rode to a vantage point for a better look, only to return to find his own campsite wreathed in smoke: Kickerterpoller had lit the grass in three separate places. Robinson couldn't believe the man could be so 'obdurate and thoughtless' as to do this when it would give their position away. Reaching Lake Echo the next day, they saw the land had been recently fired and in some places was still smouldering. There was no sign of the people.

Polare unearthed more caches containing eight guns with powder horn and some small amounts of powder, but no shot. Without ammunition, the heavy guns were useless, and they had been hidden until the people managed to steal some more powder and shot. It was unlikely that anyone would be coming back for them in the near future.

On 14 November Robinson heard dogs barking and sent his guides to investigate. They returned unanimously agreeing that there was no human presence to be seen—the barking had been a spirit that had come and gone, travelling like the wind. The next day, clearly visible tracks suggested a group of six or seven people with dogs had been close by. Before any search party could be sent to locate them, another grass fire flared, this time lit by Maulboyheener.

'I cannot effect anything without these people yet I am harassed and perplexed by them,' Robinson despaired. 'They are a peculiar people to manage.' All they wanted to do was hunt, and when not hunting were 'idling away the time' digging platypuses out of burrows or looking for the lairs of wild dogs. Even Truganini remained cheerfully indifferent to Robinson's lectures that 'the governor did not want kangaroo, but wanted us to look out for the natives'. It was a puzzle to him that his guides were not keen to meet the Big River people yet the moment they saw a settler's hut they wanted to visit despite the imminent danger, prepared to risk the settler's guns just to get some potatoes.

By late November, the party had completed a second loop of the central plateau and Robinson was now engaged in a dogged contest with Mannalargenna for control of the mission. Mannalargenna's spirit told him the Big River people had certainly gone to the east, while Robinson countered that they were certainly still hiding in the north-west. To prove his point, he took them to the top of a hill, from which smoke could be seen rising in the direction of Lake Echo. He triumphantly declared that God was directing him. Who did they choose to believe, he demanded, God or Mannalargenna's spirit guide? Everyone looked sullen and remained silent. Eventually Polare ventured to ask why he had not stayed at Lake Echo, if God told him the Big River people were there?

This was an utterly one-sided contest. Not Truganini, nor Wooredy, nor any of the other guides chose to take Robinson's part. Still, the evidence of the smoke was hard to ignore, so back to Lake Echo they trudged. Again they found no people, and again Robinson tried to assert his ascendancy over Mannalargenna. Knowing the old man had a morbid fear of snakes, he snatched up a long tiger snake, still drowsy from hibernation, swung the writhing reptile in the air and snapped it to break its back. As he threw the snake away, he challenged Mannalargenna to do the same. Instead of rising to Robinson's challenge, everyone shrank away from him in appalled horror.

Lake Echo was near the edge of the Western Tiers, and at that altitude cider gums grew profusely. With the approach of summer, sweet sap had begun to ferment in these alpine trees. Polare, who had lived in this region, showed how to bore a hole into the trunk and insert a straw of rolled bark to suck out the sweet, fermented sap, or else let it drain into their tin cups. They ran from tree to tree, sucking the honeyed liquid till they were giddy with intoxication.

Unseasonably, the advent of summer also brought horizontal sleet and snow to the highlands. The wide expanse of the once tranquil lake took on the appearance of a stormy sea with cresting waves depositing mounds of brown foam on the shores. Robinson thought the view of the dramatic snow-covered peaks to the south-west was sublime, but at night he could not sleep for the cold. As they walked north, Mannalargenna led the party, beating against the wind with his smouldering firestick, and behind him the other men made as if they were spearing the snow.

Their blankets, and even the additional kangaroo-skin cloaks Truganini and the other women had made, were inadequate covering against the cold. Discontent festered. Mannalargenna led the party north-west along the edge of the Western Tiers and down to the Meander River Valley where the climate was milder. This was bad country. There had been massacres in 1828 in which local stockmen and the 40th Regiment had all but extinguished the local Pallitore clan. Mannalargenna was keen to get through this tainted country and kept heading west along the edge of the highlands till Robinson became suspicious of the direction they were headed with such evident purpose.

Mannalargenna explained they were going to get red ochre from a deposit about three or four days' walk away. Robinson pleaded with them not to 'fritter away time in such a manner', but no one was prepared to go back over the Western Tiers until, much to Robinson's surprise, Kickerterpoller took up his case. 'What would the governor think of it?' Kickerterpoller scolded. 'If the governor asked Mr R, "Where was the blacks?" Mr R must show him the red ochre and say, "There, governor, there is the natives."' He was playing to their powerful attachment to the idea of pleasing the governor. They understood only too well that it was the governor, not Robinson, who would determine how they were to live into the future. They walked back into the snow towards Lake Echo.

On 30 December, smoke was seen once again and all the guides went to investigate. The following morning Robinson had just begun his daily journal entry when he was interrupted by a great racket: his guides were returning with the Big River people, who were indeed the remnant of the Lairmairermener and Pardarereme clans. It was not a large group—only sixteen warriors, nine women and a child, with more than a hundred dogs. In his excitement, Robinson did not return to his journal, so he wrote no contemporaneous account of what happened at this longed-for meeting.

In the report he later wrote for the governor, Robinson implied that he single-handedly fell in with the Big River people. According to this vainglorious account, a band of warriors suddenly advanced on him, rattling their spears in a warlike attitude, but he calmly walked towards them and invited them to sit down and take tea with him. After distributing some of the trinkets he kept for this purpose, he promised a meeting with the governor to discuss their grievances. In return, or so he reported, they 'placed themselves under my protection'. He did not care to explain how he could speak to them in their own language.

Of course, Robinson wasn't alone as his report implied. His guides were present and so was at least one convict, Alexander McGeary, who wrote his own account of the momentous meeting. In McGeary's telling, there was never any danger to Robinson. The Big River people knew many of the guides and were happy to join them. Both groups of people 'kissed and hugged one another—all we had to do was bring them together', he wrote.

A week later, the Big River people were paraded through the streets of Hobart with their great army of dogs for the jubilant populace to gawk at. Most of the town turned out. At Government House they were met by a full military band, which greatly alarmed them. After being briefly addressed by the governor, the men performed a spear-throwing competition on the grass under the trees. When this circus was over, they were taken to the harbour and put aboard a small ship to be kept securely until the government cutters *Tamar* and *Charlotte* arrived from George Town ten days later.

Truganini and her companions were embarked on the *Charlotte*, and the Big River people on the *Tamar* on 17 January. The Big River people embarked sedately, but once the ship set sail they erupted into cries of distress, darting about the deck or clinging to the gunwales, and had to be subdued by the crew. The fate of these people might have been the cause of some disquiet for the mission guides—and more evidence of Robinson's bad faith—yet they seemed quite satisfied to see their traditional enemies sent into exile. For Truganini, it offered further proof of her own special standing. She and her companions did not go to Flinders Island; instead, they were disembarked at George Town and sent to Mr Whitcomb's house in Launceston, to await Robinson and another mission.

Robinson was not eager to join them. The colonists' exuberant displays of gratitude for bringing in the Big River people had not translated into the generous financial reward he was expecting. Before he would agree to venture into the wilderness again, he drove a hard bargain with the governor. Three months were spent haggling to secure a further land grant, as well as £1000 in cash, of which £300 would be paid upfront with the balance due when all the people were removed. He put in a good word for his 'sable companions', who were awarded a flock of sheep. These animals were not sent to an area outside of Campbell Town supposedly set aside for the guides but straight to Flinders Island, leaving no doubt that this was already where Robinson intended his companions to live out their days.

As Truganini waited for him at their protector's house in Launceston, she could not have guessed that he had negotiated to be appointed commandant of the Flinders Island establishment and would take up the role just as soon as he had cleared the colony of every last one of the original people.

Flinders Island was no better than Gun Carriage Island: dreadfully exposed and barren with inadequate water. The clans of the north-west believed that the distant islands of the Bass Strait were the islands of the dead, and Flinders Island must have looked to them like that prophecy fulfilled. The chosen site for the establishment was on the west coast of Flinders Island opposite Green Island, where there was good anchorage for ships. Known as the Lagoons, it was on a narrow sandbank adjacent to a swampy tidal lagoon, with no protection of hills or trees, leaving it exposed to the violent winds of the Roaring Forties, which brought driving rain and sleet. The only water came from sinkholes dug above the tideline, and was decidedly brackish. The forty people transferred from Gun Carriage Island were living close to the shore in three large A-frame huts, constructed from tea-tree branches and rush thatch. A fence made from saplings was the only protection from the wind. Many people were desperately ill.

Robinson did not hold back in his denunciation of the place when he took his guides for a short, unhappy visit to the island in February 1832. In his report to the governor, his only positive assessment of the site was 'its remoteness from the main territory'. Indeed, it was remote; not even a faint outline of the mainland was visible from the Lagoons. Only from the high peaks of the Mount Strzelecki range that rose up behind them could the people have sighted the land they had inhabited for forty thousand years.

It was with great relief that the mission party left Flinders Island a few weeks later, on 12 March, on the next expedition to remove people still known to be living in the north-west corner. By then, Robinson had added two Tyreelore to the party: Plorenernoopner, who was now the wife of Peevay, and Nollahalleker, also known as Kit, who was originally from Cape Grim and had relatives still in that country. He had also managed to extract Karnebucher from McKay, as well as a Pallitore woman McKay had captured in an ambush in the Hampshire hills. Her name was Semiramis, known as Jenny, and she was soon to become the wife of Maulboyheener. Police constable Anthony Cottrell, with the seven New South Wales trackers transferred from Batman, was also included in the party.

The brief exposure to institutional life in exile proved disastrous for the mission. Nearly everyone was ill with dysentery or influenza. Umarrah died of dysentery in the Launceston hospital on 24 March. Two days later, his body was put into a plain coffin to be placed in a hole in unconsecrated ground. Following the coffin, his wife Polare and his companions did what they could to pay him the respect due to a great leader. While they were forbidden to discard all their clothes, they painted their bodies with charcoal and ochre. A curious settler asked why they painted their bodies in this way and received a curt answer from Kickerterpoller: 'What do you wear fine clothes for?'

The devastated party left Launceston on 4 April, heading into the eastern holdings of the Van Diemen's Land Company. Most remained ill, and by the time they reached the company outpost at Hampshire two weeks later, Kickerterpoller and Polare could not walk, requiring a cart to carry them. Three others were also very ill. Cottrell took all five invalids by boat to Emu Bay, while the rest of the party rested at Hampshire.

During this hiatus, Mannalargenna was determined not to miss the chance for a trip to the ochre mine. He was completely confident of the way, leading the party across a series of rock-strewn hills with steep ravines into country that Robinson described as 'a riot of wilderness'. They had to negotiate a passage through moss-covered myrtle rainforest and a horizontal scrub of sassafras so tight that they were obliged to crawl on their bellies, surrendering to the slimy, mouldy leaf litter infested with leeches. Robinson had a horrible time of it, but Mannalargenna refused to stop until they reached a spot where rocks of iron oxide were breaking through the ground. The people dropped to their knees, patting and kissing the earth.

For millennia, people had been coming here for ochre—from the east as far as Cape Portland and Oyster Bay, from the west from Cape Grim and Sandy Cape, and south from the Great Lakes. The exposed rocks were not the best for ochre as they had been scorched by many fires, so the women got to work with their digging sticks to make deep holes. They pulled out big lumps of ore that Robinson guessed weighed five or six pounds each, filling their knapsacks to overflowing.

Returning the next day with the heavy knapsacks, they followed a track that Semiramis showed them through Pallitore country. Although the land showed signs of having been burnt maybe the year before, there were no people left. She took them to a secluded forest, where the debarked trees indicated there had been an encampment. This was the spot where McKay and two

Van Diemen's Land Company employees had killed her husband when they shot at a group of five adults and a boy as they sat by their fire. Her husband, another man and a woman were killed, and one woman managed to escape. Semiramis had surrendered with the boy and had been forced to become a guide for McKay's party. She did not know what had happened to the boy.

Lying on the ground were shattered remains, including the skull of the murdered woman with her perfect teeth intact. When Robinson bent down to collect the skull, his guides howled in such outrage that he had to leave it where it lay.

The mission party arrived at Emu Bay in early May to find their sick companions were no better. Kickerterpoller was in extremis. Robinson pushed on, after instructing Cottrell that when the invalids recovered they were to be forwarded by boat to the Van Diemen's Land Company headquarters at Circular Head. To replace them, he added four of the trackers from New South Wales. He scorned these fellows as useless drunks and worried about how their wanton behaviour might affect his guides, but, having observed their skill in making sturdy ribbed canoes from peppermint gums, he could see they would be very helpful to him. He need not have worried. His guides were antagonistic towards the four alien men, except for Karnebucher, who liked having them around as a link to her son kidnapped by Batman. Their news of her boy helped to assuage her bitter grief.

Wooredy was out hunting on the coast, west of Rocky Point, on 13 May when he encountered two company workers riding horses along the beach. The horsemen were friendly enough, offering him a pipe and tobacco and asking if there were any more like him. Wooredy spoke passable English and replied that, yes, there were more with Mr Robinson's party. As the men parted from him they called out, 'See you tomorrow at Circular Head.

We give you plenty flour.' That night, as the party slept around their fire, they heard horses' hooves and men call, 'Here they are. Cut away, cut away!' They leapt up to see a group of mounted men approaching at a gallop with guns raised, shooting wildly as they pounded through the camp. By some miracle no one was hurt, although one of the riders was shot in the knee by mistake. Suddenly, the protection of the Van Diemen's Land Company did not seem like much protection at all.

When they reached the company town at Circular Head, Robinson prudently established his camp around the timber cottages near the wharf that housed the bookkeeper and the indentured workmen. He went out of his way to curry favour with the manager, Edward Curr, sending him some of Truganini's woven baskets and a shell necklace.

He even organised entertainment in two large tents where Curr and his officers were supplied with grog and cigars to watch the people dance naked. In preparation, the guides ground their ochre and mixed it with animal fat to dress their hair, and the New South Wales trackers covered their naked bodies in white clay. Together they made an imposing spectacle: those in red ochre chanting and rhythmically stamping their feet and those daubed with clay clashing boomerangs against their distinctive bark shields. The entertainment was so well received that Robinson repeated it several times, each time with more elaborate staging.

Pagerly, Richard and Karnebucher rejoined the group at Circular Head. Polare had died of dysentery at Emu Bay in May. So too had Kickerterpoller, leaving Pagerly a widow for the third time in as many years. Kickerterpoller had been baptised, and was given a Christian burial at Emu Bay on 16 May. Robinson took the news of his death as a blow, indulging in a sentimental memory of a devoted and loyal retainer. Conveniently, he suppressed the memory of the 'obdurate and callous' fellow whose persistent subversion of his authority had caused him so much exasperation. Robinson never comprehended that it was not to him that Kickerterpoller gave his loyalty, but to Mannalargenna. Equally, he failed to appreciate that Mannalargenna was even now orchestrating a campaign of resistance within the mission party.

The party arrived at Cape Grim in the far north-west corner in early June to find a party of sealers from Robbins and Hunter islands with several Tyreelore, including one of Mannalargenna's daughters and Tanleboneyer's sister. Mannalargenna was much animated to see his daughter and demanded that Robinson take the women away, as the governor had promised. He also wanted the sealer arrested who had shot him years before. 'These poor creatures imagine that I possess power to redress their grievance,' Robinson moaned. 'Alas I have no such power, I can only listen to their complaints and promise to enquire about it.' Mannalargenna perfectly understood that in order to gain his assistance Robinson had boasted that he possessed just such powers; this present demurring did not please him one bit.

Cape Grim was Peevay's country. His clan was the Parperloihener from Robbins Island, and his eldest brother, Wymurric, had gathered together the remnants of clans whose coastal territory stretched along the north coast from Table Cape to Cape Grim, and down the west coast to West Point. These were the people the mission party was looking to meet. Just how many still survived in the north-west corner, Peevay could not say.

There had been a drastic decline in the original population during the past few years. Incursions by the sealers had severely weakened the clans and triggered internecine warfare over women, although it was punitive action by Van Diemen's Land Company employees that did the most damage to an already fragile population. A common practice was for lonely shepherds to kidnap a woman to hold as a sex slave—sometimes chained out the back of the hut—inviting retaliation by the clan. The occasional spearing of a shepherd would lead to brutal reprisals in which dozens of people, perhaps not even from the same clan, were wantonly killed. Spearing sheep would invite the same response.

Peevay led the party over miles of grass-covered sandhills that provided sweeping views of the stretch of sandy beach that ran from Cape Grim all the way to West Point. Beyond was the quilted blue of the endless Indian Ocean. Not until they reached West Point on 19 June was Peevay able to make contact with his brother. Wymurric was an impressive man, six and a half feet tall, and with the same expressive face as Peevay. He had been expecting Robinson.

The previous summer, a group of Lowreenne and Ninine people had visited Wymurric, among them Dray, from Robinson's first mission. She had told him of Robinson's good intentions, but Wymurric had remained wary. Only months before, Alexander McKay had shot dead one of his warriors and captured his third brother, Pendowtewer, who was brutally beaten. Wymurric was also currently engaged in a debilitating war with the Tarkiner and Peternidic clans from the west coast. Peevay sought to persuade him that Robinson could provide protection.

About a week later, Wymurric and another brother, Pend-eroin, came to Robinson's camp. They were very friendly, until Wooredy and Mannalargenna crept up to steal their spears. The two warriors tried to wrest back their weapons and a scuffle ensued. Eventually Robinson intervened, insisting that the spears be returned. Grim and resentful, Mannalargenna and Wooredy handed over the spears and stomped away. The damage was done: Peevay could not get his brothers to stay at the camp a moment longer. Robinson grumbled that his old companions were 'bad politicians' who only understood force, rather than the tricks of persuasion.

His own tricks of persuasion appeared to be working. On 16 July, Wymurric agreed to accompany the mission party to Cape Grim, and brought with him nine men, five women and eight children. They were all quite at ease, hunting at every opportunity and singing as they walked. Carefully maintaining a stance of disinterested friendship, Robinson sought to learn their language and customs and was fascinated to be told that they would quiet their children by saying '*num lagger*', meaning 'the white man is coming'. This phrase could frighten a child into silence. He believed the terror implicit in this phrase was inspired by men like McKay, never himself. All the while he was considering how best to get these twenty-three people to nearby Hunter Island, which was far enough offshore to serve as a holding depot. From there he could arrange a government ship to deport Wymurric and his people to Flinders Island.

The generous and unwitting Peevay was used as a decoy to trick his two brothers onto a boat, on the pretence that they were all going hunting on Hunter Island. Wooredy did his best to foil the plan by loudly proclaiming that there were no kangaroos on Hunter Island and they would do better to hunt on the shore. Meanwhile, Robinson pretended to be unconcerned about whether Wymurric and his people came or not. Wymurric hesitated but eventually accepted Peevay's entreaties and climbed aboard. Once he was seated the others were prepared to follow, even though the women still evinced unease about going to the island where the sealers lived. They never came back.

Almost as soon as they were encamped on Hunter Island, Wymurric's people began to sicken. The first to expire was a nursing mother who died on 30 July, followed the next day by an old man, who was cremated over the ashes of the woman, and the day after that by the motherless baby. Each day, the grieving people coated their bodies with the ashes of the dead as a sign of mourning. Every dawn, a woman would begin the song of lamentations, then others would join in and continue to sing on and off throughout the day. Never again did they mention the names of their departed.

By the end of the month, Robinson was referring to these people as captives and organising for a ship to take them into permanent exile. 'I practise no deception, nor indeed have I at any time,' Robinson told himself defensively, 'to my having acted faithfully toward them I attribute under God my success.'

In August, Peevay's older brother Penderoin told Robinson about a large group of people from the Peternidic, Tommigener, Tarkiner and Ninine clans camped at the Arthur River. Robinson received this information with glee, delighted at the prospect of adding more people to those already on Hunter Island. In his journal on 3 September, he congratulated himself on having negotiated with the governor to remove *all* the people of Van Diemen's Land: 'By taking the whole I gain not only the reward but the celebrity.'

CHAPTER 6

In late August 1832, Mannalargenna's spirit guide was offering dire premonitions to the mission party as they travelled down the west coast in search of the Tarkiner and Peternidic clans, whose territory ran from Sandy Cape to the Pieman River. The mood was decidedly sour. Truganini, Wooredy, Peevay and Pagerly—still mourning the loss of Kickerterpoller and Polare—were unsettled by Mannalargenna's vivid vision of Tarkiner warriors spearing Robinson on the banks of the Arthur River.

Robinson was aggravated to have the cranky old man envisioning his death and he increasingly sidelined Mannalargenna, deliberately excluding him from the advance party sent across the Arthur River on 1 September. Instead he relied on Peevay to lead the group, along with his brother Penderoin, who had close kin connections to the Tarkiner and Peternidic.

Two days later, Peevay and Penderoin, together with Truganini, Wooredy, Lacklay and Maulboyheener, appeared on the far bank of the river standing among a large group of strangers. They signalled for Robinson to come over and join them. Strategically, he took Penderoin's wife Nollahalleker, whose brother was among the newcomers on the far bank, and Pagerly to swim his raft across. On reaching the opposite bank, he was greeted by a group of twenty-nine people from various west coast clans. The group included Peevay's sister, with her Tarkiner husband, and several Ninine people, one of them a relative of Truganini. The dominant man in the group was a very tall Tarkiner warrior in his forties named Wyne.

Wyne appeared to be very affable. Enthusiastically accepting Robinson's ribbons and baubles, he encouraged the others to come closer. Once satisfied there was no danger, he took all the men hunting, leaving Robinson to wait on the riverbank with the women, who were in mourning, covered in the ashes of their dead. Truganini eagerly sought information on the whereabouts of her friend Dray, and was told that she was no longer on the coast and had taken all the remaining Ninine people to Hobart in a two-masted boat. When this was translated, Robinson thought it a plausible enough story, but did not believe a word of it. He was sure it was 'a *ruse de guerre*', concocted to prevent him from going further south to find them.

As evening fell, the whole group walked back to a camp in the forest, with Robinson carrying Wyne's youngest daughter on his shoulders. Cheerful and relaxed, Wyne indicated to Robinson that he should make his bed in the middle of the camp. As Robinson laid out his bedroll, Wyne sat at its end with his wife and three daughters, while everyone else settled around the fire.

A secret warning was conveyed to Peevay that he should keep watch that night because the Tarkiner intended to kill Robinson and any of his guides who were not their kin, with the exception of Truganini, whom they wanted to keep for themselves. With much agitated whispering, this plot was communicated to Robinson, who shrugged it off. A second dire alert, sounded by Truganini's relative, was also cursorily dismissed. Robinson was determined not to be made to look foolish by giving credence to Mannalargenna's delusions.

That night's corroboree was the usual high-spirited affair. The Peternidic danced, then the Ninine danced, then all the guides danced. The Tarkiner men just watched, maintaining a sullen reserve. Robinson was surprised to see them begin to sharpen their spears. 'If they meant to go with me they did not require spears,' he reflected, uneasily. He felt a flicker of foreboding as he rolled out his blanket and prepared to go to sleep, even as the dances continued around him. Wooredy hissed that he must not sleep, because he would be speared. Robinson merely smiled and replied that his old friend was speaking nonsense. Wooredy snapped back, 'You see, by and by.' With half-closed eyes, Robinson lay on his bedroll observing Wyne hardening his spear in the fire and straightening it between his strong white teeth. Occasionally, Wyne turned to look at his guest 'with a strange savage grin'.

The attack happened just as foretold in Mannalargenna's vision. At dawn, Wyne and his Tarkiner warriors surrounded Robinson with raised spears, while everyone else raced into the bush. Wooredy implored Truganini to come with him, but instead she ran in the opposite direction, towards the river. Utterly defenceless against the Tarkiner, Robinson sprinted after her, assuming that she intended to escape across the water. He was determined not to lose sight of her, because he could not swim. This was a dangerous strategy, given that she was the woman the Tarkiner especially wanted. Frantically, Truganini called over her shoulder that he must leave her and hide in the bush. She shouted that Wooredy, Lacklay and Maulboyheener had already been speared and that he would be next. Paying no heed to Truganini's pleas,

Robinson feverishly gathered buoyant pieces of driftwood that he bound together with his garters. He begged her to swim his makeshift raft across the fast-flowing river.

In that moment, Truganini was faced with a stark choice: would her future be better served by an alliance with Robinson or a tenuous freedom among the Tarkiner? Making a snap judgement, she dived into the water, took hold of his raft and with powerful kicks pushed the flimsy contraption against the strong current that kept threatening to roll Robinson into the turbid water.

Mannalargenna was surprised when Truganini brought Robinson back to camp, trembling in shock and dripping wet but with no spear wounds. Having recovered enough to return to the river the next day, Robinson saw his guides, quite unharmed, on the opposite bank, standing among the towering warriors who were shaking their spears. Shouting across the breach of water, he implored them to come to their senses and return to his care. He could tell they were inclined to remain where they were, but they showed some signs of wavering. They were now facing the same choice as Truganini. Robinson was not dead as foretold, so they must either return to his protective custody, or risk the precarious freedom offered by the Tarkiner.

For Wooredy, the choice was easy: he wanted to be with Truganini. Maulboyheener and Lacklay had no connection to the west coast people and every reason to worry for their future safety. After some hesitation, they began to construct a raft of driftwood bound together with vines. When Pagerly stepped forwards to swim the raft across, nobody tried to stop them. Further down the riverbank, four young women dived into the water and helped her to push.

Among the defectors was Wyne's adolescent daughter, Ryenrope. Her enraged father shook his spear and screamed across the water and still she kept swimming to the other side. The Tarkiner men yelled across the river that they would trade their dogs for the return of the women, at which Robinson's guides laughed heartily and began a victory dance. Robinson ordered them to stop, fearing it would bring the infuriated Tarkiner across the river to make another attack. Peevay might have told them he was travelling without firearms.

Peevay and Penderoin hesitated on the far bank much longer. They had family ties that bound them to the Tarkiner, but also to Robinson. Their eldest brother, Wymurric, was in Robinson's charge at Hunter Island, and another brother, Pendowtewer, was on Flinders Island. Peevay was especially torn because his wife, Plorenernoopner, was with Robinson on the other side of the river. Eventually, Peevay gathered up Robinson's cloak and knapsack and, together with Penderoin and Nollahalleker, came across the river on the original raft. Robinson could not help but observe of Peevay that 'if he had influence sufficient to prevent them from taking those things, he must necessarily have had influence to prevent the attack'. This was an insight he chose not to dwell upon, any more than he would reflect on Mannalargenna's extraordinary prescience.

Wooredy had suffered a terrible loss of face at Arthur River when Truganini ran away from him during the Tarkiner attack. He was a much-changed man. A dark shadow was cast over their relationship. Within a week of their return to Hunter Island, a fearsome quarrel erupted during which Wooredy snatched up a stolen spear and swore to kill Truganini. He would not be calmed, even when Mannalargenna tried to take the spear away. Robinson had to threaten him with a loaded gun in order to compel him to relinquish the weapon. Robinson claimed to be at a loss to know what had caused this uncharacteristic outburst from his most reliable guide, even though he was well aware of Wooredy's agitation at the proximity of the tall young men from West Point and Cape Grim. Wooredy was nearing fifty, whereas Truganini was just twenty-one, which was reason enough to fear that she would desert him. She excited a great deal of interest among the Pennemukeer and Peerapper men, just as she had among the Tarkiner, and Robinson had overheard Mannalargenna's wife Tanleboneyer openly reprove Truganini for 'going with the wild black fellows'.

There was a catastrophic scarcity of women throughout the west because the sealers had abducted nearly all of them. Conflict over women was the reason for the war between the clans. A young woman like Truganini was a great prize. Wooredy may have appeared supine when a man like McKay took sexual liberties with Truganini, but he would not submit to a loss of status among his own. He persisted in stealing Wymurric's men's spears and became incensed every time Robinson gave them back. He could hardly wait for all those tall, handsome warriors to be shipped off to the islands of the dead.

The government cutter *Charlotte* was expected at Hunter Island in September but it failed to arrive—an aggravation for Wooredy and an opportunity for Truganini. For Robinson, it was a full-blown crisis. By October, the supplies were expended and he had no rations for all the people in his charge. Apart from the twenty-seven captives and his eleven guides, Robinson had to feed Anthony Cottrell and his four New South Wales trackers, seven convicts, himself and his son George. Over fifty people had to subsist on the occasional kangaroo killed by the few hunters allowed back to the mainland, as well as penguins and mutton birds supplied by the sealers. Truganini and Pagerly dived for shellfish when they could cajole a sealer to take them to Three Hummock Island, where caves heaving with abalone and crayfish were only accessible at low tide. Such was Robinson's need for food that he allowed the women to bargain with these debauched fellows.

Without adequate sustenance, people fell ill. Their precious dogs were starving. Robinson rebuffed Wymurric's repeated requests to take his people back to the mainland so they could hunt. Robinson was sure that what they really wanted was their liberty, given that they were 'under a sort of restraint they don't fancy'. He suggested that Wymurric take his people hunting on Three Hummock Island, where game was said to be plentiful. They came back empty-handed, vigorously denouncing the further island as a bad place. Robinson was convinced they deliberately came back with no game because they were afraid he was going to send them there to live.

To again reassure Wymurric, Robinson told him that a big boat would soon come to take his band to visit the huge rockeries on Flinders Island, so they could hunt mutton birds to their heart's content. This was a blatant deceit, but he was 'satisfied that they are in the situation of children not capable to judge what is best for themselves'. Wymurric was suspicious at the mention of Flinders Island, as he had heard that the place was even worse than where they were. As an additional inducement, Robinson promised Wymurric that he and his brother Penderoin would have a meeting with the governor in Hobart. Robinson wrote to the colonial secretary to secure an audience for them, and he ordered the Van Diemen's Land Company tailor to make trousers and jackets for the men and printed cotton dresses for their wives so they would be presentable at Government House.

In the meantime, the search for food continued. A sealer was contracted to take Robinson, Truganini and Wooredy by boat to a tiny island where thousands of albatross were nesting. As they approached the island they were assaulted by high-pitched screeching as the birds swooped overhead in massed profusion. Buffeted by waves that pounded the perpendicular rock face, they entered a narrow inlet between deeply eroded cliffs; here the sealer hauled his boat up the rocks using ropes. Truganini, Wooredy and Robinson pulled themselves up on hands and knees to reach a deep tunnel leading into a large subterranean cave. It was eerily beautiful, with stalactites hanging from the roof, but stank from the huge piles of putrid carcasses of plucked birds.

The boatman explained that the sealers drove the birds in here from the top of the cliff and then blocked the cave mouth. When the birds were weakened from starvation, the sealers would send their women captives in to pluck the feathers. They plucked many thousands of birds every year, he boasted, yet still the albatross came, inexhaustible like the mutton birds. Robinson knew these majestic birds were not inexhaustible, and he despaired that they would soon be gone, like the seals, whose brittle skeletons crunched beneath his feet.

At the top of the island the surface of the rock was coated silver with sun-baked guano so slippery it was like walking on glass. Everywhere, raised nests made with mud and grass held a huge white bird with bright black eyes and a long orange-tipped beak. Wooredy scrambled over the rocks, bashing the birds on the head with his waddy, until he was bent double under the enormous load of dead birds stuffed into his knapsack. Trying to get eggs, Truganini threw rocks at the nesting birds, and even got Robinson to help her to push them, but they would not stir off their nests. It was easier to suffer being pecked by the brilliant beaks while reaching underneath to snatch the giant eggs. Their haul of dead birds and eggs helped the people on Hunter Island to keep starvation at bay for another three weeks.

On 30 October, a sail was seen coming from the south-east. It was the *Charlotte*, at last. On board was Ensign William Darling, who had taken temporary charge of the Flinders Island establishment. With Darling were three young men from the south-east clans, whose job was to persuade the reluctant people on Hunter Island that they had nothing to fear in going to Flinders Island. Robinson made himself scarce as the captives were embarked so that he would not have to witness their confusion and distress. Leaving his son George and Anthony Cottrell in charge of his mission party, he took the Van Diemen's Land Company boat to Circular Head.

Robinson rejoined the *Charlotte* on 9 November and sailed as far as George Town, from where he continued overland, alone, to Hobart, leaving Darling on the *Charlotte* to take the majority of the captives to Flinders Island. Darling was instructed to then proceed to Hobart with Wymurric and family, and Penderoin and Nollahalleker.

On the morning of 26 November 1832, Truganini found herself once again at the site of her perilous escape at the Arthur River. Wooredy was standing beside her, with Peevay and his wife Plorenernoopner. They were the advance party of the new mission led by Cottrell, come to capture the Tarkiner.

Facing them on the opposite bank was Wyne, surrounded by about thirty adults and children. Peevay shouted for everyone to cross over, but no amount of cajoling could induce them. The people on the opposite bank had still not moved by the late afternoon when Cottrell arrived with the rest of the party, which included three New South Wales trackers and several convict retainers. Wyne was deeply suspicious to see that Robinson was not among them, sure he must be concealed somewhere with guns, waiting to massacre Wyne and his people when they came within range. Peevay laughed at these fears, inviting Wyne to send envoys to look for signs of an ambush.

After some disputation with Wyne, two men among his group constructed a raft and brought it across the river. They were Tommigener men from Table Cape, who had no clan loyalty to Wyne. On inspecting the knapsacks and tents and finding no weapons, they decided to stay. A definite incentive for these young men was the presence of young women in the mission party. Later that day, a third Tommigener warrior came across the river to join them. The presence of three strange men made Wooredy decidedly edgy.

When it was apparent that no one else was going to cross, Peevay and Wooredy took a raft to the opposite bank, pushed by Truganini and Plorenernoopner, and were permitted to bring Peevay's sister and her husband and child across the river. No one else showed any inclination to leave Wyne's side.

Early in the evening, Wyne shouted a request for Truganini to swim a raft over one more time, which Cottrell suspected was a ruse to capture her. Instead, one of the men from New South Wales known as Stewart paddled his canoe across. He had nearly reached the far bank when a volley of spears rained down on him. Stewart dived off his craft and swam away beneath the water, surfacing briefly for gulps of air. Wyne pulled the abandoned canoe from the river and tore it to pieces, shouting that they would kill any *num* who came within range, and if Peevay tried to cross they would spear him as well.

Dawn revealed the opposite bank to be empty. Wyne and his people had vanished into the forbidding tangle of myrtle, sassafras and tree ferns beyond the river. The party returned to Cape Grim, where the six defectors were sent to Launceston on a Van Diemen's Land Company boat. Peevay grieved to see the last of his family sent away from him, while Wooredy was highly gratified.

A little over a month later, Truganini and her companions crossed the Arthur River again, travelling down the west coast with Cottrell to rendezvous with Robinson at Macquarie Harbour. They crossed the river without incident, seeing no evidence of Wyne or any local people. Days later, they reached the turbulent Pieman River, swollen from heavy rain and seemingly impassable. A viable crossing was located further upstream, where Stewart and his two compatriots from New South Wales constructed a couple of canoes to carry the party across.

Even though each canoe was reinforced with internal ribbing made from pliable saplings, two of the convicts baulked at getting into such a flimsy craft. Taking Truganini, Pagerly and Plorenernoopner back downstream to the mouth of the river, the convicts made a raft from the huge logs thrown up onto the banks. Rather than carry the heavy contraption upstream, the convicts required the women to swim them across the swirling waters, even though the tide was running out. The current was so strong that when the raft reached the middle it was pulled towards the seething ocean, where huge breakers were smashing onto a sandbar at the river mouth. Pagerly and Plorenernoopner lost hold, while Truganini hung on, calling to the men to jump into the water so she and her friends could swim them to shore. They were too terrified. Begging Truganini not to leave them, they tore off their clothes, knelt down and locked their bodies together as the raft was torn from her and swept onto the sandbar to splinter into pieces. In seconds, the two men were swallowed by the foaming water and their bodies swept out to sea. Truganini was distressed to witness the final moments of these men, who had accompanied her on several missions and had always been kind to her. She was deeply regretful that she had lost her hold.

The very next day the Tarkiner reappeared. This time Wyne reverted to his affable persona, accepting eight blankets from Cottrell and requesting flour, tea and sugar. Cottrell had to refuse the rations as they were in short supply, yet despite the rebuff Wyne and his people stayed that night. The next morning, he gave Peevay to understand that he and his people would accompany them to Macquarie Harbour after all. Truganini distrusted the Tarkiner and refused to walk anywhere near Wyne and the other men. When, after a few miles, they melted back into the bush, no one made a move to stop them. Cottrell was sorely disappointed. No more people were sighted for the rest of the journey.

On reaching Macquarie Harbour, in January 1833, a boat was hailed to take the party to Sarah Island, where the fearsome penitentiary was about to close. Only a few convicts remained, guarded by a skeleton staff. Truganini and Wooredy had visited the grim prison on at least three occasions, and a great fuss had been made over them, so the prospect did not terrify them. Their companions were horrified by the place. Cottrell tried to ameliorate the unpleasantness of the penitentiary by moving them on to a large offshore rock called Grummet Island, where there was an empty stone dormitory originally built for the women convicts.

Nevertheless, Stewart and his two fellow New South Wales men would not stand for it. They swam back to Sarah Island, where they made canoes, crossed to the mainland and then disappeared into the wilderness. Unlike the many hapless convicts who had perished attempting a similar escape, these three men proved their exemplary bush skills by getting all the way back to Batman's property at the opposite end of Van Diemen's Land.

By early February, Robinson had still not arrived, so Truganini persuaded Cottrell that she could find the Ninine herself. She led the mission party from the southern end of Macquarie Harbour towards the coast. After nine days struggling through obdurate rainforest, Truganini reached a cleared area where stood a group of beehive-shaped huts made from saplings, bark and mud, insulated inside with down and feathers. The huts housed five women, a child and two men, all of whom were known to Truganini. She had little difficulty persuading them to come with her.

They could never have envisaged where she would take them. The clans of the west coast believed that the desolate penitentiary on Sarah Island, with its dreadful smell, was the lair of Raegewarrah—a place of terror, of no return. Cottrell was concerned about keeping these frightened people in such a terrible place, but he believed it would not be for long, as Robinson's boat was expected any day. However, Robinson was disinclined to travel any further west than Bruny Island, where he was arranging for Richard Pybus to act as agent for the sale of his land grant. It was a hundred days before he put in an appearance.

Robinson arrived from Hobart on the *Charlotte* on 28 April, bringing his second son Charles as well as Penderoin and Nollahalleker. By this time, three women had escaped by swimming to the mainland and the remaining captives were distraught to the point of stupor. Robinson was furious to discover that most of the people had somehow been allowed to escape. While his son George was exempt from the full brunt of Robinson's fury, the disgraced Cottrell was sent off in the *Charlotte* in charge of the paltry five captives he had managed to hold on to.

The west coast was as wild and untamed as Robinson had found it three years before, except that now the prison was closing down. There was still no settler presence in the region from Cape Grim to Port Davey. The Van Diemen's Land Company had abandoned the idea of extending its enterprise into this wild country, deciding that the place was uninhabitable even for sheep. At the same time, the Ninine, Peternidic and Tarkiner were still vigorous and independent, well adapted to the rugged west coast and living much as they always had. Left alone, these tall, confident west coast clans could have survived as a viable community. That was not Robinson's plan for them. He fully understood their profound attachment to their country, yet he convinced himself that they would readily accept Flinders Island as their adopted country, even though he would have to use deception and intimidation to get them there.

Robinson's journal entries were always saturated with self-delusion and duplicity, but nowhere was his dissimulation more reprehensible than in his account of his return to the south-west coast. Gone was his delight in a romantic immersion into a wild and sublime landscape. After more than three years in the conciliation business, he was impatient for the job to be finished so he could get his reward money and become the commandant at Flinders Island. Everything he craved was embodied in his prospective position: a title, authority, status, official recognition, a good salary and the promise of a handsome pension. All that stood between him and his just deserts were the three clans that remained on the west coast. He was prepared to use force to get them. Wooredy would not have to endure any more lectures about making friends, not taking captives, and the guns would not be concealed in the knapsacks. 'The sooner we got them the sooner we should be done,' Robinson wrote on 19 May 1833.

Coalescing in his imagination was the idea of a book about these last people. He had received fulsome encouragement from a friend in London, who told him to 'have some clever editor to revise your journal and get it into the hands of educated critics'. Though he wasn't settled on the form, illustrations would be essential, that much he knew. He had already commissioned the emancipated convict Thomas Bock to do some drawings, and luckily for him the penitentiary at Sarah Island still housed another felon artist, William Buelow Gould, who was directed to make portraits of Robinson and some of his guides.

In early May, Truganini led Robinson and the rest of the mission party to search for the remaining Ninine. She knew it was the season for the Ninine to go to the sea, to fish and trap seabirds, and that she could find them at a temporary camp on the rocky coastline just north of Port Davey. As they walked down the exposed coast they were buffeted by unkind westerly winds off the ocean. The nights were bitterly cold, and they had to travel without any fires to avoid advertising their presence.

All along the coast, huge stalks of bull kelp had fastened onto the rocks, sprouting long amber-coloured tentacles that undulated in the surge of the ocean, catching shoals of small fish. Torn from their stalks, the leathery tentacles were tossed upon the rocks in tangled heaps to feed cawing conspiracies of glossy black ravens. Just above the tideline, ingenious traps were baited with tiny fish to catch these birds. Ducks were trapped in a similar fashion, Truganini explained, except that the ducks were lured with worms.

On 20 May, wisps of smoke were seen and fresh footprints found in the sand. Truganini was confident that the people they sought were close by. It was so cold that the party made camp within a forest of peppermint gums, where a comforting understorey of tea tree provided shelter from the wind, yet they were still close enough to the beach for the women to dive for abalone and crayfish. At last they were allowed the luxury of a fire to cook their catch.

The next day, Robinson waited at the camp, writing up his journal, while Truganini and Wooredy went into the surrounding forest to reconnoitre. He had all but given up hope of making contact that day when Wooredy walked out of the forest carrying a small child on his shoulders. The child was the daughter of Towterer, the senior man among the Ninine, Wooredy explained, and he would definitely want to get her back. Soon, five women with two children emerged from the forest, followed by three men, each carrying a brace of ducks they had caught in their traps. They shouted out greetings to 'Mister Robinson', who warmly welcomed them with bread and tea, before handing out the beads.

Truganini was disappointed to see that her friend Dray was not among them, nor the child's father, Towterer. Truganini spoke with them at length and was able to ascertain that Dray and her new husband, Dewoorady, together with Towterer and his wife, were camped on the coast about ten miles away. The remaining group of Ninine seemed happy enough, dancing and singing late into the night. To induce them to stay, Robinson gave them his tent and kept watch all night, thrumming with anxiety that he might lose them.

In the morning, Truganini tried to persuade the group that they should go back to Macquarie Harbour with their friend Mister Robinson. They agreed to go, but not without the rest of their clan, offering to take Robinson to meet with Towterer so they could all go together.

Wooredy was firmly against this idea. The *toogee* could never be trusted, he insisted—their offer was a trick to allow them to escape. A show of guns was the only way to make them go, he said, as they were terrified of guns. Robinson protested that he did not want to intimidate these trusting people. Then why did he carry the firearms? was Wooredy's scornful rebuke. Was he planning to throw the guns away? Robinson conceded to Wooredy's blunt logic.

Determined that the Ninine would not slip away into the surrounding forest, Wooredy hatched a plan to get these people onto open ground, instructing them to make a fire to signal to the rest of their clan that they were coming. Then Mannalargenna hustled them out of the bush and onto the heathland. Once they were clear of the cover of trees, Robinson ordered the two convicts and his sons, George and Charles, to uncover the fuses of their muskets ready to fire and walk on either side of the Ninine. Wooredy then led the people in single file across the heath, with armed guards walking beside.

For the next five days the captives walked under guard, reluctantly and ever more slowly. Every night, Robinson and his sons took turns to keep watch, their guns at the ready. Reflecting on the enormity of his betrayal, Robinson rationalised that the people could have escaped if they really wanted to. 'What signified firearms if God had not made them willing to go?' he wrote with a heavy heart.

After three days, the rations were exhausted and Robinson permitted Wooredy, Peevay and Mannalargenna to hunt. They managed to get one wombat and a kangaroo, to be shared between thirty people and twenty dogs. Everyone was at the point of starvation when they reached the wharf at Macquarie Harbour on 25 May. Robinson signalled for the boat, noting that the Ninine were 'very low spirited' as they embarked. He liked to think they would cheer up once they reached Sarah Island and got some food in their stomachs.

On the island, the new people were all kept on the lower floor of the main penitentiary, in what had been the prison hospital. They were issued blanket frocks for the women and convict jackets and trousers for the men. George and Charles Robinson were stationed inside the stone hall with their guns to keep watch. Guarding them 'required the strictest vigilance', Robinson wrote on 1 June. Despite being well fed and provided with warm clothing, the eight captives were very agitated. Wooredy taunted them by saying that they would be sent a long way off, never to return. Their loud wailing caused Robinson to double the guard until the penitentiary boat was ready to take them away.

On 5 June, Robinson embarked the eight adults with four children, two of them infants. All appeared to be in good spirits, or so he chose to think. No doubt they were hugely relieved to be leaving the hideous penitentiary. One woman was too sick to walk and needed to be carried aboard. A man also claimed to be ill, but Robinson believed this was a pretence to avoid being sent into exile. He had the prison doctor bleed the man, which must have scared him witless, then sent him on his way. Towterer's four-year-old daughter was carried on board. If she cried out for her parents, Robinson made no mention of it.

It was only a matter of time before Truganini met Towterer and his group. They were no longer trying to hide and were actually lighting fires to attract attention. She found them on 17 June, when Towterer explained that he had followed after his daughter for two days, making smoke signals. Truganini had been so focused on moving ahead she had not seen the smoke.

Robinson was amazed at how attached these people were to their children. He had come to the startling realisation that if their children were taken from them they would probably die of grief, writing in his journal that night that it was essential that the people should never be separated from their children. This entry was written just days after he had sent Towterer's young daughter away to Hobart. She was subsequently taken to the Orphan School and never saw her parents again.

Dray was delighted to see her old friend Truganini and said she was tired of living in the wilds and would happily go with her, although her husband, Dewoorady, did not want to leave. The tension between them was palpable. As they were setting off for Macquarie Harbour, Dewoorady abruptly walked away. Mannalargenna ran after him and grabbed his arm to pull him back, but he sat down on the forest floor, stubbornly refusing to budge. Robinson brusquely ordered that one of the armed convicts uncover the fuse on his gun and aim at the man. Evidently terrified, Dray's husband rose to his feet and went to join his wife. 'I would not be trifled,' Robinson later boasted in his journal.

On reaching Macquarie Harbour a few days later, Robinson was gratified to see that the government cutter *Tamar* was across the water at Sarah Island. He prevailed on the captain to delay leaving so Gould could draw a portrait of Towterer. Once it was finished, Towterer's group was put aboard the *Tamar.* So great was their desire to be reunited with the rest of their clan that they were almost eager to sail away. Only Dray, who had promised Robinson to locate the last of her people, was allowed to stay in her country.

Dray was as good as her word. On 21 June, she and Truganini led the mission party down the long southern tail of Macquarie Harbour known as Birch's Inlet to the coast, where they found a settlement of beehive huts with sixteen Ninine, including the three women who had escaped from Grummet Island. Dray assured Robinson that these people were indeed the very last of the clan. Robinson immediately recognised the man he had seen on the previous visit, whose daughter had leapt into the sea—neither his wife nor his daughter were with him. Dray explained that the missing women had been taken by the men who worked the pilot boat at the head of Macquarie Harbour. These men had taken a number of women over the years.

Dray proved to be a persuasive go-between. She was trusted absolutely by her clan and she passionately urged the people to leave their country and go with Mister Robinson to Macquarie Harbour. Although they were far from happy at the prospect, they agreed to go with her because they did not want to continue living alone when the rest of their clan was gone. As they approached Macquarie Harbour, they showed signs of reluctance to proceed, walking more and more slowly. One man ran off, apparently chasing a dog. Mannalargenna ran after him, catching the dog, but the man disappeared into the forest.

Robinson reflected that past experience should have told him not to rely on Dray when she promised the people would not run away. He was also angry at Mannalargenna, Wooredy and Peevay for being too concerned with hunting to keep a close watch. His sons and the convicts were told to uncover their fuses and cock their pistols, with an armed man directed to march alongside each of the Ninine men. In this way, they were hurried out of the forest and onto the boat waiting at the wharf.

Once on board with their captives, Mannalargenna, Peevay and Wooredy stuck the boat's faded red bunting on the tips of their spears and chanted in triumph. Their singing was heard across the expanse of water at Sarah Island, where the entire population of the penal settlement came to the jetty to meet them. Officers, soldiers and convicts were all there to applaud Robinson's achievement. The Ninine were petrified by such large numbers of *num*, particularly the soldiers in uniform. Robinson had his sons hurry them into the lower floor of the penitentiary and instructed the commandant that there must be no communication between his captives and the soldiers or convicts. With only a slatted wooden ceiling to separate them, the convicts above found ways to communicate: they stamped and shouted, and urinated on the people below.

The lone man who had run after the dog was brought to the penitentiary on the pilot boat the next day. He had been found at Birch's Inlet making smoke signals. As he sorrowfully explained to Dray, it was unbearable to stay alone in his country without his family. Robinson was doubly pleased to get this man because otherwise he might have gone north to warn the Tarkiner and Peternidic that Robinson was coming for them.

Dray was a regular visitor to the Tarkiner and Peternidic. She knew their movement patterns and was expected to be the guide for Robinson's next excursion. However, in her eagerness to be reunited with Truganini, Dray had not envisaged being imprisoned in the lair of Raegewarrah. As days went by at Sarah Island, she became more and more morose. When the mission party left to find the Tarkiner on 19 July, Dray was not in a fit state to accompany them. This was no real problem: Truganini and Wooredy were now very familiar with the country they had walked over several times.

On this mission there was no dawdling or leisurely hunting parties. It was the depth of winter, with the biting winds of the Roaring Forties whipping across the coast, bringing fierce intermittent rainstorms. Fording numerous creeks and rivers in water up to their thighs left them near freezing, with only a jot of rum to revive them. On reaching the Pieman River on 21 July, they were greatly relieved to see tracks on the southern side of the heads of Macquarie Harbour, meaning they would not need to ford it. Truganini and the rest of the guides set off to follow the tracks, leaving Robinson to endure an anxious night of waiting.

At dawn, a sullen-faced Wyne appeared with his youngest daughter on his shoulders, his pregnant wife and an older daughter walking beside him. Following them was a man with his son and three women. Wooredy explained that there had been a bit of a tussle between Wyne and Mannalargenna; however, Wyne had been grossly outnumbered, with little choice but to accompany the guides back to Robinson's camp. Later that day, two young men who had been away hunting came of their own accord.

The return trek was fraught. Heavy rain had swollen one of the rivers so much that it had changed course. At the place where they had previously forded, the water was now over their heads, with a current that rushed and swirled like a millrace. It took hours for the guides to find enough sodden driftwood to construct a raft that they bound together with rope Robinson carried in his knapsack. Though not completely buoyant, the raft floated well enough to convey one person at a time. Over the rest of the day, Truganini, Pagerly and Plorenernoopner swam across the frigid river, back and forth, towing the raft, until all twenty-nine people, the dogs and the baggage were brought over.

No amount of rum could mitigate the shock to Truganini's exhausted body. That night she had a severe fit. She was seriously ill and still had days to travel through thunderstorms with wind-driven hail like tiny points of glass. The wind gusts were so strong, Robinson wrote, they almost lifted him off his feet, and he was a big man whereas Truganini was small and slight. The wonder was that the whole experience did not kill her.

It was still blowing a gale on 24 July when the party reached the boat at Macquarie Harbour. Robinson refused to wait for the storm to pass. As the heavy seas broke over the boat and his guides frantically bailed water, he embarked his captives. To the amazement of the convicts and soldiers watching from the penitentiary, the boat did not capsize. 'Providence had certainly crowned my labours with abundant success,' he boasted to the astonished commandant, 'with me the motto *veni*, *vidi*, *vici* was applicable.'

The Ninine captives came down to the jetty to welcome their Tarkiner allies. Towterer lifted Wyne's daughter from her exhausted father's shoulders to place her on his own, and then solemnly conducted the Tarkiner to their accommodation. The Ninine were coated in mourning ashes: a woman had died, and they had been permitted to cremate her body behind the prison. In the next two days, another woman and two men died, all with the same symptoms: a rasping cough, difficulty breathing, and a thick discharge of mucus from the nostrils. These three were buried in pine coffins without any ceremony.

Right away the Tarkiner began to sicken. Robinson could not understand why. The place was clean, warm and comfortable, the people were not crowded, and they had a fenced yard in which they could exercise. Granted, the doctor was an incompetent alcoholic who made matters worse by attempting to administer treatment to people when they were beside themselves with fear. They shrieked when he approached and sank their teeth into his hand, convinced he was Raegewarrah trying to catch them. Wyne attempted to break down the prison door, and when that failed, he set it on fire. He died a week later.

In the face of such suffering, Robinson insisted that the sick and dying be isolated on Grummet Island. Here, a Tarkiner warrior plunged forty feet down the cliff trying to escape. By 5 August, every single Tarkiner adult had died except Wyne's pregnant wife; she died after suffering a miscarriage on 11 August, leaving her two orphaned daughters as the last survivors. Robinson blamed the doctor, he blamed the weather, and he blamed the convicts. But he steadfastly refused to admit any culpability of his own.

With all the adult Tarkiner dead and several of the Ninine, Robinson conceded he would have to remove the survivors as soon as the next boat arrived from Hobart. So keen were the people to get away from the island of death that it scarcely mattered to them where they went. Waiting agitatedly at the water's edge to embark, they were sobbing with fear that they might not be able to leave. These fourteen traumatised people were taken to Hobart with a brief stopover at the penal station at Port Arthur, which must have horrified them all over again. They arrived in Hobart on 18 October, where they camped around Robinson's house for a month before they were sent to Flinders Island on 20 November.

Sixty-six people were captured on the west coast between January and July 1833, and within a year nearly all of them were dead.

CHAPTER 7

Beneath the lowering bulk of Ben Lomond, Truganini and Wooredy and their usual companions camped on a bend of the meandering Nile River during the first week of January 1834. This part of the north-east was the country of Maulboyheener's mother, although he would not have been happy to be back in the region where John Batman had initiated several massacres. Their camp was painfully close to the site of Batman's surprise dawn raid on a large group of Pyemairenerpairnener and Plangermairener people in the early spring of 1829. By Batman's own account, fifteen men were shot dead and he subsequently executed two wounded male prisoners. Maulboyheener escaped that attack, but three weeks later he was taken in another surprise raid on nine families. Batman never admitted to killing the men on that occasion, reporting only that he shot about forty dogs, burnt the huts and rounded up nine women with their children. He kept the infant Rolepana, and the rest of the captives were sent to the Richmond jail, from where Robinson had rescued them.

The mission party was camped a few miles away from

Batman's homestead, because Robinson was determined to rescue Rolepana, now known as Ben Lomond, as well as Karnebucher's son Meelerleeter, now known as Jack Allen. Rather than confront this loathsome man himself, Robinson directed his son George to take Karnebucher to Batman's home to retrieve both boys. They returned without them; Karnebucher was beyond inconsolable. Batman had been very belligerent, George reported. He had refused to release the boys, and on being shown a letter from the governor, he had insisted the boys 'were as much his property as his farm and he had as much right to keep them as the government'. An official letter was never going to compel Batman to surrender the boys, a local settler informed Robinson; they were too useful to him. One boy looked after the pigs, the other milked the cows and was often seen ploughing. Batman flogged the boys with a whip to make them work, Robinson was told.

About a mile in the other direction was a large farm belonging to the distinguished landscape painter John Glover. Robinson took this opportunity to visit Glover to commission a frontispiece for his proposed book. Glover gossiped to Robinson that Batman was 'a bad man' who had turned his wife out of doors and had lost part of his nose to syphilis. Whatever Glover said in private about Batman, in public he maintained friendly relations with his neighbour. He had recently walked to the top of Ben Lomond with Batman and one of the captive boys—probably Jack Allen—whom he had drawn in his sketchbook.

After viewing Glover's landscapes, Robinson took the celebrated painter to meet his companions at the river camp. The people danced while Glover sketched them. Delighted, Glover repaid the honour by inviting them to visit his studio. Modestly clothed in their dresses, or trousers and jackets, they walked to Glover's farm, where they were shown landscape paintings of the surrounding Ben Lomond country. Maulboyheener was astonished to see the familiar trees and hills of his country, and especially the picture depicting a corroboree. Captured on a piece of canvas was the life he had lost forever. This painting elicited an animated response from all the people. They could not stop looking at it and exclaiming in wonder.

In turn, Glover was fascinated by Robinson's guides. Over the next two days he visited their camp to make sketches that he would later incorporate into a number of paintings, such as *The River Nile*; *Van Diemen's Land, from Mr Glover's Farm*; and *Natives in the Eucalypt Forest on Mills Plains, Patterdale Farm.*

The mission party left the Nile River on 6 January to walk to Launceston, where they prepared for what Robinson hoped would be the last mission. Karnebucher was extremely reluctant to leave Ben Lomond without her son; she remained disconsolate during the nine days they spent at Whitcomb's house in Launceston. She was 'much dejected' on 14 January when the party headed off for the Van Diemen's Land Company lands in the north-west, so Robinson noted. Five days later, when they reached the Mersey River, he was furious to find that she and Pagerly had both disappeared. He could understand that Karnebucher was distracted to the point of madness at being taken further away from her son, but the defection of Pagerly, who had been with him from the very beginning, hit like a hammer blow. He took it as a personal betrayal.

Truganini was close to both women: she shared in Karnebucher's loss and grief, while Pagerly had been her companion since childhood. When soldiers captured the pair two days later, Truganini expected they would be sent by boat to Emu Bay to rejoin the mission. However, Robinson made no such request. Instead they were sent to jail in Launceston and subsequently transported to Flinders Island three months later, in late April 1834. Truganini never saw her friends again. Pagerly and Karnebucher were among at least twenty-five unidentified people who died on Flinders Island between May 1834 and November 1835.

The summer of 1834 was unseasonably hot. Every day they walked under a baking sun that turned the landscape parched and brittle. Though it was late in the season, the people continued their practice of burning the country. Passing through the empty country of Maulboyheener's wife Semiramis, they set fire to tinder-dry bush that flared into a wall of lurid flames, which raced across the landscape generating stifling heat. Robinson described the scene as apocalyptic. Despite the soaring temperatures, he could not prevent them from setting fires. The land might be empty of people, but it still demanded their attention; it was their cultural obligation to burn.

On reaching Circular Head, the party stayed two weeks at the Van Diemen's Land Company headquarters, where they camped around the cottages of the dozen young men the company employed. These bored bachelors came often to the camp, going hunting with the men and providing an audience at the nightly dances. In return for this entertainment, they staged two theatrical performances of their own, one of which went on past midnight. Many years later, two of these young men, Samuel Anderson and Robert Massie, would again play host, in very different circumstances.

Leaving Circular Head, the mission party travelled through Peevay's country. It was bone dry from drought, but that did not deter Peevay and his brother Penderoin from firing it. Fanned by a hot wind, the flames sped across the coastal plain, with gathering fury, to reach the coast. The party was forced to make camp on a small offshore island to escape the conflagration. It seemed as if the entire country was ablaze. Only a dramatic change in the weather made it possible to proceed to Cape Grim.

By late February, they were once more camped on the banks of the Arthur River on the trail of the last remnant people from Cape Grim, relatives of Peevay, Penderoin and Nollahalleker. These three were sent off to find their kin and returned five days later accompanied by Nollahalleker's brother and another man, with their wives and three children. These people came willingly. A debilitating war with the Tommigener had already killed several of their men, and without the rest of their clan these few were lonely and vulnerable. They were resigned to removing to Flinders Island, welcoming the prospect of being reunited with their relatives. They walked back to Cape Grim to wait for the transport to Flinders Island.

Robinson believed that a few Tommigener and Tarkiner were still at large, whereas Mannalargenna was emphatic that there were no more people to be found. Cold westerly gales were sweeping in from the ocean and he could not bear the idea of another winter on the exposed west coast. Robinson pretended not to hear his complaints and pressed on. None of the guides was happy about this. 'Few people would believe the vexation and trouble I have with them,' Robinson moaned on 13 March. Two days later, he was confronted with an alliance of disobedience from his most important guides when Wooredy and Truganini, as well as Mannalargenna and Tanleboneyer, refused to proceed. Their resistance was so formidable that he was obliged to leave these two couples on the northern bank of the Arthur River while the rest of the party crossed the river to proceed south.

On 9 April, Robinson reappeared on the opposite bank with twenty captives, including five children. He was exceedingly anxious to cross and untied the raft he had left moored here, instructing a convict to steer him over. Heavy rain had swollen the river in the intervening weeks and the strong current swept the raft towards the river mouth. Watching the disaster unfold from the opposite shore, Truganini leapt into the water. She swam to the raft and managed to pull the two men safely to the bank. Small as she was, Truganini had twice saved Robinson's life on that treacherous stretch of water, something he would long remember as testament to her unwavering loyalty.

As the winter closed in, the mission party travelled inland below the Western Tiers towards Cradle Mountain, looking for the last of the Tommigener. The weather was brutal. 'I am wearied of life travelling around the country,' Robinson wrote to his wife on 6 July. 'It is a *wretched* existence; perhaps *vegetating* would be a more appropriate word.' He might have spared a thought for his guides, especially Truganini, who was required to swim across swollen and freezing rivers time and time again. She and her companions were as fed up with this mission as he was, but for Robinson to get his reward they must stay in the bitterly cold highland wilderness until the last people were found. He himself would not be staying: on 1 August, he rode back to Hobart, leaving his son George in charge of the mission.

After four cruel months, they finally located the Tommigener on 28 December. The pitiful remnant of the clan was located about thirty miles east of Cradle Mountain, near Western Bluff. The group consisted of one man, four women and three boys, all of them ill from the unremitting cold. Two men had died of illness, and a third had been shot by a shepherd. Exhausted and depleted, they wearily accepted the harsh reality that they were to be sent into exile.

If Robinson's guides had ever needed evidence that an independent life was no longer viable, this miserable group provided it.

The Tommigener were a coastal people who had been driven into the brutal conditions of the highlands to barely subsist without adequate shelter or food. By contrast, the mission guides could move about freely under government protection, they could hunt wherever they found game, and they were otherwise well supplied with meat rations, tea, sugar, tobacco, shots of rum, and blankets. Without Robinson's protection and support they too would be in the same dire straits as the Tommigener.

On 3 February 1835, Robinson could claim that he had cleared all of the original people from the colony, a boast that met with almost universal acclaim. The *Hobart Town Courier* was especially enthusiastic about his great achievement and promoted a public subscription to raise money to reward his efforts. Robinson had assiduously cultivated the editor of this paper, who did sterling duty as his mouthpiece. Actually, Robinson's claim to have cleared Van Diemen's Land of its original people was somewhat wide of the mark, since a small family group of Tarkiner remained at large for several more years. For the purposes of the colonial authorities, however, Robinson's claim was good enough. The domestic hearth was quiet, and property values skyrocketed.

The time had come for Robinson to claim his dues. He had already received £400 of his promised £1100, and a land grant, which he had sold for £1280. Now, after a protracted negotiation with the governor, he secured the £700 balance in cash and a lifetime pension of £200 per annum. A grant of 1000 acres was made to his son George and another 500 acres to his son Charles. In addition, a considerable amount of money and silver plate was raised by public subscription. By any measure, his years in the wilderness had proved lucrative.

Truganini had been Robinson's stalwart companion for five years. Could she have known that his ultimate triumph would bring an end to her nomadic life and quasi freedom? Despite the unruly and uncooperative attitude she and Wooredy had sometimes shown, they understood that their safety depended on him and their future lay in his hands. They had time enough to ponder their future as they waited for Robinson to collect his rewards, organise his finances and draft the book he expected to publish. There was some talk of going with him over the sea to England. Wooredy found this an interesting prospect, but Truganini smartly put him right—an excursion to England would mean they would be away for a good many summers. Only one thing were they sure of: wherever he went they would go too.

It was by no means settled that Robinson would go to Flinders Island. The role of commandant was no longer enticing. His idea of moulding dislocated and traumatised people from different clans and language groups into a community of dutiful Christians looked less viable with every passing month. News gleaned from visitors to Flinders Island was not encouraging. Ensign Darling, currently in charge of the Flinders Island establishment, had moved the site further north to a slightly more sheltered spot on the south-western side of the island, which he had named Wybalenna, because he thought it meant 'black man's houses' in one of the various languages. The people never used that name to describe where they were forced to live. Nothing Robinson heard about Wybalenna suggested things had improved with the new location.

Brighter prospects beckoned in the as yet uncolonised southern part of New Holland. In November 1834, the Henty brothers had moved from Launceston across Bass Strait to Portland Bay and helped themselves to a large swathe of the traditional country of the

Gunditjmara people. There they remained, squatting on the land while petitioning the British government to grant them freehold title. Batman and his friend John Helger Wedge had followed their example, putting together a consortium of settlers to occupy the land of the Kulin around Port Phillip Bay.

Alarmed at the prospect of squatters from Van Diemen's Land moving into the unregulated territory across the Bass Strait, Governor Arthur wrote to the Secretary of State in London in January 1835 to request that Robinson be authorised to extend his friendly mission into the uncolonised region of New Holland, taking the survivors from Van Diemen's Land to assist in the conciliation process. According to the *Hobart Town Courier*, 'the finger of Providence' pointed to the moral justice of Robinson's making an early intervention in the region across Bass Strait and taking the people of Van Diemen's Land as 'a nucleus for mediating with and ultimately civilising the yet harmless natives of that vast continent'. Such a move would also have the advantage of removing those on Flinders Island even further away from the inquisitive gaze of critics of the government like the editor of the *True Colonist*.

Robinson was much taken with this idea. Removing the people from Flinders Island to New Holland would be of great benefit, he explained to the colonial secretary on 11 February 1835. It was so far away from their own country that they would be less liable to the 'mental irritation' that was exacerbating illness and hastening their death at Wybalenna. On Flinders Island, where their country was still visible from high points, the people were giving themselves up to excoriating grief that was invariably proving fatal. Removing them to distant New Holland would give them something to live for. He assured the colonial secretary that he had discussed the idea with his guides and was confident that all of the people would be pleased to go to New Holland.

This was not true for the disaffected Mannalargenna, who still had the expectation that the governor would honour his promise to return him to his own country. For Truganini and Wooredy, crossing the water into alien country was not so different from what they had been doing for years. New Holland was not as many moons away as England. Peevay and Maulboyheener were keen to take their extended families to any place where they could continue to live in the traditional way, where settlers were scarce and game was plentiful. For the time being, Robinson showed no inclination to take them anywhere. For most of 1835, he was preoccupied with the production of his book, for which they were necessary props. He needed them close at hand.

Prolonged rest at Robinson's house might have been welcome after the severity of the last two expeditions, except that these people were temperamentally unsuited to a long confinement in town. Truganini had caused a public outcry the last time they had lived in Hobart—she had taken several other women to the river, where they had stripped off their clumsy blanket dresses to go for a swim. As a consequence, they were not allowed to walk about the town or go to the river. Their only sanctioned outings were to the studios of various artists.

Truganini and Wooredy were well used to being models for artists. They had sat for portraits by a convict artist in Launceston in October 1831, and again in 1833 for William Buelow Gould at Sarah Island, and then for Thomas Lempriere at Port Arthur. Late in December 1833 they sat, or rather stood, for Benjamin Duterrau, an English artist recently arrived in Hobart whose first exhibition featured three-quarter-length portraits of Truganini and Wooredy. Each was posed in kangaroo skins strategically draped over their intimate body parts. Truganini, her hair shaven so close she looked bald, was posed with arms folded across her belly and several strands of her trademark necklaces around her neck. Wooredy, with a dark beard and his long coiled woolly locks splendidly coloured, was holding a spear. Suspended around his neck was a jawbone encased in fibre as well as two strands of his wife's shell necklaces.

While Duterrau boasted that he had exhibited at the Royal Academy in London, he was a poor draftsman—his pictures were as stolid and inanimate as blocks of wood. It was evident to Robinson that Duterrau's lumpen portraits would not make good engravings for his book. He turned instead to the recently emancipated convict Thomas Bock, a far superior artist, who had already executed a commission for Robinson in January 1832 following the capture of the Big River people. Bock had hurriedly produced wonderfully expressive head-and-shoulder drawings of the warriors Tongelongeter and Montpelliater, so Robinson now commissioned Bock to produce a portrait of each of his twelve guides, with a studio sitting for each subject.

A set of twelve portraits in pencil and watercolour on thick beige paper was completed by the end of April 1835. Several sittings were necessary for each subject, to enable Bock to capture subtle detail in the sketches that he finessed into watercolour portraits. One portrait remained in a preliminary state, that of a man with ochred locks, almost certainly Penderoin. His sitting must have been curtailed by the measles epidemic that swept through Hobart in autumn. Penderoin and his wife Nollahalleker were admitted to hospital in April, and Tanleboneyer in early May. Apparently they all died, although their deaths were not recorded, nor any burial.

The portraits of Truganini and Wooredy were the finest. Bock's portrait of Wooredy captured a proud, handsome warrior whose muscular body was stained with ochre, his gaze resolute beneath a rusty mop of oiled ringlets. He looked determined but not unfriendly, a self-contained man who knew his own worth.

The portrait of Truganini sounded a different note. Bock captured a woman with dark curly hair cut close to her scalp, wearing a kangaroo skin draped over her back to expose firm, round breasts and five strands of luminous shell necklaces that glowed against her reddish-brown skin. Her pronounced brow and high cheekbones framed sorrowful brown eyes and her hollowed cheeks emphasised a sensuous but unsmiling mouth. This was a portrait of a fragile woman, bone-weary and disengaged. Bock produced several copies of the couple's portraits for Robinson's friends, two of which were sent to employees of the Van Diemen's Land Company.

About the same time as Truganini and Wooredy were sitting for Bock, the sculptor Benjamin Law arrived in Hobart looking to set up business. He sought permission from Robinson for 'a native chief' to sit for a sculpted bust. Law intended to mass-produce inexpensive plaster casts to sell as mementoes. It was a measure of Robinson's disillusionment with Mannalargenna that he chose Wooredy for the sitting.

For several days, Wooredy sat patiently in the stable that Law had been loaned for the purpose. His hair and beard were carefully dressed with oil and ochre and he wore the same kangaroo skin and sinew necklace he wore for Bock. The bust was finished at the end of March and exhibited in Robinson's house, where visitors were encouraged to compare it with the original. Working in three dimensions, Law had portrayed the same proud warrior as Bock, only his Wooredy looked older, more like a man in his forties, which gave him even greater dignity and authority. All agreed the likeness was so remarkable that even a person who had only glimpsed the subject would immediately recognise the bust as Wooredy.

Casts of the bust of Wooredy were in high demand, selling for four guineas each. Law's wife reported to her family in England that the attorney general had purchased one, as well as the governor, who ordered a second to send to the Home Secretary, 'and indeed all or nearly all the great people . . . so that we begin now to be very comfortable indeed'.

Wooredy had become a colonial celebrity, now referred to as 'His Majesty'. It made good economic sense for Law to produce a companion bust of Truganini, although she was not promoted as a significant historical actor in her own right, merely as the wife. Mrs Law provided a rare insight into the relationship between the artist and the model in one of her letters to England, in which she expressed her admiration for Truganini, describing her sitting on the carpet in the Laws' comfortable new home and singing for them, intermittently demanding a reciprocal gift of a glass of wine. The finished bust of Truganini deployed the kangaroo skin more modestly, with a partly exposed breast revealing one erect nipple, and a double-looped strand of shells. Appearing to be more robust than in the Bock picture, her gaze was nonetheless slightly downcast; she looked pensive, even sad.

Both Bock's and Law's representations were admired for their likeness to Truganini, yet neither resembled the vivacious young woman described in Robinson's journals. This was not just an artistic convention at work, presenting the female subject as sorrowful victim. Bock's portraits of Peevay's wife, Plorenernoopner, and Maulboyheener's wife, Semiramis, depicted them as vibrant and robust, with generous, open gazes. Plainly the extreme rigours of the last two expeditions had taken a physical toll on Truganini. No doubt she was also feeling the separation from Pagerly, and may have already learnt that the friend of her youth had died on Flinders Island.

The dismal news of Flinders Island that trickled into Hobart suggested that the place was an unmitigated disaster. On 8 May 1835, the *True Colonist* newspaper reported that a visitor from

Wybalenna told 'a melancholy tale about the condition of these poor creatures . . . one-half of them are dead, and the survivors are in a most wretched condition'. Robinson was gripped by anxiety that the adulation in which he basked as the 'great conciliator' would be entirely extinguished by the ignominy of being the agent of the extinction of an entire race of people.

Robinson's consternation at this story, so gleefully reported by his enemy at the *True Colonist*, was further exacerbated by a report on 15 May by his sycophantic friend at the *Hobart Town Courier*. This story concerned another of his enemies, John Batman, who had taken an advance party across the Bass Strait to Port Phillip, including the two boys that Robinson sought to remove. The paper reported that Batman's intention was 'to purchase from the Chiefs of that part of the country such a territory as he may require, of which he will himself become the Chief, with the best of all possible titles, that of the real proprietor'. Batman returned alone to Launceston in triumph a few weeks later, having gained possession of 6000 acres of land around Port Phillip Bay.

Batman had negotiated a 'treaty' with the Kulin clan elders on behalf of the Port Phillip Association, agreeing that the association would pay a yearly tribute of one hundred blankets, one hundred knives, one hundred tomahawks, fifty suits of clothing, fifty looking glasses, fifty pairs of scissors and five tons of flour, in return for the use of their land in perpetuity. To a jubilant crowd in the Cornwall pub in Launceston, Batman announced that he was now the greatest landholder in the world. On hearing Batman's boast, the canny publican quickly convened another syndicate of investors and wasted no time in loading ships with chattels and livestock to sail across the Bass Strait. By August 1835, they were squatting on Batman's land and building the rudimentary settlement that would become known as Melbourne.

This was exactly the problem Governor Arthur had outlined to the Secretary of State: unregulated occupation that would put the original people at risk of wholesale destruction. Robinson seized his chance, proposing that instead of going to Flinders Island he should go directly to Port Phillip, where his experienced guides could initiate contact with the resident clans and prepare the way for conciliation. In the meantime, he would select a suitable site to which the people on Flinders Island could be transferred.

The governor took the view that Robinson should wait for approval from the Secretary of State, and proceed immediately to Flinders Island to take charge of Wybalenna. This was a directive Robinson was keen to deflect. He argued that he should wait in Hobart until the approval came from London. It would be unwise to go to Flinders Island, he explained, because the people there had somehow got the idea that as soon as he took charge they would all be repatriated back to the mainland of Van Diemen's Land.

Governor Arthur had grown very testy over the eight months that Robinson had remained in Hobart, on full salary, with his twelve guides all rationed at the government's expense and domiciled in the annex of his house, for which the government was billed rent. By September 1835, the message coming from Government House was unyielding: if Robinson wanted to keep his £500 annual salary he had to go to Flinders Island and do the job for which he was being paid.

What of his 'sable companions'? Robinson had all but promised they would not go to Flinders Island and that they could continue to live as they had been for the past five years. He wanted to keep faith with them, because they were the people he was most determined to save. Furthermore, he would need their loyalty if he were to succeed in New Holland. He sought to persuade the Aboriginal

Committee that rather than send his guides to Flinders Island they could go to the remote north-east corner of the colony, presumably with one or both of Robinson's sons. This proposal was tailored to placate Mannalargenna, whose accusations of bad faith were aggravated by his grief at the death of his wife Tanleboneyer, to whom he had been deeply attached.

The committee paid Robinson's suggestion no heed. It was not the first time the Aboriginal Committee had proved an impediment to his plans: he had been furious at their demand that the children at Wybalenna be sent to the Orphan School in Hobart. He himself had admitted two boys he had found working for a gang of thieves on the streets in 1832, and Wooredy's two sons in 1833, but Karnebucher's and Towterer's intense grief had taught him the powerful attachment the people had to their children. He had come to see that separation was the worst thing he could do to them.

When a large group of nine boys and girls arrived in Hobart to be admitted to the school in February 1835, he wrote a strongly worded letter to the committee, protesting that this was breaking a solemn promise he had made to their parents. His mouthpiece at the *Hobart Town Courier* sought to influence public opinion in his favour. 'We have no right whatever to take away their children without the leave and consent of their natural parents and guardians,' the paper thundered, 'and we know that the parents and relations of these children daily and hourly lament their removal . . . [which] is not unlikely to accelerate their death.'

Stiff opposition to Robinson came from the Anglican dean, who believed the children's future would be best served by their being schooled in Christian values and kept well away from the heathen lifestyle of their parents. After half of the children died of measles in rapid succession during April and May, the dean relented.

When Robinson wrote to him on 14 September demanding the release of eight children who had parents on Flinders Island, he offered no further argument. The children were embarked on the *Tamar* for Flinders Island on 1 October, along with Robinson's nine surviving guides.

Any assurances Truganini and Wooredy had been given that they would be able to continue a life of freedom had come to nothing. They could have no illusions now about what their future would be, having seen how very far away the island was from their own land and heard the stories of terrible suffering and death. It was an awful moment for Mannalargenna too, as he absorbed the magnitude of Robinson's betrayal. When the *Tamar* sailed past the north-east coastline he was visibly distressed and requested a spyglass so that he could have a last look at his country. He tied a strip of kangaroo skin around his head and paced back and forth along the deck.

Mannalargenna had come to the end of the line in his attempts to find accommodation with the invaders. He had lost his two wives, his four daughters, and now he had lost his country. As the *Tamar* moved away from the outline of Cape Portland and into the Bass Strait he solemnly cut off his long ochred hair with a piece of glass. A few weeks later he was buried in a Christian ceremony at Wybalenna. No songs or dances were permitted for the departed spirit of this great man. There were no relics of bone, no ashes, by which the people could remember him.

Pea Jacket Point was a forested hill on the western coast of Flinders Island, running down to a jagged point of bare granite rocks, stained vermillion with lichen, jutting into the marbled blue of the

Bass Strait. Some eighteen miles north of the Lagoons, it was utterly exposed to the fury of the Roaring Forties. Tucked beneath the hill on the southern side, the white crescent of Lillies Bay offered some shelter from the prevailing winds, and here a jetty had been constructed as a safe landing place. About half a mile inland, in a depression between Pea Jacket Hill and the range of hills to the east, was the Wybalenna site. The tea trees had been cleared to create space for a rudimentary settlement consisting of a chapel, military barracks, hospital, tannery, bakehouse, storehouse, cottages for the officers and a few wattle-and-daub huts for the people. The centrepiece was the commandant's substantial quarters.

Wybalenna was no better than the Lagoons. It had even less protection from the winds and no proper anchorage. Supply ships had to stop at Green Island and transfer people and rations into whaleboats for the last leg to the jetty at Lillies Bay. There was no freshwater stream or spring and the water supply taken from wells was brackish. The game had been quickly exhausted, and the people were dependent on rations whose high salt content caused chronic illness, and came close to famine when the supply vessel failed to arrive.

When the *Tamar* anchored at Green Island, Robinson went ashore to discover that nearly everyone had decamped from Wybalenna and was living on Green Island, where they could hunt for birds and eggs. He was pressed on all sides by people clamouring to be taken back to Van Diemen's Land. 'We don't want to live here. Let us go to our own country and we can live,' they pleaded. 'Why keep us here to starve?' He had nothing to offer to reassure these unhappy souls. The *Tamar* sailed back to Launceston and he had the people returned to Wybalenna by whaleboat.

If this place was to be his domain, Robinson was determined to make it a fitting conclusion to his glorious achievement in saving the original people of this distant British outpost—in his prospective book, if not in actuality. Constructing his journal entries to fit the story he hoped to publish in England, he created a heroic role for himself and arranged a plot to take place around it. His predilection for manipulating events to fit his preconceived vision was so intensified by his literary ambition that his journal entries became little more than imaginative constructs.

The first project he described was the Elysium Walk, a winding road he had the people cut through a dense thicket of casuarinas and melaleuca to the landing place at Lillies Bay. He planned for rustic seats and flowerpots along the verges. In his report to the governor about his beautification project, he made much of the willingness and aptitude of the people, reporting that they had accomplished in hours what would have taken convicts a week. Similar rapturous sentiments coloured his descriptions of men reaping corn as if they were born to the sickle, or the women in the sewing circle dutifully making dresses out of sackcloth. None of this bore any relation to reality.

Robinson was fictionalising his charges into the parts he had made for them, miraculously transformed from nomadic hunters into meek Christian serfs. In keeping with his literary delusions, Robinson gave his charges new names. Henceforth, Wooredy became Count Alpha, possibly signifying that he was the first among them, and Truganini became Lalla Rookh, named after the great oriental beauty celebrated by Thomas Moore.

At his first Christmas at Wybalenna, Robinson chose Count Alpha and Lalla Rookh to be his special guests for the formal Christmas luncheon. They were seated at a table with King George, as he had renamed Woreternaterlargner, and Tongelongeter, now known as King William, with their wives Luggenemeener, now Queen Charlotte, and Droomteemetyer, now Queen Adelaide.

They were all decked out in proper European clothes, which must have been an imposition for the men, who usually walked about semi-naked, wearing only an open pea jacket. Their table was presented with a bottle of wine, from which each was poured a glass. Robinson was pleased to report that they 'conducted themselves with great propriety'. At the commandant's table were the doctor, the catechist, the storekeeper, the military officers and their wives, one of whom approvingly remarked of the adjoining table: 'This . . . was civilisation.'

Even as Robinson performed for his imagined readership, he could not avoid seeing the despair and disintegration of the people he had professed to save and for whom he alone had responsibility. It was one thing to fantasise in his journal and fabricate fraudulent reports for the governor; it was quite another to contend daily with evidence of serious malnutrition and neglect. For his own psychological health, it was not enough to imagine the process of civilising his captives; he needed it to be true. He was not so deluded that he could not see the awful impossibility of the place.

After burying yet another body on that same Christmas Day, Robinson sat down to his journal in deep despair. Bitterly, he finally acknowledged that he had been an unwitting agent of extermination. His new role was to stand watch over an unremitting cascade of misery and death. He cast his mind back to when he had first known these proud vigorous people in the wilderness, and could only 'weep in silence'. It was a rare day. Ordinarily, thoughts of his own moral culpability did not engage him for more than a fleeting moment.

Truganini was greatly dissatisfied with life at Wybalenna. She disdained the sewing classes under the direction of the storekeeper's wife, with whom Robinson was having a clandestine affair. She was restless and bored. Wooredy also had little to do, as there was scant game to hunt. However, he drew great comfort in being reunited with his sons Davey and Peter, as they were now known. Aged twelve and eleven respectively, the boys had lived apart from him for most of the past five years and still were not permitted to live in the hut he shared with Truganini. Instead they were compelled to live with all the other children in a dormitory in the house of the puritanical catechist Robert Clark, employed to teach religion, who shamefully neglected them and was a great believer in exemplary punishment. Years at the Orphan School had already conditioned the boys to that Christian tradition.

Alone of the guides, only Maulboyheener managed to please Robinson, by digging a garden outside the hut he had been allocated to share with Semiramis and erecting a fence around it. Now that Maulboyheener had Semiramis as his wife, and Peevay had Plorenernoopner, Lacklay was obliged to also take a wife. Under Robinson's watchful eye he chose Maytepueminer, also known as Matilda, who had recently been rescued from the sealers. Robinson had them married according to the rites of the Church of England. Failing to appreciate the solemn vows she had taken, Maytepueminer refused to stay with Lacklay any longer than one day.

Truganini and Wooredy got away from Flinders Island five months after they arrived. Together with Peevay and Plorenernoopner, Maulboyheener and Semiramis, and the rejected Lacklay, they were dispatched on a mission to locate the last defiant group of Tarkiner still at large in the north-west. Robinson's son George was nominally in charge and he had as little desire to be on Flinders Island as they did. For sixteen carefree months they enjoyed a pleasant reprieve, roaming about the empty country, hunting as they liked and visiting the ochre mines wherever possible. Occasionally they got close enough to farms for their dogs to wreak havoc among the sheep, raising the ire of disgruntled settlers who complained to the colonial secretary that they were supposed to be rid of this nuisance.

While they were gone, Robinson managed to cajole the colonial authorities into providing materials and convict labour to build weatherproof houses for the people. It proved a bigger battle to ensure a regular supply of food. He had expected a measure of generosity and goodwill towards these dispossessed people from the government. 'They are the lawful owners, not us,' he wrote in another rare moment of sombre reflection. 'We have desolated them, despoiled them of their country, the land of their forefathers, and having placed them on an isolated spot the least we ought to do is abundantly supply their wants.' Any fool might have foreseen that as far as the self-interested colonial authorities were concerned, out of sight was out of mind.

George Augustus Robinson was not just any fool. For all his posturing as the antipodean Caesar, Robinson had truly believed that his removal of the original people of Van Diemen's Land was for their own good. He had wanted to protect them from murderous settlers, to bring them into God's grace and to bestow the great benefits of civilisation, as he understood it. Never did he think that his beneficent God would permit them all to die. Now the inescapable reality was that his intended sanctuary would become one great graveyard.

He had no intention of bearing witness to the end of the race. With renewed vigour, he set his sights on a position in New Holland, with the hope that he could take the survivors with him. It was a severe blow when word finally came from the Secretary of State in London that he would not be permitted to transplant the people from Van Diemen's Land to New Holland.

Now he fixed his attention on the new colony proposed for Spencer Gulf, which would eventually become the colony of South Australia. In September 1836, he travelled to Hobart for a meeting with the new governor, Sir John Franklin, who had persuaded the Secretary of State to offer Robinson the position of Protector of Aborigines at Spencer Gulf. This looked promising, if he could get permission to take the people from Van Diemen's Land with him. He spent several months in Hobart, haggling with Franklin, only to find that the administrative meanness extended to him as well as his captives: the job offer came to grief on the matter of salary and compensations. The offered salary of £250 rubbed salt into his wounds. 'My business is now a matter of pounds, shillings and pence,' he complained with uncharacteristic perspicacity.

He was more determined than ever to transfer to New Holland. In late December 1836, he accepted an offer from the Port Phillip Association to visit for several weeks, taking with him Mannalargenna's son Neenhepeerminer. While at Port Phillip, they were approached by a dirty, ragged child who was revealed to be one of Batman's captives, Ben Lomond. Neenhepeerminer was overwhelmed to see this boy, who was kin to him. Robinson was profoundly moved as he watched Neenhepeerminer weeping and repeatedly caressing the boy, who begged to be taken away from Batman.

Robinson was gratified to discover that Batman no longer held sway in Port Phillip; his so-called treaty had been dismissed by the British government as an impertinence with no legal standing. Captain William Lonsdale had taken charge, armed with the legal apparatus of the statutes of New South Wales, and Robinson told Lonsdale he must remove the boys from Batman. Lonsdale, who came from Launceston, did not care to take orders from Robinson. He bluntly replied that Batman made good use of both of his captives so he saw no reason to deprive him of their service. Robinson returned to Wybalenna even more embittered about Batman and more determined than ever to get himself to Port Phillip.

It was not until July 1837 that Truganini and Wooredy and the other guides returned to Wybalenna. They had no captives to show for their long absence, but they did have a lot of fresh red ochre. Their rude good health was not lost on Robinson, who had witnessed the deaths of nineteen people while they were gone. When he boasted to them about the new houses he had had built, he was stung by Truganini's curt observation that soon there would be no one left to live in them.

Truganini found nothing tolerable about their new home, whereas for Wooredy there was compensation: always impressed by the power of written language, he was keen for his sons to teach him how to write. He laboured at forming letters so he could write to the governor. Peevay and Maulboyheener showed no interest in Wybalenna. They would take their wives and go hunting in the north of the island for weeks at a time. Lacklay sometimes went with them, although he was still trying to couple with Maytepueminer, who continued to spurn him. He was formally remarried to her in January 1838, although she remained largely indifferent.

For all his displeasure at their disrespect, Robinson still had a special regard for his long-time companions. In December 1837, he went with them on a five-day expedition to explore the eastern section of Flinders Island, revelling in the freedom and challenge of being in the bush for the first time in more than two years. At the same time he was shocked to observe a fundamental change in their relationship with him: their sense of mutual obligation had evaporated. They treated him with total disinterest and disregard, forcing him to fend for himself. Not even Truganini lifted a finger to help him. 'They had four swans, an abundance of kangaroo, ducks, teal etc. and never prepared me a morsel nor made me a shelter wherein to sleep nor made my tea nor damper bread,' he complained sourly.

Robinson returned to Wybalenna without them, 'exceedingly displeased at their negligence, their careless indifference and their ingratitude'. He did not pause to consider what they might have made of the negligence, indifference and ingratitude he had shown them: to Truganini, the constant ally who had twice saved his life, or Wooredy, who had stuck by his side with stoic resignation, or the three young men who had grown into adulthood in his service.

It was only too apparent to Robinson that his long-term guides were not going to fulfil the roles he had envisaged for them of an elite leadership for his civilisation program. They continued to live the way they wanted to and were stubbornly resistant to his Christian indoctrination. Try as he might—and he tried mightily—he was unable to stamp out their traditional rituals, which he knew persisted out of his sight and hearing.

It was the children in whom Robinson now placed his hopes, as they had already been indoctrinated from their time at the Orphan School in Hobart. Two young men showed particularly great promise: Walter George Arthur, one of the boys he had found on the streets of Launceston, and an orphan he called Thomas Brune. He took them to work in his office and appointed them as the editors of a newsletter, the *Flinders Island Chronicle*, although he maintained overarching editorial control. Since the adult residents of Wybalenna could not read or write, the audience for this publication must have been Robinson's colonial masters.

The first edition was published in September 1836. The two editors wrote, 'We date our history from the month of October 1835 when our beloved father made his appearance among us dispelling the darkness and cheering us with a dawn of hope, freedom and happiness.' The *Flinders Island Chronicle* repeatedly printed stern warnings not to vex the commandant or make him angry. After Robinson returned from his failed hunting expedition in a fury, Thomas Brune warned that the commandant 'don't let the people be master over him while he is on the island and he will certainly not be given them things any more'.

The *Flinders Island Chronicle* did not always maintain such a deferential tone. As the settlement disintegrated in the face of ration shortages and mounting deaths, the reporting of events took a more critical edge. 'The Bible says some or all shall be saved,' wrote one of the editors in November 1837, 'but I am much afraid that none of us will be alive by and by, as there is nothing but sickness among us.' This editorial ended with an incendiary plea that was removed from the final draft: 'Why don't the blackfellows pray to the King to get us away from this place.' Soon Walter George Arthur and Thomas Brune joined the others at the whipping post, or in the stocks, or clapped into irons, as punishment for their recalcitrant and unchristian behaviour.

Actually, it was Robinson who was doing the most praying to get them away from this place. He was frantically lobbying Governor Gipps of New South Wales to be appointed Chief Protector of Aborigines for the Port Phillip District. The governor finally and wearily agreed that Robinson was indeed the man for the job. He was instructed to proceed to Port Phillip as soon as practicable, if this was agreeable to Governor Franklin in Van Diemen's Land.

For the moment, Robinson had Franklin's confidence. The governor had visited Flinders Island in February 1838 along with his intrepid wife, Lady Jane, when Robinson had supplied 'curiosities' for their collection. As a keen observer of autopsies, Robinson had been systematically obtaining skulls by decapitating corpses and boiling down the flesh, and soon after their visit, he sent Lady Franklin the skulls of Peevay's brother Pendowtewer and his wife. Robinson was more than happy to gratify Lady Franklin's request to 'get a black boy for her'. In January 1839 he sent her the son of Wymurric, now baptised as Adolphus, who was about eleven years old. Since his father was dead, this boy had the same relationship to Peevay as a son. A month later, Robinson also sent one of the very few children born on Flinders Island: the four-year-old daughter of Towterer, baptised as Mary. Towterer had died on Flinders Island two years previously, but his wife Wongenneep was still alive when her only child was sent away to Lady Franklin, who called the little girl Mathinna.

So confident was Robinson that he could take everyone from Wybalenna to Port Phillip that, while he was in Hobart negotiating with Franklin, he arranged a mass assembly of the people with the establishment officers to witness their 'unequivocal consent agreement' to the transfer. Whether the people at Wybalenna understood where they would be taken, or if they even consented to go, was another matter. A petition sent to the colonial secretary with a list of names of those who agreed to go to New Holland had an identical mark, made in the same hand, beside each name, even those of people like Walter George Arthur who were perfectly able to sign for themselves.

Once again, Robinson was getting ahead of himself. Governor Gipps refused to agree to the transfer, because the legislative council in New South Wales was implacably opposed to importing murderous 'savages' from Van Diemen's Land. In an abject letter, Robinson pleaded with Gipps to reverse his decision, or else 'this remnant of a wronged and much maligned people will become extinct'. Facing additional pressure from Franklin, Gipps reluctantly conceded that Robinson could bring one family as his 'personal attendants'. By family he meant one couple with their children.

It was obvious that Truganini and Wooredy, with his two sons, would be that family. But what about Peevay and Maulboyheener and Lacklay and their wives? Somewhere in his narcissistic soul Robinson felt a kind of love for all his guides and simply could not bear to abandon them. Likewise, he felt a powerful duty of care towards Walter George Arthur and Thomas Brune, who had been in his charge since childhood. He wanted to give them the best chance of survival. In his eyes he was their father. They were all family to him.

IN KULIN COUNTRY

1839–1841

CHAPTER 8

Truganini, Wooredy and Peevay arrived at Hobson's Bay in the Port Phillip District on 27 February 1839 on the cutter *Vansittart*. Robinson's landing declaration indicated that he was travelling with 'three servants and three Aborigines'. Presumably those designated as his servants were the youths Walter George Arthur, Thomas Brune and a mixed-race boy named Thomas Thompson, while his three long-term guides were passed off as the family that Governor Gipps had allowed him to bring. Maulboyheener and Semiramis were meant to come also, but they had been too dangerously ill to sail. Robinson himself was so ill with influenza that he was kept aboard the *Vansittart* in Hobson's Bay for four days before being allowed ashore.

While Robinson fretted feverishly in his cabin, Truganini and her companions were disembarked into a lighter and rowed to Williamstown's stone pier. Here they were transferred to a ferryman who rowed them down the muddy Yarra River to the natural rock ledge known as the Falls, which separated the brackish water from the deep basin of fresh water that supplied the fledgling town of

Melbourne. They were landed just above the Falls on the swampy south side of the river, where they were given into the charge of William Thomas, one of four men appointed as assistant protectors. This unappealing place, so Thomas gave them to understand, was to be their new home.

Beyond the tents of the assistant protectors there was little to see except a forlorn collection of twig and bark shelters that Thomas called *mia mia*, where dozens of the local Kulin people huddled around, barely covered by ragged blankets. They were obviously unwell. Across the river, only a ruined landscape of huge blackened tree stumps and one small wooded hill could be seen; the town of Melbourne was out of sight. At the base of the hill was a log house and vegetable garden, home of their old foe John Batman.

Batman's proximity came as no surprise. They already knew that the terrible man with no nose was living in this new place. They knew that Stewart was there also—the tracker from New South Wales who had worked with them on a mission to the west coast in 1833. It may have been a comfort to know they could find a friend in this strange new place, but the knowledge that there were two boys at Batman's house was a source of pain. Batman's oldest boy captive was Karnebucher's son, known as Jack Allen, and Truganini well remembered Karnebucher's inconsolable grief at the forced separation from her last surviving child. The younger boy, known as Ben Lomond, was close kin to Peevay's wife and to Maulboyheener. These boys might be a stone's throw away but it remained extremely unlikely they could get them. Batman still had friends in high places. He was, after all, the reason that Melbourne existed.

When Batman had declared the river flats above the Falls 'the place for a village', he had not known it was a significant meeting ground for the Wurundjeri, Boonwurrung, Wadawurrung,

Djadjawurrung and Taungurong, who comprised the Kulin nation. The village had grown to become a town of about three thousand settlers and still the dispossessed Kulin continued to visit for large ceremonial gatherings. Increasingly, they stayed around the town, since they had nowhere else to live and were on the verge of starvation: the roots they had used as a staple food were being destroyed by grazing sheep and the game had been driven away.

No land was returned to the Kulin clans when the British government assumed control of Port Phillip, and the clans were not compensated for the expropriation. No serious attempt was made to curtail the rapacious land grabs by settlers, who were now multiplying exponentially. The early adventurers from Van Diemen's Land were permitted to remain squatting on the vast areas of land they had already claimed, for the payment of a new licence fee of ten pounds. Waves of new settlers from England and Scotland followed suit, paying their fee to access vast areas of 'Crown land' to graze flocks of sheep and cattle. Many squatters believed the licence fee granted them a right to exclusive occupancy, even though they were required to provide access to the land for the original owners. Guns and poison effectively drove the Kulin clans off their hunting and ceremonial territory. Robinson's appointment as Chief Protector of Aborigines could do nothing to halt this wholesale and brutal dispossession. The powers of his lofty new position were as vague as they were ineffectual.

Mostly the people who stayed around Melbourne were Wurundjeri, whose country was the Yarra River basin, while some were Boonwurrung, whose country covered the eastern side of the bay. They subsisted on the fringes of the town by selling possum skins and lyrebird feathers, or cutting bark. More often they were selling their bodies for food and grog, or just begging for food.

To be abruptly deposited among these alien clans might have been a source of great apprehension for Wooredy and Peevay, but they faced no hostility from the Kulin. Despite the lack of a comprehensible common language, the two groups of people could dance their stories and communicate in a kind of pidgin. There was also an Englishman named Bill living among the Wurundjeri who had been at the Orphan School in Hobart with Walter George Arthur and Thomas Brune and now acted as interpreter. When the Chief Protector of Aborigines arrived in the territory of the Kulin four days later, he was expected and his purpose in their country was dimly comprehended.

With horror, Robinson contemplated the flimsy tent he had been allotted on the edge of the miserable Kulin encampment. This might be appropriate for his assistant protectors and his Van Diemen's Land charges, but there was no way the chief protector could be expected to stay there. After assessing the situation, he took the regular punt across the river to the town and spent his first night at the best hotel. The following night he made himself the guest of the acting superintendent for Port Phillip, Captain Lonsdale.

In what must have been a very irritating meeting, Robinson sought to impress upon Lonsdale the importance of his position and protest the insult that he had been provided no proper accommodation. Lonsdale had received no orders about the protectorate and had no idea what role Robinson was meant to perform. And he was disposed to distrust the man: settlers who had relocated from Launceston considered Robinson a notoriously self-serving fellow and no friend of theirs. The editor of the *Port Phillip Gazette* had already begun a sustained attack, decrying the enormous outlay of public money on the chief protector's salary of £500 plus an additional allowance of £200. To do what, no one could say.

The best accommodation Robinson could extract from Lonsdale was the use of a small wooden hut on the north bank of the river—it was to have been his office, but it could be made a place to sleep. Over the next eight days, he sought to make himself comfortable in his little riverbank hut. On a makeshift desk he placed his many books, writing materials and Benjamin Law's bust of Wooredy.

Meanwhile, on the other side of the river Wooredy himself was becoming familiar with the people whose land he now inhabited, watching and learning. Every day more Kulin were arriving to begin elaborate rituals of body painting in preparation for a large ceremonial gathering that was to last several days. Robinson was enticed across the river to watch the corroboree one night in March, but he declined to return for any further performances. Two days later, he was forced to cross the river again to deal with a large group of agitated men who had gathered around Assistant Protector Thomas's tent. Stewart, Batman's tracker from New South Wales, had been found dead on the riverbank, and a bunch of settler ruffians who hung about the Kulin camp were insisting the Wurundjeri had killed him. Terrified, the Wurundjeri crowded around, pleading, 'No kill Stewart, plenty rum, too much rum, plenty tumble about, by and by tumble in the water . . . and then plenty dead.' Remembering his own trouble with Stewart's drunkenness, Robinson found this an entirely satisfactory explanation for the drowning. He assured the Wurundjeri men that he knew they had been falsely accused. Hugely relieved, they pronounced the chief protector 'one big master', at which he was plenty pleased.

The presence of the chief protector at the Kulin camp emboldened a few women to cross the river and visit his hut. On reaching the door, they shrieked and gesticulated at the sight of a disembodied

Wooredy staring unerringly at them. Only when Robinson laid his hand on the bust to show it was not Wooredy's spirit but an inanimate object could they be persuaded to enter. One woman came back several times, always careful to lay her hand on Wooredy's bust as she entered. Eventually, she brought a group of men to invite the big master to a corroboree with a large contingent of Djadjawurrung, who had come down from the north-west.

For the next two days, Robinson was kept busy trying to stop the fighting between the local clans and the visitors, although it was not always easy for him to determine if they were engaged in serious combat or just a display of comparative strength. He spent several hours observing a highly ritualised wrestling contest, conducted in absolute silence, which seemed entirely good-natured. More serious internecine conflict erupted a fortnight later when an angry group of Wadawurrung arrived to settle a dispute with two other clans. Robinson made frantic efforts to stop the fighting, although his interventions were not appreciated by the drunken settlers who had congregated on the south bank to watch. One fellow was heard to shout, 'Are you going to drive the poor creatures away here, Mr Robinson, as you did in Van Diemen's Land?'

With more than five hundred Kulin from many different clans gathered in the encampment, Robinson saw an opportunity to build trust. A huge feast was organised so that he could personally distribute food to the Kulin. It fell to Truganini, Wooredy and Peevay to dispel suspicions that the feast was a trap to get the clans corralled in one place where they could be shot. Eventually, the offer of fresh meat was too enticing for the Kulin to stay away and the feast went off without incident, topped off with a display of fireworks. Truganini did especially well selling her baskets to the Melbourne gentry, who had been invited to attend. She earned the tidy sum of four shillings and one penny.

Robinson's wife, Maria, arrived in April with their three daughters and three younger sons, while the eldest son, George, had stayed on Flinders Island, intending to follow in a few months. Robinson's instructions to his wife had been to bring Peevay's wife, Plorenernoopner; Lacklay and his wife, Maytepueminer; Wooredy's sons, Davey Bruny and Peter Bruny; and Walter George Arthur's wife, Mary Ann. He asked that Maulboyheener come without his new Tyreelore wife, Rebecca, but she came anyway.

Maria Robinson's arrival was noted in the local newspaper, which reported that she came with her family and four servants, as well as 'an Aboriginal female and child, who had been forcibly taken from this place by one of the sealers'. This was Charlotte, originally from New Holland, with her son Johnny. There was no specific mention of the other eight people Mrs Robinson had brought over at her husband's insistence, and so it was not readily apparent that a total of fourteen Van Diemen's Land people had been transferred to Port Phillip. This subterfuge suggested that Robinson was not entirely confident that Governor Gipps would acquiesce to his curious calculation that fourteen disparate individuals could be considered one family.

The arrival of the chief protector's wife and his numerous children did nothing to bolster his claim for official housing. His large family was forced to live in tents alongside those of the assistant protectors, men Robinson quickly came to despise. When Mrs Robinson suffered a virulent attack of dysentery, he was able to secure slightly more appropriate shelter in an abandoned wattle-and-daub house on a flood-prone section of the south bank. He covetously surveyed the disbanded Aboriginal Mission Station on a bend in the river above the Falls. The mission had been shut down on his advice, yet the missionary remained ensconced in the well-appointed residence. He was determined this inept fellow must move to make way for him.

Once he had comprehended the enormity of the task of the chief protector at Port Phillip, Robinson's daily journal reflections paid next to no attention to the people he had been so determined to bring from Van Diemen's Land. His focus was now firmly fixed on the battles to get the colonial authority to pay for their keep; the people themselves barely rated a mention in his journal. He had made no real plans for how to deploy the Van Diemen's Land people in Port Phillip. Previous experience would have told him they would be of no use to him as guides or conciliators when dealing with clans with whom they had not the slightest cultural connection. His fleeting references reveal that they were camped in *mia mia* around his house but he gave scant information about how they passed their days. They were left largely to their own devices, when not serving his family.

An acute labour shortage in Port Phillip meant that able-bodied men and youths were in high demand, but there was no sign that the Van Diemen's Land men were being hired to work for settlers. They did provide free labour to Robinson's sons, going with them on expeditions to locate good land to establish stations, clearing the trees and building the infrastructure of huts, fences and stockyards. For several months in the spring of 1839, Maulboyheener and Walter George Arthur helped to drive a herd of eight hundred cattle overland to South Australia, for which they were never paid. Robinson's brief asides implied that Wooredy, Peevay, Maulboyheener and Lacklay were often away hunting in the bush beyond Melbourne to supplement the food rations. Wooredy liked to hunt with a spear and waddy, but the other three men preferred to use guns.

Since the early days of the settlement, guns had been given out to Kulin for shooting lyrebirds, whose tail feathers were much sought after by the settlers. But while guns were readily available, powder and shot could be difficult to obtain. Assistant Protector Thomas complained about the common practice of Kulin women trading sex for much-needed ammunition so their men could shoot increasingly rare game. The Van Diemen's Land men also prized their guns and were known to be exceedingly good shots. Robinson's sons procured powder and shot for them.

With the men often away, the women stayed in the *mia mia* around Robinson's house. There was little to occupy them. They were neither temperamentally nor culturally suited to laundry, sewing or cooking, although Walter George Arthur's mixed-race wife Mary Ann continued to be a domestic servant in the Robinson household. Truganini made some money weaving baskets but she was increasingly bored and restless, drawn to the company of Kulin men at the nearby encampment. Nor was Truganini the only one engaging in cross-cultural sexual exchange. Peevay contracted syphilis while on a hunting trip.

Leaving Flinders Island, Robinson had calculated that the fourteen Van Diemen's Land people would automatically continue to be charges of the colonial government, and that he would have the use of them while the government paid for their keep. By April 1839, the supplies he had brought from Flinders Island were exhausted and he had not found the appropriate moment to clarify authorisation for their rations with Lonsdale. Swallowing his pride, he put in a large order for meat from his nemesis, John Batman, who ran the Port Phillip Commissariat. Knowing that Batman was never a stickler for the rules, he hoped his order would automatically be charged to the government.

After receiving a second supply of meat, he suffered the indignity of a visit from Batman's brusque manager, who protested that there was no authority to pay for these supplies and demanded that Robinson personally sign the bills of credit before he would advance any more rations. The chief protector was suddenly forced to find the wherewithal to feed, clothe and house fourteen people in addition to his own large family. Here lay the rub: the Van Diemen's Land people were supposed to help *make* money, not cost him.

Humbling himself, he wrote a letter to Governor Gipps requesting authority for the rations for the fourteen Van Diemen's Land people and reimbursement for his personal outlay on them to date. Gipps was in no mood to accommodate such a request. He was infuriated at Robinson's sleight of hand in bringing 'a regular Scotch family, consisting of all the kith and kin', instead of the father and mother and their children he had authorised. He reiterated his stipulation that rations would only be provided for a family of four. Robinson could expect no public support for his conviction that it was the government's obligation to pay for the dispossessed people he had brought to Port Phillip. As the *Port Phillip Gazette* told its readers, the position of chief protector was taking out of the public purse almost twice what was paid for a resident magistrate, and he could have no possible reason to 'offer one remark expressive of discontent'.

Truganini and her companions from Van Diemen's Land continued to be rationed with meat and staples and Robinson continued to be hard-pressed by Batman's manager, who refused any further supplies unless Robinson put up the cash. His financial concerns greatly increased in May when Batman was finally killed by the syphilis that had eaten away his nose and confined him to a makeshift wheelchair. Robinson was at last given responsibility for the two boys whose release from Batman he had long sought. Now he didn't want them and certainly wasn't going to pay to feed and clothe them too. He set about finding employment for the older boy, Jack Allen, who was contracted to work for two squatters for £26 a year.

The younger, Ben Lomond, ran away days before Batman's death and Robinson made no attempt to find him. Months later, a merchant rescued the boy from a Geelong public house and brought him to the chief protector in Melbourne. Robinson drew up a contract for Ben Lomond to work as a shepherd for twelve pounds a year, but he ran away again in August, fearing punishment for having lost a sheep. When he again turned up at Robinson's house he was sent to Assistant Protector Thomas, who didn't know what to do with him either. Ben Lomond, aged twelve, was left to fend for himself.

On the first day of October 1839, booming cannon announced the arrival of the official superintendent for Port Phillip, Charles La Trobe. Robinson hoped his financial problems might now come to an end, and leapt astride his horse to ride to the Falls so as to be among the first to shake La Trobe by the hand. He never even got close. Over the next few days he endured the humiliation of being excluded from the reception at the Melbourne Club, and was even denied an invitation to the swearing-in. He should have known that the hostile Melbourne elite would be quick to make unflattering insinuations about him, yet despite their strident attacks he was entirely unprepared for his reception when finally granted an audience with the new superintendent. La Trobe was so hostile that Robinson was stunned into silence. Never had a colonial official treated him with such disrespect.

A few days later, La Trobe relented enough to permit Robinson to take over the missionary's capacious abode. On the matter of payment for rations he gave no ground. La Trobe's acute distrust went beyond his disdain for a man who had been promoted beyond his class expectations. Profoundly shocked by what he witnessed at the Kulin encampment, La Trobe sent Robinson 'damning and dictatorial' letters accusing him of neglect of duty and indifference to the plight of the Kulin.

La Trobe was mistaken to think Robinson was indifferent. Confronted with the magnitude of the suffering in Port Phillip, the chief protector had no idea what he was supposed to do for so many afflicted and desperate people. Sometimes there would be upwards of six hundred men, women and children from various Kulin clans congregated at the edges of Melbourne, living in what he readily conceded was 'a deplorable state of disease and wretchedness'. In his journal, he raged about the criminal theft of Kulin land, the cruelty of the colonial authorities, and the farce of the official policy of protection, but when it came to providing amelioration he could only extemporise.

He arranged for the colonial surgeon to visit the Kulin camp. The surgeon confirmed that an epidemic of virulent typhus was rampaging through the encampment, and that at least half the residents, including many small children, were infected with syphilis, which was killing dozens every day. The only action Robinson could propose in response was to move all this human suffering out of town and out of sight. Just two days before Christmas, he sought La Trobe's approval to create small areas of Crown land as protectorate stations, each one under the supervision of an assistant protector, where the dispossessed clans could be supplied with government rations in return for labour.

The first of the stations was to be in the Westernport District, where the colonial government had already secured nearly 4000 acres about twenty miles south-east of Melbourne, along Dandenong Creek at Nerre Nerre Warren in the country of the Boonwurrung. This station was to be under the direction of Assistant Protector Thomas, who was given instructions to remove all the people camped around Melbourne, no matter their clan or country. Handouts of food and blankets were to be strictly reserved for the sick and infirm, while the healthy must be made to work for their rations. The Kulin 'should be taught to feel their wants, should feel their necessities', Robinson insisted.

Stressed to the limit by his battles with La Trobe on the one hand and his despised subordinates on the other, Robinson sought to recreate the camaraderie of times past. In September 1839, he took Truganini and Wooredy on an excursion to the Mornington Peninsula. They headed south-east towards the landmark of Arthur's Seat and for several nights camped behind the coastal heath near Point Nepean. There, a natural depression had created an ephemeral wetland with a limpid lagoon that was a sanctuary for large flocks of grey herons, black swans and blue-billed ducks. The surrounding grassland provided food for mobs of large kangaroos. At one spot beside the lagoon they found a Kulin burial site where two bodies had been burnt, and in other places the trampled grass indicated the tracks of settlers' cattle, yet they saw no other sign of human activity. Ringing axes, bleating sheep, barking dogs were not heard. Apart from the honking and quacking of the startled birds, the place was silent.

Flooded with memories of their first mission together, Robinson observed to Truganini that this tranquil place reminded him of Port Davey, but she said it was more like Bruny Island. This remark prompted Wooredy to tell stories from his life on Bruny Island, nostalgic for his country now far beyond his reach. He told how his brother had been hunting seals with his second wife and child when their canoe capsized and all three had been caught by Raegewarrah, who had been summoned by the jealous first wife. Wooredy also told how his father had watched in wonderment as Captain Cook stepped onto the beach at Adventure Bay, and how he himself had seen the first white men come ashore at the tip of Bruny Island. He had been frightened by a dog that had lunged at him, barking, when he tried to touch it, and bewildered by the ship's biscuit a strange man threw at him. The hard, round object was a plaything, he had decided, not something to eat. In turn, Robinson told how Captain Cook had visited other islands in the south seas and discovered the usefulness of breadfruit. Truganini was delighted with this information. Finally, it made sense to her how white men got their bread. Of course, it came from the fruit of a tree.

Swapping stories around the fire in empty bushland under a canopy of stars was the last moment of intimacy Robinson would share with these two people, who had served him so well for so long. They were no longer of any use to him.

For Truganini, the excursion to Arthur's Seat was possibly also the last time she shared the intimacy of a couple with Wooredy. For over a decade, she and Wooredy had been cast as a couple in Robinson's daily journal, yet from the time they had arrived in Port Phillip this was no longer so, except for this one brief episode. From time to time Robinson would briefly note that Wooredy was working for one of his sons, with no suggestion his wife was with him. His one or two sporadic references to Truganini were about her running away 'to the Port Phillip men' or unknown assignations further afield. And it was not Wooredy who was dispatched to find Truganini and return her to Robinson's house—Maulboyheener always went looking for her.

Neither Truganini nor Wooredy was chosen to accompany the chief protector on the long excursion through Gippsland to Twofold Bay between January and March 1840. It was the first time he had been on a mission without them. None of the Van Diemen's Land people went with him. Nor did they go with him when he was again dispatched on a long journey, into the Goulburn region, leaving on 1 April. The very day he left, all the people living with him dismantled their *mia mia* and walked away. There were sightings of them on the Mornington Peninsula and in Westernport. It was several weeks before Robinson's sons managed to locate various individuals and bring nearly all of them back to Melbourne.

No sooner was Truganini returned to Robinson's house than she was gone again. In June, she was reported to be on a station near Mount Eliza on the Mornington Peninsula, and Maulboyheener was sent to find her with Robinson's son Charles. Eventually she was located living with two shepherds in a hut on a pastoral run at Port Nepean. She was within eight miles of Robinson's house when she slipped away from her escort again. Once more Maulboyheener was sent to bring her back. This pattern would be repeated several times.

By May, most of the people had returned to Melbourne. But not all: Thomas Brune never returned. Peevay went to look for him without success; he was only able to ascertain that the youth was with Jack Allen, who had run away from his employer. They were travelling with two Boonwurrung women across pastoral runs between Dandenong and the Mornington Peninsula. On Christmas Day 1840, all four were reported to be camped at Arthur's Seat, and by the New Year they were working on Torbinurruck run on Lang Lang River near the head of Westernport. On 1 January 1841, Thomas Brune fell from a tree while hunting possum and broke his neck. He died on 3 January, and was buried on the station. Nothing more had been heard of Jack Allen.

Lacklay simply vanished. Apparently he went as far afield as Gippsland and lived with the Kurnai for a while. In mid April 1840, he turned up with a gun on Mornington Peninsula, where he boldly announced that he had quit the chief protector because of inadequate rations. Lacklay stopped at several stations to give warnings that the Kurnai were planning an attack and the squatters had better be prepared. For a brief time he was employed by John Highett, whose huge cattle run lay between Dandenong and the Carrum Carrum Swamp. He was with Highett only a few days before heading back to Lower Westernport, having helped himself to a supply of food, blankets, clothing, pannikins and about ten pounds of buckshot for his gun.

Rumours later reached Melbourne that he was working for a man named Berry on the lower shore of Westernport between Bass River and Cape Paterson. This was Christopher Berry, the master of two small cutters that regularly traded between Launceston and Port Phillip, and who had recently left Melbourne under a cloud of scandal after running off with his business partner's wife. In October 1840, Robinson made enquiries about Berry from squatter Robert Jamieson of Torbinurruck station, who had come to Melbourne to report an attack on his station by a large party of Kurnai from Gippsland. The squatter told him that Berry had settled much further down the eastern shore of Westernport and had put to sea months earlier and drowned. Jamieson had nothing to say about Lacklay, whose whereabouts remained a mystery.

All but two people returned to Robinson, but their faithlessness in leaving him had soured his view of them as his family. He no longer had a mind to plead their case for remaining in Port Phillip. At a meeting with La Trobe on 22 June 1841, he said he wanted them all sent back to Flinders Island, a request La Trobe chose to ignore.

For the next six weeks, Robinson was entirely preoccupied with the first land sales in Port Phillip. He had his eye on a lot of 150 acres on Merri Creek, selling for five pounds fifty an acre, but he had to settle for 10 acres. In addition, he bought an allotment of 20 acres in a subdivision on the south bank of the Yarra, where he planned to build a grand house. He called his new property Turneet, using the name the Wurundjeri people gave to this part of their country.

Soon he had all the Van Diemen's Land men and boys at work clearing the ground and preparing the site for the house, although he remained determined to ultimately have them sent back to Flinders Island. He reiterated his position more forcefully in a meeting on 4 August, telling La Trobe, 'They were no use to me and I wished to get rid of them.' When the superintendent was unmoved, Robinson sent a formal request to Governor Gipps, who refused to entertain the idea. Having been deceived about Robinson's bringing these people in the first place, Gipps was not about to wear the expense of sending them back.

Given the chronic labour shortage in Port Phillip, Gipps was confident that the people from Van Diemen's Land could be used to advantage. On 2 October, he ordered La Trobe to release the chief protector from the necessity of paying for them by removing them from his control. La Trobe was more than happy to oblige. It had not escaped his attention that Robinson and his sons were in the enviable position of having unwaged workers at their beck and call. The expense of their clothing and rations would be nothing set against the value of their free labour. Moreover, he had received good reports about them from various settlers.

In January 1841, Robinson was ordered to deliver the people from Van Diemen's Land to the Protectorate Station at Nerre Nerre Warren, where they would become the responsibility of Assistant Protector Thomas. Robinson angrily protested 'they would not go', only to be curtly informed that they would not be given the benefit of a choice. Robinson knew that the strategy to employ these people was not viable and that nothing would induce them to stay at the Protectorate Station. They did not like Thomas, who in turn had a very poor opinion of them as unruly and undisciplined.

It was true they were no compliant labour force. It had long been their habit to do just as they pleased. None of them could be expected to conform to any employment contract that Thomas might negotiate. Previous contracts had been broken within months of being negotiated. Ben Lomond had run off from the employer to whom he had been contracted in August 1839 and had not been heard of since. Jack Allen had abandoned his employer, when he had been accused of killing a horse and he was last heard of roaming around Westernport with a stolen gun, living among the Boonwurrung people.

When the matter was raised again on 24 February, Robinson reiterated that his people refused to go to the Protectorate Station and that he could not compel them. By way of illustrating the difficulty, he confessed that Peevay, one of his most trusted guides and the man he had chosen to accompany him on a long expedition, had just walked away from his property in Melbourne. Peevay was away for several weeks, most likely in Westernport looking for his friend Lacklay. He reappeared just in time to join the expedition into the Western District that left on 21 March.

When the expedition returned six months later, Robinson was in no position to hand over his charges to Assistant Protector Thomas—he had no idea where most of them were. He could only vouch for Walter George Arthur and his wife, Mary Ann. These two were 'not wild blacks', he explained to La Trobe, they were his domestic servants, paid out of his own purse. He also undertook to personally support Wooredy, a man to whom he owed 'a debt of gratitude', as well as Wooredy's wife and sons, failing to mention that he had no notion where Wooredy's wife and sons might be. In other circumstances, Robinson would have sent

Peevay to look for the missing people, but Peevay was gone again as well. After staying close to Robinson for six gruelling months in the Western District, he had abruptly left the expedition to go after his wife, Plorenernoopner, who, together with Lacklay's wife, Maytepueminer, had gone to look for Lacklay.

Truganini had run off with Maulboyheener. When Maulboyheener's wife, Rebecca, died on 29 April 1841, it was inevitable Truganini would become his new wife. These two had been together since they were both adolescents. She was now twenty-seven and he was twenty-five, whereas Wooredy was an old man. Deserted by Truganini for the last time, Wooredy left Melbourne to go to the station of Dr James Allen, who at one time had been the medical superintendent at Flinders Island and had a genuine affection for Wooredy. He was there in June 1841 when Assistant Protector Thomas came to investigate the killing of sheep in the vicinity. On hearing the description of an old man with a dog rushing a flock of sheep to cut out a ewe and lamb, Thomas was sure this man had to be Wooredy. Dr Allen would not identify the culprit and further annoyed Thomas by persistently refusing to take Wooredy to the Protectorate Station.

Wooredy's younger son, Peter Bruny, was with him at Dr Allen's farm, while his elder son, Davey Bruny, was believed to be living on a squatter's run at Point Nepean with Ben Lomond. Barely had Robinson settled back into his home in Melbourne when three men called to tell him there was a Van Diemen's Land boy in a very bad way at a pub in Flinders Lane. It was Ben Lomond. He had been at the hotel for a fortnight and was 'very badly mistreated', Robinson noted, though he did not say whether at the pub or at Point Nepean. He arranged for Ben Lomond to be urgently transferred to hospital, where he died one week later, on 5 September 1841. A servant was sent to look for Wooredy's son, who could not be found.

That tragic incident was the last reference Robinson made to his errant 'family' in his journal entries. He thereafter showed not the slightest interest in knowing where they were. He could breathe a sigh of relief that they were no longer his responsibility.

Truganini and Maulboyheener left Melbourne to travel south, working for food and shelter at stations in the lower Dandenong. By mid May 1841, they were living on the Ballymarang station at the eastern edge of Carrum Carrum Swamp. This huge pastoral run included a series of waterholes that had great significance for the Boonwurrung original owners. There were always Boonwurrung people living at Ballymarang, which was a source of irritation to Assistant Protector Thomas, a regular visitor to the station.

Truganini was displeased to see Thomas arrive at Ballymarang in May and tried to hide from him, unsuccessfully. For his part, Thomas was very surprised to see her and even more surprised that she was with Maulboyheener. Believing them to be his responsibility, he insisted that the couple travel with him to Nerre Nerre Warren, where they would be supplied with rations. The resident station manager James Horsfall intervened, explaining that Maulboyheener was employed on a verbal agreement for the pay of a dollar and a half a week. When Thomas proposed drawing up a work contract, Horsfall refused, saying such formal arrangements with his workers 'made them dissatisfied'. Distrustful of Horsfall's intentions, Thomas again pressured Truganini and Maulboyheener to go with him to Nerre Nerre Warren the next day. Tentatively they agreed, but by the morning they were gone.

By June, Truganini and Maulboyheener had moved on to John Highett's Pallarangun run on the Mornington Peninsula, where Lacklay had been briefly employed the previous year. Once again, Thomas came to fetch them, and once again Truganini tried to hide from him. On being discovered, she dutifully promised that she and Maulboyheener would go to the Protectorate Station. They never arrived. Instead, they went to work for Thomas's son on his nearby station, Tuerong. The couple left this employment in early September, taking a gun, along with a good supply of powder and shot. They were heading back to Horsfall's station.

Peevay was headed in the same direction. By September, he had caught up with his wife, Plorenernoopner, and they reached Horsfall's station with Lacklay's wife, Maytepueminer, on 4 September. Reconnected with Truganini and Maulboyheener, they stayed only long enough to steal another gun. Thomas noted in his journal that two days later they were seen directly south of Ballymarang on a station at the top of Westernport Bay. He guessed they were going into Lower Westernport to continue looking for Lacklay.

Lacklay was most probably dead, in Thomas's opinion. In October 1840, Thomas had established that Lacklay—known to him as Isaac—had been seen many months earlier working much lower down in Westernport Bay. A worker at the huge pastoral station Torbinurruck, on the Bass River, told him that no more than a week after that sighting, a cutter set out from the far eastern tip of Westernport Bay. On board was the owner, Christopher Berry, with a woman and her three children. Lacklay and an unnamed German man were the crew. That night a heavy squall had swept in from the Tasman Sea and the boat was presumed to have capsized, with everyone drowned. No bodies or pieces of wreckage had been recovered. Thomas was not fully convinced, noting in the margin of his journal 'the death of Isaac supposed'.

Thomas was right to have reservations about this narrative of death by drowning—the truth, only established 176 years later, was that the cutter did not capsize. Christopher Berry sailed all the way to the remote whaling port of Kororareka in the Bay of Islands in New Zealand, where he and his bigamous wife made a new life.

Lacklay may well have done the same. The whaling industry provided good opportunities for young men cut loose from their land and culture. Lacklay could easily have secured a berth on the many American, French and British whaling ships that called into Kororareka, or else joined the shore-based whaling station being established at Hawkes Bay. Prominent among the whalers at Hawkes Bay were several Van Diemen's Land men, the mixed-race sons of sealers from the Bass Strait whose mothers were at Wybalenna. The head whaler at Hawkes Bay was Ned Tomlins, whose sister Bullyer had been a guide on some of Robinson's missions. Lacklay certainly knew Ned Tomlins.

At the time there was no conceivable way that anyone in Port Phillip could have known that Berry's boat had managed to sail across the Tasman Sea. Lacklay's disappearance was left to supposition and speculation. A story that made much more sense than drowning was that he had been shot by a settler, a narrative that everyone in Port Phillip was familiar with. Peevay and Maulboyheener had heard just that kind of story at Horsfall's station and were on their way to Lower Westernport to investigate.

During the many months that the Van Diemen's Land people were on the loose in Port Phillip, Robinson paid them no attention. His journal entries reveal not the slightest interest in establishing where they were. He had brought them to Port Phillip because he had wanted to be absolved of the dreadful burden of responsibility for their fate on Flinders Island, so starkly apparent in the crowded graveyard he left behind. He had had vague hopes they would somehow make a new life in alien Port Phillip among an alien people. Whatever the hopes, he had surely known that he was taking an almighty risk. Even so, he could never have foreseen the dramatic and tragic consequences.

CHAPTER 9

NEGOTIATING THE MANGROVES at the top of Westernport Bay was torturous. A concertina of inlets formed by creeks draining out of a huge bog of decomposing reed beds and dense thickets of swamp melaleuca, the Koo-Wee-Rup Swamp spread for miles to the north and east, making it near impossible to find a way through. Truganini, Maulboyheener, Peevay, Plorenernoopner and Maytepueminer were obliged to make a wide detour around it to find higher ground by the Lang Lang River, where Robert Jamieson and Samuel Rawson had their pastoral run Torbinurruck.

Prudently avoiding the station, the five followed the course of the river through a broad, flat terrain littered with long ribbons of bark shed by the sparse cover of eucalypts. Reaching the coast, they pushed their way through a tangle of wattle and melaleuca to the rocky shore, where massive tide fluctuations had created an extensive intertidal zone of mangroves and saltmarsh. At low tide, the wide expanse of mudflats provided a rich harvest of scallops, mussels, oysters, abalone, limpets, marine worms, crabs and burrowing shrimp.

No one noticed these five interlopers camped above the tideline. Despite the evidence of longstanding occupation in the exposed shell middens, the place was empty. From the Koo-Wee-Rup Swamp to Cape Paterson was Boonwurrung territory, originally occupied by the Yallockbulluck and Yowengerral clans. By the time the settlers from Launceston arrived, these clans were already gone, extinguished by the cumulative effect of renegade encroachments from Van Diemen's Land, endemic warfare with the Kurnai and debilitating attacks by sealers and runaway convicts come to steal women, all compounded by epidemic disease. The final blow to this fragile population had been the establishment of a penal settlement on an elevated point above the Bass River in 1826, which was subsequently abandoned in 1828.

When Samuel Anderson and Robert Massie first sailed from Launceston to the eastern shores of Westernport in 1835, they had found no sign of the original owners. Even vestiges of previous settlement were deserted, although some transient visitors had still crossed the Bass Strait to strip the bark of the blackwoods and silver wattles that grew abundantly along the lower shore. The bark was shipped to Launceston to be processed into tannic acid for medicinal use, which was a lucrative export to Europe and Britain.

Anderson and Massie landed at the Bass River, where they took up a pastoral lease to grow wheat and built a homestead using bricks from the old penal settlement. Near the river mouth, they created an agricultural settlement that included a flourmill driven by tidal power, saltworks and an orchard. A small harbour just north of the river mouth sheltered several small vessels that shipped their produce to Melbourne. In addition, they held another huge pastoral lease over coastal land from the old penal settlement to Griffith Point, opposite Phillip Island. During Anderson's indefatigable explorations of the Lower Westernport region and beyond, he located a seam of black coal that ran along the coast from his lease all the way through to Cape Paterson.

When Truganini and her companions arrived in the spring of 1841, they found the eastern side of Westernport was still virtually uninhabited all the way to Gippsland. There were no original owners, only a handful of squatters and the occasional bark cutter. On 15 September, Anderson and Massie became aware that Truganini, Maulboyheener, Peevay, Plorenernoopner and Maytepueminer had established camp on their run. They were surprised to see them, and especially surprised that they came with their own supplies of tea and sugar.

The two squatters knew Truganini and her friends very well from their time working for the Van Diemen's Land Company at Circular Head, where Anderson had been a bookkeeper and Massie an engineer. On several occasions, Truganini, Peevay, Plorenernoopner and Maulboyheener, together with Lacklay, had camped at Circular Head. They had stayed for a month during the summer of 1834, when both Anderson and Massie had been frequent visitors to their camp and gone hunting with them.

Without hesitation, the squatters handed over generous amounts of flour to make damper and were not greatly fussed when Peevay and Maulboyheener appropriated one of their dogs to hunt kangaroos. Nor were they concerned that the men were hunting with guns.

If anyone in Lower Westernport knew what had happened to Lacklay, it would be these two squatters. While at Anderson and Massie's station, Truganini and the others were almost certainly told that their companion Lacklay had last been seen in the company of a unnamed settler who lived at the end of Westernport Bay.

After a leisurely stay at Anderson and Massie's run, Truganini and her companions moved off on 29 September, taking with them Anderson's short-tailed dog. Later that day, they crossed the Powlett River and made camp close to the hut of William Watson, who was the sole settler present in the region between the Bass River and Cape Paterson. Watson had recently arrived with his wife, daughter and son-in-law, Walter Ginman, in mid May 1841—employed by a consortium of investors to work the seam of coal that Anderson had discovered. Watson and Ginman had sunk a shaft into the coal seam near the mouth of the Powlett River and built a rudimentary hut just above the high-water mark.

Watson welcomed Truganini and her friends, while his wife gave them tea and sugar and even loaned them a kettle. On 2 October, the fourth day of their visit, Watson and Ginman departed for the mine, and the five approached the hut and lingered in the yard until Mrs Watson came out to give them some more tea and sugar. Sometime later, the women began to scatter the bark from their *mia mia* and pack up their belongings, while the men came to the hut to return the kettle. Once the men gained entrance to the hut, Peevay went to look for Watson's guns while Maulboyheener took Mrs Watson and her daughter by the shoulders to propel them towards the door. The women resisted until Peevay pointed a gun at Mrs Watson's head, warning that he would shoot them both unless they went outside.

Truganini and Maytepueminer took hold of Mrs Watson and her daughter, pulling them into the bush. On reaching the river, they carried the distressed women across the water on their backs, and then pointed them in the direction of Anderson and Massie's station. Meanwhile, Peevay and Maulboyheener systematically stripped the hut of food staples, blankets, clothing, an axe, two guns and a supply of buckshot. After setting fire to the hut, the five loaded up their plunder and followed the river towards the coast, with their dogs in tow.

Early that evening, Peevay and Maulboyheener lay concealed in the low coastal heath watching Watson and his son-in-law returning from the mine. When the two men came into range, they fired a volley of shots from several guns, hitting Ginman in the calf and slightly wounding Watson in the foot and elbow. Hobbling towards their hut, the two men saw that their home was a smouldering ruin and their wives had vanished. It was well after dark when they reached Anderson and Massie's station to find their wives unharmed. The next day, Massie sent a boat to Melbourne with a message that La Trobe should send a military detachment to the region. He also supplied Watson with a brace of firearms and two of his workers for a search party.

Peevay and Maulboyheener must have known that Watson would come looking for them, and that he would likely shoot them on sight, yet they lingered at the Powlett River mouth for another four days. It was a delightful spot. The meandering river cut a wide gully through sandy hillocks of coastal heath and gnarled, wind-stunted melaleuca where they could camp camouflaged from view. Entering the bay, the river spread fingers of water across broad stretches of sand that ran south as far as the eye could see. It was a place of cornucopia, much visited over centuries by the original owners, as evidenced by the middens exposed by the mining operations. The daily low tide yielded a rich harvest of molluscs and shellfish, while the coastal heath was home to a multitude of small game, mutton birds, edible crimson berries and pigface.

Staying low, with the heath to provide cover, the five kept careful watch for Watson's search party. From a high point on the sand dunes, they had an excellent view of the flat country to the north and east, the direction they knew danger would come from. They managed to avoid detection until the evening of 5 October, when Watson caught a glimpse of Maulboyheener standing on a high dune. Several shots were fired, which failed to wound Maulboyheener, although a bullet came close enough to make a neat hole in the coat he was wearing.

Alert to the danger from Watson's party, they didn't notice six unarmed men approaching from the south, walking along the beach to Watson's mine in the late afternoon on 6 October. The six men had walked overland from the whaling station at Lady's Bay, on Wilson's Promontory, more than fifty miles away. Finding the mine deserted, the whalers assumed that the people they had glimpsed entering the dunes about two hundred yards away must be the miners. Who else could they be?

Two whalers, known as Yankee and Cook, went to look for the miners while their companions entered the hut to rest. Minutes later, two shots rang out in quick succession.

Maulboyheener and Peevay each fired, first one then the other, leaving no time between to reload with powder and shot. Having seen the two men fall, Maulboyheener kept watch from the top of the dune while Peevay, Truganini, Plorenernoopner and Maytepueminer went down to the beach with their dogs to check.

Lying on the beach were two men they had never seen before: a shot had hit one in the head, killing him instantly, while the other had entered the second man's side, leaving him grievously wounded and in agony. The four returned with this terrible information to Maulboyheener, who pulled up a couple of strong tree roots and went alone to the beach to dispatch the wounded stranger with heavy blows to the back of his head. Watching from above, the three women cried in distress.

They were not the only ones watching. Having been woken by the gunshots, two more whalers, Robbins and Evans, stepped outside the hut to look about. They could not see any sign of their comrades on the beach, because their view was obstructed by a sand dune. However, a party of four or five people, with what looked like two guns and two dogs, were visible on a high dune some two hundred yards away. It was not possible to distinguish whether these figures were male or female, white or black, but they observed some of the group go down to the beach, leaving a person with a gun watching from above. When they returned, the one who had been watching went down to the beach alone.

Believing that they had seen a group of miners hunting birds or kangaroos, Robbins and Evans concluded there was no reason to be alarmed and went back inside to sleep. Waking about an hour later, Evans was disturbed to see his companions Yankee and Cook had not returned. This time he went to search for them. He was a few yards from the hut when a shot zinged over his head. Watson's search party materialised in front of him with their guns aimed right at him.

Evans quickly established that none of these men had fired the shots he'd heard earlier. Alarmed now, he woke his fellow whalers. They enlisted Watson's party to help search for Yankee and Cook and found the bodies on the beach, their blood staining the sand. Both were readily identified: Yankee was already cold, with a bullet wound behind his ear, while Cook had a deep wound in his side and had been bludgeoned on the back of the head.

The whalers carried the bodies to a small gully between the dunes, well above the high-water mark, for burial. As the bodies were being interred, Watson noticed that a few hundred yards away about four people were watching them from atop a dune, well out of range. Pursuing them, he caught occasional glimpses of people crawling on their hands and knees through the heath. Then he lost them. Watson couldn't clearly identify the people, but he recognised one of their dogs as the short-tailed dog from Anderson's station. He'd know that dog anywhere.

What could possibly have triggered such aberrant behaviour? Never before had Truganini or any of her companions engaged in violence. Any criminal behaviour had been limited to taking firearms, food and clothes from squatters they believed had cheated them. If they had intended to exact some kind of retribution for colonial dispossession it made no sense to travel all the way to a place almost bereft of settlers. There was some other reason for their murderous action, a reason specific to that place.

After the shooting, the obvious course would have been to head westwards and make common cause with the aggrieved Kurnai in Gippsland, who had attacked the squatters in the previous year. That is not what they did. They waited a couple of days in the coastal dunes, to be sure the search party had gone, then buried much of their plunder and retraced their journey along the coast, keeping to the cover of the coastal heath. By the time they reached the Bass River, their supply of powder and shot was running low. Without powder, their stolen guns were just a useless burden. They raided a couple of empty huts belonging to Massie and Anderson's workers but found no guns or powder, although they did carry off a pair of bullet moulds.

On 11 October, they made a camp on an elevation near the site of the old penal settlement. They became aware of a boat sailing close to the eastern shore and saw beacon fires burning on cliffs to the north to guide the boat to the beach below the red bluff. The following day, the boat sailed further down the coast and pulled in at the mouth of the Bass River, disembarking a large group of men who disappeared into the scrub. The five kept moving in the opposite direction.

On 13 October, they came very close to a man named Westerway, who was cutting bark. This stranger was clearly not expecting any trouble—he was unarmed and working in the scrub some distance from his camp above the high-water mark. Keeping out of sight, they crept along the shore and stealthily stripped one of his tents, then stole away without being detected. They got food staples, but little else of use. What they really needed was guns and ammunition.

For the rest of the day they maintained surveillance of the coast, observing that the boat seen earlier was now sailing towards the nearby camp, where Westerway was frantically signalling. The boat contained fourteen heavily armed men, who were cold, tired, irritable and covered in scratches from thrashing about in the bush on either side of the Bass River. The man in charge was the commissioner for the Westernport District, Frederick Powlett, who explained to Westerway about the murders and that they had found no trace of the culprits, only a discarded shotgun. He could not stay to search around the camp, as Westerway demanded—the tide was going out and he needed to set sail immediately to return to Melbourne and organise reinforcements. It was already too late: by late afternoon Powlett's boat was still visible, stuck hard on the extensive mudflats.

Four workers from Anderson and Massie's station came to Westerway's aid that night. The following day, they had some satisfaction in recovering numerous discarded items, including a cloak taken from Westerway's tent and a pair of bullet moulds taken from one of their huts. They could tell this item had been stolen by the Van Diemen's Land men because it was stained with the red ochre they used to paint their bodies.

The next night, under cover of darkness, Peevay and Maulboyheener stealthily advanced on the sleeping men and fired a hail of gunshot, startling them awake. As they crawled away from the firelight into the shadow of the trees, Westerway sustained a flesh wound and one of Anderson's men was shot in the chest. They stayed hidden while their assailants rummaged through the second tent, taking firearms and a warm coat, as well as £22 in banknotes, which they later decided to burn.

Leaving Westerway's camp, the five travelled steadily in a north-westerly direction, possibly heading for Dr Allen's station where Wooredy was living, or even Robinson's house in Melbourne. Over ten days, no one reported seeing them, although they probably made contact with people at the Boonwurrung camp around the Banyan Water Holes. Here they would have heard the story of cold-blooded murder that was spreading like quicksilver through the Westernport District, amplified in horror with every telling. The culprits in this narrative were two Van Diemen's Land men; the three women were never mentioned.

By late October, Truganini was suffering from swollen legs and could barely walk. She needed to recuperate. They rested at Michael Solomon's Moodie Yallo station, which ran from Lower Dandenong to the edge of the Carrum Carrum Swamp. Maulboyheener knew this particular run as he had worked for Solomon in the past, and Thomas Thompson, one of the three youths who came with them from Flinders Island, was still employed there. Another draw was that it was very close to the mine where the local Boonwurrung got their red ochre.

They stayed hidden on Moodie Yallo station, with Thomas Thompson secretly supplying them with damper and meat, for at least four days before Solomon became aware of their presence on his run. As another early settler from Van Diemen's Land,

Solomon felt he had a special affinity with these people, and he tried to win Maulboyheener's trust by proposing a deal: he would buy their plunder if they brought the stuff to him in three days. Maulboyheener appeared to assent to this ruse and left to find his friends. As soon as he was out of sight, Solomon jumped on his horse and rode to Melbourne to alert Commissioner Powlett. Maulboyheener and his friends left that night, taking Thomas Thompson with them.

Truganini was limping badly as they made their way back to Westernport Bay. As they passed through Ballymarang they learnt, if they didn't already know, that Assistant Protector Thomas had recruited several senior Boonwurrung men as trackers and joined Commissioner Powlett with his party of nine policemen on horseback. Also riding with Powlett was the squatter Samuel Rawson from Torbinurruck station. Robinson had refused to join the search party and had gone on another excursion in exactly the opposite direction.

Leaving Thomas Thompson at Ballymarang, the five moved on to Balla Balla station near Tooradin on 30 October. By then they were so low on ammunition that they risked a raid on the station during the day while the workers were away. So as not to alarm the lone woman inside with her child, Plorenernoopner and Maytepueminer approached one of the huts to ask for tea and sugar. Having gained admittance, they revealed a gun and demanded the woman tell them where the firearms were kept. To reinforce the threat, Peevay and Maulboyheener came inside too. They found eight canisters of powder, two shotguns and two pistols. Running off with the firearms, they also took one of the station dogs.

They crossed an inlet on the eastern side of Tooradin, carefully stepping in cattle tracks to obscure their own footprints, and on reaching the edge of the swamp, they made camp on 31 October.

A hindquarter of kangaroo was roasting on a fire and a kettle boiling to make tea when they heard the sound of gunfire and horses. Snatching up the guns and some ammunition, they ran towards the swamp, leaving behind the remains of the kangaroo, flour, tea and sugar, as well as the blankets, a tomahawk and several canisters of powder.

The horsemen were on their heels, although never quite close enough to shoot. Entering the swamp, the horses stalled and refused to move. Several of the riders urged their mounts to plunge into the reed beds, where they were soon stuck in the bog. Dismounting, the riders tried to pursue the fugitives into a dense patch of swamp melaleuca, until they too sank into the mire. Helpless, in mud and water almost to their knees, the searchers were confronted by a seemingly impenetrable mass of ghostly trunks and were disoriented by whistling that came first from one direction, then another, and then another again. With night closing in, the search party withdrew, 'hungry, wet, tired and disappointed', as Samuel Rawson confided in his journal.

Truganini and her companions were gone long before first light. Once more they picked a path through the swamp to the Lang Lang River, where again they made camp on Torbinurruck station. Truganini rested her legs while Maulboyheener and Peevay went to replenish their food supplies. While they were hunting on 2 November, they came across two convicts assigned to work for an absent squatter, and engaged them in affable conversation. Having established that the convicts were the sole occupants of the sturdy slab hut near the mouth of the river, Peevay and Maulboyheener returned that night to make an audacious raid.

Cowering inside, the convicts attempted to return fire through chinks between the timber slabs until their ammunition was almost finished. When the moon disappeared behind clouds, the shooting ceased. At dawn, Peevay and Maulboyheener renewed their attack and met with no answering fire. Cautiously, they approached the hut, dispatching the barking dog with one shot. A missing slab from the base of the back wall revealed how the occupants had wriggled out and escaped up the river. Using the same technique, Peevay and Maulboyheener removed a slab from behind the fireplace to get into the hut. It was hardly worth the effort. The guns were gone and all the shot expended. All they could find was some flour, a pair of trousers and a kangaroo-skin rug.

Two days later, a boat with nine policemen, Rawson, Thomas and four trackers approached the river mouth, where it became stuck on the mudflats about a mile from the shore. As they walked across the mud they could hear dogs barking and guns firing, much to Rawson's chagrin. On reaching the site of the besieged hut, the policemen became very nervous about following the tracks that led away from it. One policeman told Thomas that the nine of them would not be strong enough against two Van Diemen's Land men, especially if they had double-barrelled guns, since the women also knew how to use firearms. They chose to wait till Powlett arrived with reinforcements.

Thomas and his four trackers did follow the tracks of Peevay and Maulboyheener for several days and were puzzled that they could identify the tracks of two men and two women and that these people appeared to be moving around in circles. One woman must be laying low somewhere. They could get no closer to her or any of her companions. By 8 November, it became clear that all five had moved further down the coast towards Anderson and Massie's run on the Bass River. The Boonwurrung trackers refused to go any further south, deathly afraid of attack from their traditional enemies, the Kurnai of Gippsland.

Peevay and Maulboyheener hunted around the Bass River for a week until they were again low on ammunition. That was when their attention turned to the Anderson homestead. Throughout the morning of 17 November they kept watch and established that only three servants were at home. An old man and a woman were in the main building, with another young woman in the kitchen. After midday, Peevay and Maulboyheener crawled through the long grass to the homestead. Maulboyheener went into the main building and sent the two servants outside, while Peevay stood guard with three guns on his arm. The woman from the kitchen ran towards Peevay, distraught, to get her infant. Peevay told her the child would not be harmed and, pointing one of his guns, made her stay with the others. Searching the homestead, Maulboyheener found three shotguns, a pistol with bayonet attached, three bags of shot, bedding and clothes, as well as flour and sugar.

That night, even as Anderson's brother and the other male workers kept watch at the homestead, Plorenernoopner and Maytepueminer made a return visit, silently digging up potatoes and robbing the henhouse of two birds and six eggs.

Carrying considerable baggage, the five took the bridge over the Bass River and walked a few miles across the flat coastal plain before heading into a low range of hills, where the thick bush provided protective cover. The hills gave them an expansive view of the whole of Lower Westernport. They observed Commissioner Powlett arrive at the Bass River with reinforcements from Melbourne. His search party now consisted of Rawson and three other squatter volunteers, Thomas, nine soldiers and nine policemen, all on horseback. Seven men from various Kulin clans accompanied them on foot. The entire party was armed.

Watching the search party cross the Bass River, it was obvious to the five that the trackers had finally relocated their trail. They decided to go back to the site of the killing at the Powlett River mouth. They moved slowly over the hilly ground, possibly because of Truganini's painful legs, making camp every few miles. They were carrying a very heavy load of food, including a large sack of potatoes, several bags of flour, sugar, tea and tobacco. They also carried cloaks and blankets, at least six shotguns—single- and double-barrelled, weighing between ten and twelve pounds each—and numerous smaller pistols. For the guns, they also needed to carry canisters of powder, bags of shot, ingots of lead and bullet moulds. They soon abandoned the heavy sack of potatoes, and then the clothing and at least one shotgun. On 19 November, they reached the river mouth as the tide was rising, and managed to get across about an hour before Powlett's party arrived.

Behind them, the mounted searchers had made good time over the flat plain, coming close enough to hear the gunshots of Peevay and Maulboyheener hunting. When the search party arrived at the river mouth in the late afternoon, Powlett found the incoming tide made crossing impossible and was forced to wait till morning. The trackers, examining marks in the sand, gave the opinion that their quarry was exhausted. They could tell that Maulboyheener was dragging his two guns, one on either side. Not only were the fugitives tired, they were also running out of ammunition. That same day the search party had come upon a fire still burning, the ashes containing discarded pieces of lead from casting musket balls.

The fugitives had made camp a few miles further down the coast, at the bottom of a gully between two sand dunes, well hidden by thick coastal heath. It was a bitterly cold night and they lit a fire, even though the smoke was visible to the Kulin trackers watching on a high dune at the river mouth. Surely they knew the fire would reveal their hiding place. Maybe they no longer cared. It was only a matter of time before they were found. They slept soundly.

Franklin Sound from Gun Carriage Island, attributed to Henry Laing, 1831

Residence of the Aborigines on Flinders Island, by John Skinner Prout, 1845

Courtesy Allport Library and Museum of Fine Arts, State Library of Tasmania

Mathinna, by Thomas Bock, 1842
Courtesy Tasmanian Museum and Art Gallery

Truganini (Lallah Rookh from the Huon), by John Skinner Prout, 1845

John Batman's House, by W.F.E. Liardet, c. 1875
COURTESY STATE LIBRARY OF VICTORIA

Melbourne (Port Phillip), engraved by J. Carmichael, 1841
COURTESY STATE LIBRARY OF VICTORIA

Aboriginal Station, by Annie Benbow, n.d.
Courtesy W.L. Crowther Library, State Library of Tasmania

Tasmanian Aborigines at Oyster Cove Station, by Annie Benbow, n.d.
Courtesy W.L. Crowther Library, State Library of Tasmania

Truganini, studio portrait by Charles Woolley, 1866;
printed by Alfred Winter, 1876
COURTESY TASMANIAN ARCHIVES AND HERITAGE OFFICE

Truganini, Billy Lanne and Bessy Clark, studio portrait by Charles Woolley, 1866; printed by J.W. Beattie

Courtesy Tasmanian Archives and Heritage Office

John Woodcock Graves and Truganini, photographer unknown, n.d.
COURTESY ALLPORT LIBRARY AND MUSEUM OF FINE ARTS, STATE LIBRARY OF TASMANIA

A single gunshot woke them at dawn. Twenty-three armed settlers and seven armed trackers were cautiously moving towards them, each man positioned several feet apart with guns at the ready. Peevay and Maulboyheener sprang to their feet and sprinted into the scrub, with Plorenernoopner and Maytepueminer fleeing behind them. Truganini, in no condition to run, stayed hidden in her *mia mia*.

All thirty guns were discharged at once. Rawson fired off his double-barrelled shotgun, having stocked each barrel with five pistol balls. In a hail of fire from all directions, Rawson was confident all the fugitives would be shot, yet there was only one injury, which he claimed as his achievement: his pistol ball had grazed Maytepueminer's head. Amazing as it was to all participants, no life was lost except for that of a dog, who had had the misfortune of raising his head at the sound. Thomas was astonished that the dogs had not barked, and decided they had been overawed by the thunderous volley of exploding gunpowder.

Maulboyheener was quickly grabbed by Powlett and handcuffed. Peevay could be heard running through the undergrowth, although no one could see him. The searchers took hold of Plorenernoopner and Maytepueminer, her face bloody, while Thomas found Truganini hidden under a blanket in her *mia mia*. Thomas promised that Peevay would not be shot, at which the women were persuaded to climb a dune to call out to him. In response to their cooees, he emerged from the bush.

Searching the camp, Rawson found two double-barrelled guns and one single-barrelled, and a brace of pistols, in addition to a considerable stockpile of flour, sugar, tea and tobacco. The famished searchers rekindled the fire and made a large quantity of damper from the stolen flour, which they shared with their prisoners, who appeared to be in remarkably good spirits despite being chained at the legs, calmly smoking their pipes. For Commissioner Powlett, the compelling question was where the whalers were buried. Truganini told him that it was several miles back, near where the searchers had left their horses at the river mouth.

Released from the chains, Truganini went with Powlett to point out the exact place. On locating the grave, she explained that the sticks lying about had been used to kill one of the men. Peevay had fired first, then Maulboyheener, she explained. Only one shot had been fatal and Maulboyheener had used the sticks to beat the wounded man's head. Soon afterwards, Corporal Johnson of the border police brought up Peevay and Maulboyheener, handcuffed and their legs chained.

Only Maulboyheener spoke when Powlett questioned the men. Maulboyheener accused Peevay of firing first and threatening to shoot him if he did not also fire. He then made motions to show how he had beaten the wounded man about the head. Truganini became more voluble, explaining that she and the other women had been distressed at seeing Maulboyheener and the strange man struggling and that they had stayed on the dune, hiding in the heath. 'What could make you do it?' Powlett demanded. 'We thought it was Watson,' Maulboyheener volunteered, and then fell silent.

Truganini and her companions arrived in Melbourne in chains on 26 November. They were taken to the watchhouse, where committal proceedings commenced almost straightaway. Robinson attended every day of the committal hearing. He could hardly have done otherwise, as all the Port Phillip newspapers held him responsible for visiting these murderers upon the settlers. He had shown not the slightest interest in them until then, entirely unaware that his long-term companions had been roaming around Westernport. Even when the news that they had committed a double murder reached him one week after the event, he did not stir himself to try to find them.

Statements were taken from the whaler Evans, from Watson and his wife, from Samuel Anderson's brother, and several of Anderson's employees, from one of the assigned convicts, from Commissioner Powlett and from Corporal Johnson. When this display of damning evidence concluded, Peevay remained stoically silent while Maulboyheener made a garbled attempt at a defence. The day before the murders, Watson had tried to kill him, he explained, and when he saw the whalers he thought it was Watson and that was why he fired his gun.

Maulboyheener and Peevay were committed for trial for murder, while Truganini, Plorenernoopner and Maytepueminer were charged as accessories before and after the fact. On 2 December, Robinson went to speak with the accused men, who were being held separately from the women. He came in the company of the Methodist minister Reverend Joseph Orton, who was taking a close interest in the case. Peevay continued silent but Maulboyheener gave an explanation that provided some coherence for their otherwise inexplicable actions. Both Robinson and Orton recorded in their journals that Maulboyheener said James Horsfall of Ballymarang station had told them that Watson had shot Lacklay.

On 20 December, Redmond Barry rose to speak at the Supreme Court in Melbourne as the government-appointed counsel for the defence. Barry argued that the five accused were not naturalised subjects of the colony of New South Wales and therefore they must be considered aliens, who were entitled by common law to be judged by a jury that was half comprised of the same alien people, able to speak the language of the defendants. Unsurprisingly, the judge overruled Barry, making it clear that he considered the accused were not aliens and it was proper they be tried as civil subjects in the colony. He had ascertained from Robinson that they all had knowledge of the existence of God, knew right from wrong and could speak English. Even so, none of the accused were permitted to give evidence, because they were not Christians. It was apparent to several reporters in the court that when asked how they pleaded to the charges, they did not understand the question. Barry had to supply a plea of 'not guilty' on their behalf.

The following day, the jury heard almost the same evidence as that given at the committal hearing, except that instead of Evans, the whaler Robbins gave an eyewitness account of the moments after the shots were fired. Like Evans, he said he saw figures in the dune, with guns and dogs, and he could not 'distinguish whether white or black men or women'. William Watson reiterated that he had seen people in the dunes with Anderson's dog the day before the killings. He was emphatic that there could be no other black people in the whole area between the Bass River and Cape Paterson. 'I never saw any blacks but those I saw that evening,' he swore. 'I never saw any but the prisoners at the bar.'

Powlett and Johnson repeated the confessions Truganini and Maulboyheener had made at the whalers' graves. Neither mentioned that Maulboyheener also said he and Peevay had shot the whalers by mistake, thinking it was Watson. Barry's cross-examination did not draw attention to the matter of mistaken identity either, nor did he raise the accuseds' belief that Watson had killed their friend Lacklay. An admission of clear motive and murderous intent was the last thing he wanted the court to hear. The prosecutor had privately warned that 'shooting . . . slugs at Watson would hang them'. In the punitive penal code of the day a man could hang for stealing a horse.

Robinson then spoke to the character of the two men. He told how they had been in his service for eleven years or more and their behaviour had been exemplary. Both were loyal, honest and industrious. 'I have never found these persons wanting in humanity,' he said. The main thrust of his evidence was to exonerate the women, especially Truganini, who had saved his life. Careful to distance her from men he knew to be doomed, he insisted that Truganini was married to Wooredy and not Maulboyheener, as had been implied in the evidence. He then made the remarkable assertion that the women could not act according to their own will as they were 'in entire subjection to the men, in absolute thraldom'.

The jury took Robinson at his word. After half an hour of deliberation they pronounced the three women not guilty of any charges. But they were not swayed by Barry's argument that the evidence against the men was circumstantial and of dubious quality. Both men were found guilty of murder, with the jury making a strong recommendation for mercy 'on account of general good character and the peculiar circumstances under which they are placed'.

On 22 December, the sentence was handed down that Peevay and Maulboyheener be 'hanged by the neck until dead'. The next day, the judge sent his notes of the trial to La Trobe, noting the jury's recommendation for mercy and adding his own opinion that the case 'is one of great atrocity'. In forwarding the appeal for clemency to Governor Gipps, La Trobe made it clear he was not in favour. It was promptly rejected. The execution date was set for 20 January 1842. This would be the first execution in Port Phillip.

Truganini, Plorenernoopner and Maytepueminer were discharged into Robinson's care and strictly confined to the precincts of his house, to his considerable annoyance. He grumbled that to be expected to keep these people 'was not the way nor was my residence the place', but he still managed to secure clothes and rations for them on the government account. When the judge chose, 'in a mean way', to strike out the allowance of tobacco, Robinson was furious. He knew he would never keep the women at his house without this necessary commodity and that he would have to supply it to them himself. He was very relieved when La Trobe agreed that they could soon be repatriated back to Flinders Island.

While Robinson sympathised with Plorenernoopner as Peevay's legitimate wife, he never took her with him on his visits to the prison. Perhaps he feared she might be an impediment to his plan to have Peevay and Maulboyheener baptised before they died. He was encouraged that Maulboyheener had requested prayers after the sentencing, and he took Walter George Arthur as the one devout Christian among his charges, to read prayers with the men. Robinson made several subsequent visits with the Methodist preacher Reverend Orton, and the night before the execution he arranged for the Anglican chaplain to baptise the distraught Maulboyheener. Peevay remained entirely indifferent. Sullen, was the term Robinson used.

Before leaving to visit the jail on that last evening, Robinson asked Plorenernoopner if she would come with him to see Peevay before he died. It was a heart-wrenching decision for her. At first she said she would go, but then was so overcome with grief that she couldn't, sorrowfully telling Robinson 'no my like to see his face'.

By all accounts Maulboyheener was distressed and confused on the night before the execution, almost hysterical at the idea of the divine wrath he would suffer after death. The chaplain stayed to pray for his soul till the early hours of the morning, and subsequently reported that Maulboyheener reiterated he had had no part in the murders until threatened by Peevay with a loaded musket. He said he acted then only because the women urged him to remember the murder of their relatives at Port Arthur. If

Maulboyheener did say this then he was confused indeed. Peevay remained silent, as he had throughout his arrest and trial, making no admissions and showing no contrition.

For the fledgling town of Melbourne this first execution provided compelling theatre—all three Port Phillip newspapers published long, vivid accounts of the drama. According to the *Port Phillip Gazette*, Peevay's indifference marked him as a hardened sinner 'sceptical of the simplest truths of Christianity, [who] doggedly retained his firmness to the moment of death'. The papers reported that the condemned man slept soundly and woke to eat a hearty breakfast and calmly smoke his pipe, whereas the petrified Maulboyheener was cast in the role of the penitent who confessed his sins and refused to eat or smoke, 'affected at the last by the terrors of his situation'.

To meet their death the men were instructed to wear a symbolic outfit of white trousers, a white shirt and a white cap, personally supplied by the judge. The Reverend Orton was horrified that they should be dressed up in this way; he and Robinson both wept for the pity of it. As the two men shed their filthy jail clothes to wash and shave, Peevay suddenly became voluble, at least according to the jail attendant, who supplied an account. In his telling, Peevay laughed and said that when he was dead he would be reunited with his father and together they would hunt kangaroo. He also said he had three heads: 'One for the gallows; one for the grave; and one for Van Diemen's Land.' Almost certainly Peevay never said any such thing, but perhaps this florid invention was an attempt to capture the insouciance of this young man with the wonderful smile.

Peevay and Maulboyheener travelled in Robinson's cart to the gallows on a grassy hill at the north-eastern edge of the town. Painted sheeting was stretched around poles fastened to the corners of the cart, to shield the two men from the throngs of rowdy people, who merged into a festive crowd of four to five thousand packed around the gallows base or perched on the half-built stone walls of the new jail. Straddling the tree branches were a number of silent Wurundjeri men.

The temporary gallows was a flimsy affair; two upright posts about twenty feet high joined a crossbeam from which the ropes dangled to a narrow plank below. The plank was fastened to the gallows at one end by a hinge and supported at the other by bricks, which would be knocked away to let the platform drop. Peevay remained impassive throughout the ritual that preceded the execution, and he managed to climb the unsteady structure unaided, despite his arms being bound. At his own request, his eyes were left uncovered, and the *Port Phillip Gazette* noted that his gaze was fixed on the watching Wurundjeri in the tree nearest to the gallows, 'the only sign of interest or anxiety he had expressed'. Maulboyheener was beside himself in terror, moaning and trembling so much that he had to be pushed and pulled to the execution platform.

Robinson was not present to witness this horror, having gone straight to the graveyard to receive the bodies, but Assistant Protector James Dredge did provide an eyewitness account in his diary. 'Such an affecting, appalling, disgusting, execrable scene my eyes never saw—God forbid they should ere behold the like again,' he wrote. The mood of the crowd became angry when the gallows malfunctioned and the drop failed to completely release, leaving the men struggling. Once the drop fully released, Peevay died instantly without any struggle. But Maulboyheener's noose had been partially dislodged; he was left struggling for several minutes, 'his fine athletic frame dreadfully convulsed, it was an awful sight', Dredge observed. After an hour the bodies were taken down, placed in coffins and carried in Robinson's cart to the burial ground, where a special section had been set aside.

After the burial, the Reverend Orton went to offer condolences to 'the wives of the two blacks', finding them sitting forlornly outside their *mia mia* in the grounds of Robinson's house. When he expressed his pain at the awful circumstances, they 'wept bitterly', and one woman, most likely Truganini, who had the best English, provided a personal insight into the terrible moment on the beach when they had first seen the men who were shot. She said that they had expected to see Watson and Ginman, who had shot at Maulboyheener the day before, not two strangers. She said the wounded man had begged to be killed, because 'he could not survive and it served him right as he has killed many blacks'.

Orton's brief journal entry provides the only insight into Truganini's grief and bitterness. Robinson never mentioned her. From when it had first become apparent that Truganini had run away with Maulboyheener, she had been a profound disappointment to him. As far as he was concerned, she remained the wife of his old faithful companion, even though Wooredy was many miles away on Dr Allen's station. Her name never again appeared in his journal. Effectively, he had closed the book on her.

THE WAY THE WORLD ENDS

1842–1876

CHAPTER 10

TRUGANINI WATCHED WOOREDY'S body being wrapped in a shroud as the ship dropped anchor at Green Island. They had just come within sight of Flinders Island when Raegewarrah finally caught this proud Nuenonne warrior. Even before they left Melbourne, Wooredy had been desperately debilitated—Robinson expressed alarm that his old companion had become an 'imbecile'. The official reason for Wooredy's death was given as 'general decay of nature', yet he was a very strong man in his mid fifties. Less than a year before, Wooredy had been hunting and cutting out sheep from a flock with his dog. The final stage of syphilis was a more likely explanation for his rapid decline and death.

Wooredy had been Truganini's intimate companion for twelve devastating years, during which they had shared an agonising accretion of unspeakable loss. Although she no longer looked on Wooredy as her husband, it was her obligation to cremate his body, then collect ashes and relics of bone to give to his sons. Instead, he was unceremoniously put into a hole in the ground on Green Island. It was a cruel affront that she was not permitted to perform any ceremony for his departed spirit.

The next day, 8 July 1842, Truganini was landed in a whaleboat at Lillies Bay with Plorenernoopner and Maytepueminer. At Wybalenna, she found the people even more diminished and demoralised than when she had left. The newly arrived commandant, Dr Henry Jeanneret, was the latest in a string of inappropriate authoritarian men to churn through that role, and he looked to be the worst of the lot. He had previously been catechist at the boys prison at Port Arthur. Jeanneret insisted his charges abide by Christian teaching, go to school to learn to read, and speak proper English instead of the pidgin they used to communicate between language groups. Above all else, he was determined to make them learn to work in return for rations and clothing.

At first Jeanneret was impressed with Truganini, mistaking the quietude of mourning for compliance. She was enrolled at the school, as they all were, where her efforts were described as 'indifferent'. She was not interested in learning to read any more than she was interested in learning to sew the shapeless dresses she was obliged to wear. Within a matter of weeks, Jeanneret had completely reversed his opinion of her disposition. In his report of September 1842, Jeanneret complained of the 'shamelessly immoral conduct' of Truganini and her friend Maytepueminer, who were undermining his every effort to create an environment of modesty, monogamy and sexual restraint.

Soon after arriving from Port Phillip, Truganini and Maytepueminer made contact with the sealers who regularly came to Flinders Island from nearby Cape Barren Island. Jeanneret was unable to prevent the two women from running off and staying away for days, sometimes weeks, due to 'some collusive arrangement' they had with the sealers. Truganini's refractory conduct intensified after October, with the arrival of four people repatriated from Port Phillip.

Superintendent La Trobe had insisted that all the Van Diemen's Land people be returned, except the mixed-race youth Thomas Thompson, who was allowed to keep working on Solomon's pastoral run, and Wooredy's younger son, Peter Bruny, who stayed on Robinson's farm.

Jack Allen was the first youth to be sent back, arriving in Hobart on 12 July 1842. He stayed there for more than two months, under the protection of the Quaker missionary George Washington Walker, who had a keen interest in the welfare of the original people. In early September, he was joined by Wooredy's elder son, Davey Bruny, as well as Walter George Arthur and Mary Ann. As these four tarried in Hobart, they heard rumours about the harsh regime instituted by Jeanneret at Wybalenna and urgently expressed concern to their Quaker guardian. Walker sent a letter to Jeanneret's wife in the hope that she might persuade her husband that kindness was the best tool for the management of his vulnerable charges. Walker's cautious advice was entirely lost on the new commandant.

Jeanneret was determined to bend the people to his will. He considered his charges inherently lazy, unwilling to lift a finger without the inducement of tobacco, and even then doing little beyond seeing to their own basic needs. His predecessors had faced the same intransigence, although they had recognised that these exiled people were not lazy—rather, the people believed the government was obligated to provide for them. They were free, not prisoners, and would not be made to work as the degraded convicts were.

Those returned from Port Phillip were the most intractable, in Jeanneret's view, perpetually undermining his efforts to establish labour routines. Truganini and Maytepueminer were licentious and uncontrollable. Walter George Arthur spent his time playing marbles and fomenting discontent. Davey Bruny and Jack Allen were the most indolent, using their experience of paid employment at Port Phillip to insist that free people must be paid for their work, and giving 'exaggerated accounts of the value of their services'. These two young men also undermined Jeanneret's ideas about moral improvement by bringing fresh supplies of ochre, obtained from the Boonwurrung in Westernport, which encouraged a resurgence of ceremony.

Jeanneret was horrified by 'the dirty custom they have of besmearing themselves with red ochre and grease' and, worse still, of stripping naked for nightly corroborees that involved 'scenes scarcely equalled in the spheres of greatest depravity'. He bullied them into promising to cease this disgusting behaviour, only to find they were sneaking away to hold their ceremonies deeper in the bush.

Like Robinson, Jeanneret placed great store in formal marriages as a path to moral improvement. He pushed the people returned from Port Phillip into Church of England marriages, even though he could not legitimately perform weddings. He married Jack Allen to a recently widowed Lairmairermener woman known as Wild Mary, and Davey Bruny to Clara, the last surviving daughter of the Tarkiner warrior Wyne. Not long after the wedding, Clara gave birth to a mixed-race child who died soon afterwards. She would not say who the father was, if indeed she knew. She herself died of syphilis a few months later. Jeanneret then married Davey Bruny to Maytepueminer.

In another of his sham wedding ceremonies, Jeanneret married Truganini to Mannapackername, the most senior man of the Big River people, now called King Alphonso. Jeanneret described the groom as 'the steadiest of men', on whom he placed much reliance. A big man in every respect, King Alphonso towered over his diminutive wife. Jeanneret expected he would exert patriarchal control to curb Truganini's transgressive behaviour, but that was not how things turned out. Truganini instead took her new husband with her to visit the sealers, causing Jeanneret to 'growl at him with his pistol in his hand', as King Alphonso later recounted, and curtail his sugar and tobacco ration. Jeanneret's nasty retribution only served to turn 'the steadiest of men' into an aggrieved adversary, ready to make common cause with the intractable young men returned from Port Phillip.

Simmering grievances among the exiled people, and among the military stationed on the island, led to Jeanneret's dismissal in November 1843. He was replaced by Dr Joseph Milligan, who had previously been an inspector of convict discipline in Hobart. Jeanneret fought to be reinstated, and both men sought to influence the colonial office in London with an absurd series of charges and countercharges. It was Jeanneret who triumphed, in December 1845.

Reaction to the news that Jeanneret would return to Wybalenna was intense. Walter George Arthur, Davey Bruny and Jack Allen took the extraordinary step of organising a petition to Queen Victoria to pray that he not be permitted to return. At their request, the catechist Robert Clark drew up the petition, and those who could write a little signed their name to it. The petition asserted that 'we are your free children, that we were not taken prisoner but freely gave up our country' and that 'Mr Robinson made for us with Colonel Arthur an agreement which we have not lost from our minds since and we have our part of it good'. What followed was a litany of complaints about how Jeanneret threatened them with a gun, withheld their rations, made them work for their clothing and put people in jail 'because we would not be his slaves'. One passionate complaint was that 'he had shot our dogs before our eyes and sent other dogs of ours to an island where we told him they would starve and he said they might eat each other'.

Significantly, one of the eight signatures was that of a very senior man, King Alexander, brother of King Alphonso. The two brothers were regarded by Jeanneret as the most compliant and reliable of the captives at Wybalenna.

The petition was received by the colonial office in London and may have reached the Queen. If Victoria read it, she made no response.

Jeanneret returned to Flinders Island on 14 March 1846, incandescent with rage about the petition. He 'growled at them plenty', Walter reported, and bullied all those he saw as complicit in this heinous act of rebellion. He even threw King Alexander's son Washington into the jail. Outraged at the treatment of his brother's son, King Alphonso demanded Washington's release and threatened to write to the governor. On 19 June, he made good on that threat. In an extraordinary joint letter, King Alphonso and King Alexander accused Jeanneret of gross intimidation. They wrote that he had threatened the petitioners by saying, 'Queen take care of him and hang white man [Clark] and black man together' and that he refused to issue the warm winter clothing sent from Hobart unless they worked in his garden. This last was a particular concern for King Alphonso, who was 'a sick man plenty to much cold come and what he do to keep him warm he no able to work'. Determined they not be seen as pawns of Jeanneret's rival Milligan, they proudly signed the letter 'Me write myself King Alphonso' and 'Me write myself King Alexander'.

Truganini appears to have played no role in her husband's political activism. This was men's business. Certainly she wanted to be rid of Jeanneret and refused to bend to his will, but her preferred mode of resistance was more covert.

Tension grew when Jeanneret threatened libel against Walter George Arthur for sending yet another letter of complaint to the governor and confined him to jail for seventeen days. This was a step too far. The governor immediately sent the harbourmaster from Launceston to investigate. He found that there was no basis for Walter's imprisonment, that the people fully understood the purpose of the petition, and that their sense of grievance was very real. The mood was best summarised by Davey Bruny, who explained to the harbourmaster, 'I told the Queen that we had given up our country and we expected in return to have what we wanted.' What they wanted was so very little. 'I have asked for clothes,' he elaborated. 'Dr Jeanneret said I must work for it.'

Jeanneret's final dismissal came in May 1847, and Joseph Milligan returned the following month. By that time the governor had received the colonial office's response to the petition. Rather than address the petitioners' complaints, or consider the government's obligation to recompense them for the loss of their country, the colonial secretary advised that Wybalenna should be closed. It became Milligan's responsibility to dismantle the establishment and supervise the transfer of twenty-three women, fourteen men and ten children, together with their many dogs, to an abandoned penal station at Oyster Cove, south of Hobart.

Truganini came to Oyster Cove on 18 October 1847, one of nine single women. King Alphonso had not survived the 'plenty to much cold' that he so feared at Wybalenna, dying on 7 July that same year. She had no reason to be sorrowful about the loss of another husband or the move to Oyster Cove. She was back in her own country, at last.

The old convict station at Oyster Cove was beside a small rivulet that trickled into the broad D'Entrecasteaux Channel.

It was a place of great significance to her, as the cove held a stone quarry where the Nuenonne had made their flaked-stone implements. At low tide, layers and layers of shell middens were exposed on the southern arm, testimony to a timeless heritage of gatherings of Truganini's clan. Across the variegated blue water of the channel she could see the knobbly fist of North Bruny, then the long sandy ribbon of the Neck, and in the far distance the mauve majesty of fluted cape at the end of Adventure Bay.

The site for the station was certainly picturesque. It was also low-lying, sitting on a saltmarsh that extended into wide mudflats at low tide, which made it perpetually damp. In winter it was wreathed in morning fog, and in summer it became a humid haven for biting insects. The place had proved to be so damp and the land so infertile that it had been abandoned as a convict station after less than three years. The quadrangle of brick and timber-slab buildings had been empty for eight months and was already falling into disrepair, despite a quick application of whitewash and a new watercourse.

Milligan chose to reside in Hobart, leaving day-to-day control to the catechist Robert Clark and the constable Jack Russell, who had both come from Flinders Island as part of the transfer. The children were sent to the Orphan School in Hobart to be educated 'in a manner to fit them to mingle with and to be ultimately absorbed into the community', so the colonial secretary told the public. Another reason may have been to remove them from the none-too-tender care of Clark and his wife, who continued to face serious accusations of brutality in the management of the children, especially the girls.

At Oyster Cove the people were expected to dress and live as the settlers did. Truganini was issued a blue serge petticoat to be worn under an ankle-length woollen sack dress that fastened around the neck and was tied at the waist with rope. Over that she wore a loose-fitting knitted jacket, a scarf, and one of her luminous shell necklaces. Sometimes she wore a blanket as well. She used broken bottle glass to keep her hair close-cropped and often covered her head with a red peaked cap, although she also liked to wear a silk scarf wound around her head like a turban, with a tobacco pipe tucked into the fold. Her hut had a fireplace in which a fire was kept burning day and night against the cold and she had a cooking pot, plates and utensils. It was furnished with a table, chairs and a bed. Truganini preferred to leave the bed to her dog Trumpy and sleep on the ground in front of the fire.

Any attempt to inculcate a work ethic at the station was soon abandoned. Milligan had already discovered that he could not use people's craving for sugar and tobacco as an inducement to make them work. The people were 'intelligent enough to perceive they have a fair claim to support and good treatment without any exertion on their part', he told the colonial secretary. They would readily work for themselves, gathering firewood to keep fires roaring inside their huts to fend off the insidious chill, and sourcing traditional foods so they did not have to subsist entirely on the substandard meat ration. Somehow they were still able to get red ochre that they would grind and mix with grease to paint their bodies for ceremony, well away from disapproving eyes.

There were three boats at the station; the men were experienced boatmen who had become expert at fishing with lines on Flinders Island. They fished day in and day out. The women would take the dogs and beat through the scrub surrounding the station to catch the small, shy marsupials known as kangaroo rats. Using sticks they had sharpened with glass, the women would dig under the bark of the wattle trees to hook out fat oily grubs. Truganini remained especially adept at climbing trees to catch possums.

Truganini would often go out to the rocky point at the end of the cove, where she would tuck her cumbersome dress into the rope at her waist and dive for oysters and scallops that lay on the bottom, picking up the shells with her powerful toes and storing them in woven bags hung around her neck. Settlers who saw her would marvel at her grace and ease in the water, how she could stay under for maybe five minutes, bobbing up like a bottle to take a breath and then diving down headfirst again.

Truganini was so impressive in the water that in local settler lore she was believed to have swum from Oyster Cove to Bruny Island, a tribute to her extraordinary ability as a swimmer and her deep attachment to country. However, it was pure myth—the distance was too great. Nor could she swim down the channel to visit Alexander McKay at Peppermint Bay, also in Nuenonne country, as some settlers thought. Truganini undoubtedly did visit her one-time paramour, who was now married with a brood of children. She loved being around children, and she and McKay could reminisce in her language about the two years of her early life spent in each other's company. She must have walked the six miles to get there.

As often as she could get a boat to take her, Truganini would cross the channel to Bruny Island, most likely accompanied by her kinswoman Dray. Truganini knew every inch of North Bruny. After landing at Woodcutters Point, she would be seen walking across Richard Pybus's grant, and then William Davis's, to get to the southern section of the island where there were no settlers. At the long narrow stretch of the Neck, on the channel side, were hillocks of shells not yet covered by the undergrowth, indicating where Nuenonne families had made camp before the settlers came. Here, Truganini and Dray would cast off their long sack dresses to walk about naked. They would wade into the water to scoop up mussels, oysters and scallops that they opened on their fire at night. After feasting on this harvest, they threw the shells over their shoulder, just as their families had done in that lost world of only forty years earlier.

Crossing to the ocean side of the island, Truganini would dive for the succulent crayfish she knew hid in the rock crevices behind the waving kelp forests. She would comb the fine sand of Adventure Bay for tiny marineer shells to polish and string into long necklaces. If it was egging season, she might walk to the grassy point at the far southern end of the bay, where James Kelly's whaling station was now a tumbledown ruin, to reach the rocky island where the penguins nested. Or else she might follow the brackish creek inland to find swans' nests. When the mutton bird chicks hatched in the burrows at the Neck, most of the people from the station would come to the island with her. The settlers on North Bruny always knew when Truganini and her friends were on the island, and no one was disturbed by their presence. The Pybus and Davis families remembered Truganini and Dray as young women and it pleased them to give them tea, tobacco and potatoes, just as they had all those years before.

Truganini and Dray would also take the people and their dogs on extended trips into their country, to the Huon River and beyond, to Recherche Bay, and even to Port Davey on the south-west coast. At these times, usually in late spring and early autumn, they would be away for at least a month, and occasionally several months.

At Oyster Cove it was impossible to be insulated from the intrusion of settlers. Grazing sheep were irresistible quarry for the people's cherished canine companions, and dog attacks caused endless complaints. Milligan had to order that some dogs be shot after the governor received a hefty claim for damages. Milligan's greatest concern was not the dogs so much as the disreputable men who had built rough-hewn huts on the Crown land beside the station in order to trade liquor for sex. To get rid of them, the governor was reluctantly persuaded to grant them land three miles away. The move made little difference: three miles was no distance when it came to sourcing the alcohol that had become a potent addiction.

Prostitution became a feature of life at the station. The exchange of sex for grog was the kind of reciprocal relationship Truganini understood only too well. There was also a brisk exchange in government-issue blankets, clothing, meat and flour. Robert Clark did nothing about it. Milligan thought him too indolent to exercise even a modicum of control—not that Milligan was much bothered to go to Oyster Cove to correct Clark's dilatory oversight. The gross neglect became apparent when Davey Bruny died in October 1848 after a lingering illness during which Clark made no effort to call in medical assistance. Wooredy's treasured elder son was thirty when he died, and had no children.

Clark himself was felled with a heart attack at the end of 1849 and died in March the following year, leaving Jack Russell in charge. Russell had worked for years at Wybalenna and he got along with the people just fine. He could easily communicate in their pidgin language. He was also an alcoholic. In October 1850, Russell got into an altercation with a local settler when he was 'beastly drunk', in the company of several men from the station. The argument escalated and Russell made a signal to one of the men—maybe Jack Allen—who drew a knife, causing the settler to flee in terror and subsequently write an outraged letter of complaint to the colonial secretary.

The official response was to install Keith Davie as resident overseer and storekeeper at a pay grade above Russell. Like Russell, Davie had known the people for years, as the coxswain at

Wybalenna, and he had no interest in trying to manage their lives. He was more than happy to facilitate their drinking, since he was a drunk as well. As the storekeeper, his job was to distribute the rations, and when people were away from the station on hunting expeditions Davie was pleased to appropriate their rations to trade for spirits.

The closest neighbour was Richard Pybus's eldest son, Henry Harrison Pybus, who had a house and orchard at the adjacent bay, known as Little Oyster Cove. He also acquired large tracts of land in the hills above the station, facilitated by the colonial surveyor, James Erskine Calder, who was married to Henry's sister Margaret. Here he established a timber business in partnership with the colonial surgeon, Dr William Crowther. A jetty was built on the arm of the cove that marked the southern boundary of the station, and in 1855 a tramway was constructed to carry the milled timber from the hills directly to the jetty. By then, most of the men in the vicinity of Oyster Cove were transient ex-convicts, employed as sawyers and woodsplitters for Pybus and Crowther's timber operation.

In April 1851, Henry Harrison Pybus had played host to George Augustus Robinson, who was about to permanently leave the colonies for England. He had returned to Van Diemen's Land briefly to finalise the sale of his land grants. After visiting Richard Pybus on Bruny Island, he stayed at Little Oyster Cove for a weekend while waiting for the boat that came four days a week from Hobart. On 26 April, he made an unexpected visit to the station to say goodbye to Walter George Arthur, from whom he had been receiving letters. Robinson's journal entries for that weekend were very sparse; he only recorded interactions with Walter George Arthur, Mary Ann and her sister Fanny. Both women gave him a shell necklace as a keepsake.

Robinson thought the station an unhealthy place, too low and damp, with a bitterly cold wind that swept 'like a tunnel' off the mountain. He wrote that everyone was in residence on Sunday, 27 April, when he read prayers, and noted that several had grown fat. If he saw Truganini he made no mention of it. He copied down a list of the names of those in residence from a list that Davie provided, and drew a rough map of the small graveyard in a cleft in the hills to the south of the station, on which he marked the places where ten people were already buried. Given that he was about to leave for England, it was strange that he wanted to identify the graves. Perhaps William Crowther had asked him to do it. The colonial surgeon was a man of science with a keen interest in the original Tasmanians.

As for Milligan, he didn't visit the station often enough to judge the state of affairs for himself. His annual reports between 1852 and 1855 document a rising percentage of people dying each year, without bothering to record individuals by name or cause of death. No one kept a record of when people died or the date of their burial, or even if they were buried; their names were just removed from Davie's ration inventory. Milligan ventured the opinion that the people had themselves to blame for their fatal illnesses, by moping about inside their overheated huts 'like hothouse plants obnoxious to the breeze that promotes health and vigour'. Another contributing factor he identified was the sly grog shops that had begun to proliferate in the vicinity with the influx of splitters and sawyers, 'with whom it is understood they are far from straight laced in their intercourse'.

Grog certainly proved fatal for Mathinna, the child sent from Wybalenna in February 1839 to live in the pampered inner sanctum of Government House with Sir John and Lady Franklin. She was very much a young lady when Thomas Bock painted her portrait in 1842, but the following year, when Sir John and Lady Franklin returned to England, she went to the dreadful Orphan School. In July 1851, when she was sixteen, she was unceremoniously discharged from the school and sent to live at Oyster Cove.

As Towterer's daughter, Mathinna was kin to Dray, but she had no language or cultural knowledge to help make that connection meaningful. In the dysfunctional environment of the station she quickly learnt to make carnal connections with the itinerant workers in the neighbourhood, becoming a regular at a disreputable public house about four miles away. On 1 September 1852, seventeen-year-old Mathinna was stumbling back to the station in a drunken stupor when she fell into a puddle, passed out and drowned. Only because of a brief coroner's inquest was her death documented at all. There was still no record of her burial.

On a rare visit to the station early in 1855, Milligan found only twelve people living in the dilapidated huts. Tanganutura's other mixed-race daughter, Fanny, had married one of the local splitters and moved away in 1854, and soon after her young half-brother Adam went to live with her. Jack Allen, with another young man known as Augustus, had joined the crew of a whaling ship. Of the people who remained, Milligan reported favourably on the industrious Walter George Arthur and Mary Ann. He noted that their 'adopted son' Billy Lanne, aged about fifteen, had recently returned from the Orphan School and was helping Walter grow potatoes. Milligan suggested that these three, 'whose manner and sympathies are to some degree European', should live apart to insulate them from the 'irregular and profligate' behaviour of the rest. He exempted 'two women from the bush'—meaning Truganini and Dray—from his dismay at the others, who were in thrall to 'the maddening excitement of strong liquors'. Although Milligan did not point the finger at his subordinates, there could be no mistaking that Russell and Davie were acting as conduits and pimps to facilitate the debilitating traffic in grog.

The dissolute life of the station was a cause for concern among its respectable neighbours, and especially the absence of any spiritual guidance for these benighted souls. Henry Harrison Pybus had a particular concern for the condition of the people living adjacent to his jetty. He was a pious man who fondly remembered his family's dealings with the people on Bruny Island in his youth. He persuaded his influential brother-in-law, the colonial surveyor James Calder, who was also churchwarden at St David's Cathedral, to visit the station to see for himself how bad things were.

Calder arrived at the station on a sunny day in April 1855, having walked there in the company of a young friend, James Kirwan, who was the assistant police magistrate for the district. Calder wrote an account of it for a Hobart newspaper. While passing along the edge of North West Bay, he and Kirwan spoke with the licensee of a public house beside the North West Bay River and another at Snug Cove. Both publicans gave distressing accounts of women from the station in shocking states of intoxication engaging in 'disgusting scenes of immorality . . . with white men in open day'.

After thrilling to the panoramic glory of the channel landscape, Calder received a visceral shock at the 'vile contrast' of the dank, derelict station. If there were people within 'that desolate-looking shealing', they had made themselves invisible by the time he began to look around the huts the people shared with their many dogs. The rooms were inherently unhealthy, with low ceilings, tiny windows that let in little light, and no ventilation. The bedding was filthy and covered in lice, while the dirt floors were strewn with litter and scraps. Calder was especially dismayed that the former convict chapel appeared to be unused and he could find no evidence of any religious instruction. He noted that Supervisor Milligan was drawing a salary of £600, yet he 'might as well be in Spitzbergen' for all he did to protect the vulnerable people in his care.

Indignant, Calder determined that 'even at this late hour', something must be done to improve the conditions of life for a people 'we have forcibly dispossessed of everything but mere existence'. It never occurred to him that he might surrender his own substantial land grant on Bruny Island for that humane purpose. He made informal representations about the dereliction of the station, reinforced by the swingeing formal report submitted by Kirwan. Finally, the government was stirred to action.

Parsimony rather than benevolence drove the reorganisation of the station management. With an eye to the cost to the newly self-governing colony, now named Tasmania, funding was cut to a bare minimum. The positions held by Milligan and Davie were abolished, with Russell expected to retire the following year. The duties of the three were collapsed into the role of a resident supervisor, at a fraction of Milligan's salary. Milligan himself stayed on the government payroll in another capacity and remained as secretary of the Royal Society of Tasmania until he retired from government service in April 1860. Returning to England, he supplemented his pension by surreptitiously selling skulls he had collected from the original people of Van Diemen's Land. Later in life he donated several skulls to the Royal College of Surgeons.

New regulations were promulgated for the station, reminiscent of the penal establishment it had once been. Henceforth, the people were to be mustered each day so their persons, clothing and rooms could be inspected. Any infringements of the rules, such as bartering rations or getting drunk, would cause the tobacco and sugar ration to be suspended. Kirwan was ordered to make unannounced inspections of the station and submit a report at least once a month. Prayers must be read every morning and evening and a visiting clergyman was to hold monthly services in the convict chapel. An amendment to the *Licensing Act* instituted a penalty of £50 for 'supplying with any liquor any native'. This would make no difference, Kirwan ruefully observed, as they could always get liquor from timber workers in the bush.

Rumours that draconian changes were in train reached Walter George Arthur soon after Kirwan's report was submitted. Reprising the strategy that had rid Wybalenna of Jeanneret, he wrote to the governor, saying that if Kirwan were given management of the station he and his wife would have to leave. He begged the governor not to place Kirwan in control of the people as 'they have got bad disliking for that gentleman'. Walter got his way. He and Mary Ann were permitted to live separately on a Crown lease adjacent to the station, while a man genuinely committed to the welfare of the people was appointed as resident supervisor on a salary of £100.

John Strange Dandridge had just turned thirty when he took on the challenging role of supervisor of the station at Oyster Cove. He was the son of an Anglican minister from Oxfordshire, and his wife, Matilda, was the daughter of the artist John Skinner Prout, who had visited Wybalenna in 1845 and made portrait sketches of several of the people, including Truganini. The Dandridges arrived in July 1855 with several young children, who provided a source of delight to Truganini. She doted on the children and carried them around on her shoulders.

Almost immediately, Dandridge sought to have the decaying buildings repaired and made watertight, although it was nine months before any work began, and the people had to endure another winter with gaping holes in the roof and next to no glass in the windows. The accommodation for Dandridge and his family was scarcely any better. Dandridge also objected that the government contract for supplying the station was so stingy that no contractor could afford to supply decent meat. The meat rations were invariably sourced from animals that had died from illness rather than those freshly slaughtered, and often had to be returned. The meat ration was of most concern to Dandridge and his family. The people could always find other sources of protein for themselves, if not for their army of dogs. Truganini found the ration supply was a problem only if the boat from Hobart was long delayed and she ran out of flour or tea and sugar. She couldn't go a day without sugar.

Dandridge taught himself to row in order to take Truganini and Dray across the channel to Bruny Island so they could gather protein-rich abalone, or young mutton birds, or swans' eggs, depending on the season. In the spring and summer months, most of the people would disappear into the Huon district with their bedding and as much flour, tea and sugar as they could carry. Four to six weeks later they would return, looking sleek and healthy after enjoying a steady diet of possum and wallaby, supplemented with the subterranean fungus known to the settlers as native bread.

To attend to their spiritual welfare, a chaplain visited every month to give Sunday services. Dandridge reported that the people so detested this meaningless ritual that the moment they knew he was coming they would disappear into the surrounding bush, and 'not one of them would make their appearance till he was gone'. To be sure they could make their getaway, one person would lie down, hand under cheek, pressing an ear to the ground to pick up the vibrations of horses' hooves up to two miles away.

The colonial bishop finally found the time to make a visit to the station in April 1858. He came by boat so the people did not have a chance to escape. The reason for the visit was to take their photographs. His subjects stood or sat in front of the slab wall of their huts, staring blankly into his camera, each face a study in sullen defiance. The bishop was unimpressed with their want of spiritual yearning, and after that the chaplain never visited them again. The bishop himself returned once, the following January, to take more photographs.

In May 1858, an opportunistic settler was granted a licence to run a public house called The Aborigine at Little Oyster Cove, despite opposition from Pybus and Crowther, who warned of the deleterious effect it would have on both their workers and the people at the station, tacit acknowledgement of how these two groups intertwined. By then, rampant alcoholism at the station was causing serious problems for Dandridge, especially in trying to contain the younger men, like Jack Allen and Billy Lanne, who were volatile and violent when drunk. Billy Lanne was twenty and already sexually involved with Truganini. In March that year, she suffered an unexplained fracture of her arm. On another occasion the doctor had to be called to tend Jack Allen's wife Emma after she suffered a severe beating. Dandridge was greatly relieved in June 1859 when Jack Allen went back to whaling, taking Billy Lanne with him, both signing on for a long voyage.

Walter George Arthur had become a serious problem. He had shown a good deal of initiative when he had first arrived at Oyster Cove. He and Mary Ann had proudly taken on the mantle of leadership, greeted as the king and queen by the occasional visitors to the station. When they were given the lease on a separate parcel of land, Walter George Arthur paid for labourers to clear several acres to plant potatoes; however, a formal request for an assigned convict to work on his farm was refused. It was made apparent that he was not, nor would he ever be, considered the equal of a settler. While he was in Port Phillip, Walter George Arthur had become a heavy drinker, and in his humiliation and defeat, he now reverted to alcoholic oblivion.

He could be nasty while drunk, violent and abusive to everyone at the station. Mary Ann, who also drank heavily, bore the brunt of it, although she was a big strong woman who gave as good as she got. When Walter gave up on trying to farm, Dandridge arranged for him to be employed at the station, getting firewood and meeting the steamer from Hobart. This employment had to be suspended in 1858 because he and Mary Ann continued to drink and cause havoc with their fighting, 'exhibiting a violence of conduct impossible to describe', a despairing Dandridge reported to the colonial secretary. When drunk, which was much of the time, they physically attacked others at the station and subjected Dandridge to 'most virulent abuse, conveyed in disgusting & disgraceful language'.

In April 1858, Walter went to Hobart to ask the colonial secretary if he and his wife could be removed from proximity to the station. He requested land in the Huon region, closer to Mary Ann's sister Fanny, now married to William Smith. His request was never even considered because the couple refused 'to take the pledge against drinking'. In October 1859, the doctor was called to treat Mary Ann for 'injuries caused by ill usage', by which time her abusive husband had signed on for a long whaling voyage. He returned to the station early in 1861, 'looking much worse than when he left'. A few months later, he fell from a boat belonging to the publican of The Aborigine and drowned. His body was never recovered.

Surviving the winter in the bleak conditions of the station was a challenge. Four people died of influenza in the winter of 1860, and by 1862 only eight remained, described in the *Royal Kalendar and Guide to Tasmania* as 'uncleanly, unsober, unvirtuous, unenergetic, and irreligious, with a past character for treachery, and no record of *one* noble action . . . the race is fast fading away and its utter extinction will hardly be regretted'.

The prospect of the imminent extinction of a race of people had the scientific community scrambling for memorabilia. By some mysterious circumstance, not explained in Dandridge's correspondence with the colonial secretary, nor in the visiting magistrates' reports, members of the Royal Society of Tasmania were given access to the body of Augustus, a relatively young man who had died on 29 August 1860, as well as an older woman known as Caroline, who had died weeks earlier, on 10 July. Moulds of their faces were made within days of their death and their skulls were removed to be stored in the society's museum collection. In 1861 the Ethnological Museum at Oxford wrote to the governor to request a male and female skull be obtained 'without injuring the feelings . . . of the few survivors'. Dandridge refused to contemplate such a request. Three years later, the Oxford museum acknowledged they had managed to get the skulls from 'another source'. This was the prominent Hobart solicitor Morton Allport, who was vice president of the Royal Society of Tasmania. As a longstanding friend of the Dandridges, Allport was an occasional visitor to the Oyster Cove station.

There was money to be made from the neglected burial site above the station; it was ripe for pilfering, so overrun with bracken that the graves were barely distinguishable from the scrub and a number of graves had collapsed. Who would know if skeletal remains were being exhumed?

Sensitive to accusations of wasting public money on the people at Oyster Cove, the government had no intention of repairing the graveyard or the dilapidated station, which had become basically uninhabitable. At this point Henry Harrison Pybus weighed in with a proposal: he would look after the eight survivors on his adjacent property and keep them from 'intimacy of an objectionable nature'. For relieving the government of the continuing responsibility for the people he requested £500 a year, which was less than the current government outlay.

Pybus was a pious man, keen to do good works; he had established a school for local children and he had nostalgic memories of Truganini. His curious gesture was also possibly prompted by his business partner, William Crowther, who understood how valuable the skeletons of these last people would be. He had already approached the colonial secretary about securing their skeletal material. As the joint owner of the property to which the people were being invited to move, Crowther would have prime access to the bones and skulls he so coveted. Nothing came of it. Pybus's price was considered too much to spend on a small group of 'dipsomaniacs', and the settlement was allowed to continue in its deplorable condition, under the despairing supervision of Dandridge, who did what he could with his meagre provisions.

Truganini suffered a profound blow when Dray died in the winter of 1861, said to be not less than 75 years old. Losing her intimate friend and the last connection to her clan caused her to become somewhat isolated within the station. For friendship and emotional warmth she was dependent more than ever on the Dandridge family and one or two settler women at Little Oyster Cove who had been the children of government employees and had spent their childhood with her at the station. She continued to go to Bruny Island with Dandridge, and every year in late spring she and the other women took the dogs on hunting trips into the Huon.

She was not immune to the contagion of alcohol that had overwhelmed the station. In 1863, when Billy Lanne and Jack Allen were in residence at the station, Truganini was one of the seven people from the station reported to the police for being 'senseless drunk' at a hotel at North West Bay. Truganini and the others were kept in the lockup overnight because of the very real fear they would come to harm trying to walk the six miles back to the station.

Truganini's two-room hut was in a shocking state of disrepair. The partition wall was damaged, part of the roof had caved in and the windows had no glass. The visiting magistrate had requested repairs that were never made. She shared the hut with Billy Lanne whenever he was back from a whaling voyage. According to later reminiscences from one of her settler friends, Truganini was very proud to have a husband more than thirty years her junior. Bessy Clark, one of the three other women at the station, was much closer to Billy Lanne in age and she also claimed him as a husband. Mrs Dandridge vividly remembered having to protect Truganini and Bessy from Billy's drunken rages. They would both run into her house and hide under her bed while he banged on the door to get them.

It was nearly impossible to contain this volatile and very strong young man, no matter how far gone in drink he was, and Billy resented Dandridge's attempts to keep him out of trouble. Just before shipping out in December 1864, Billy lodged a complaint against Dandridge with a magistrate in Hobart. He accused the superintendent of expropriating clothing and food rations for the private use of his family and the neighbours, as well as forbidding the use of the station boat. 'I am the last man of my race and I must look after my people,' he was reported as saying.

An inquiry was held to investigate the accusations. Truganini and the three other women at the station were interviewed, as well as Mary Ann who lived on adjacent land. Dandridge was completely exonerated. It was found that when the steamer had failed to arrive he occasionally lent supplies of flour to local families, and none of the women seemed to mind. Truganini explained that should she 'suffer a little short when the boat not come' she could always 'eat plenty kangaroo rat', and if she wanted fish or oysters she could always use the boat. As for Dandridge, he was 'kind fine fellow', she told her inquisitor. 'Mrs Dandridge fine fellow too.'

The decay and dissolution that surrounded Truganini was belied by photographs taken in 1866, when the women were dressed up in silk ballgowns and put on show at Government House. A newspaper social columnist reported them to be 'charmed beyond measure by the position they occupied'. On the contrary, they look grumpy and uncomfortable in the photograph, as though they would much prefer to be someplace else.

Having once been a model for painters and sculptors, Truganini was now regularly called upon to pose for photographers. While Billy Lanne was again in residence at the station in June 1866, the government requested a photographic record for posterity. Truganini, Bessy Clark, Patty Clark and Billy Lanne had portraits taken in a Hobart studio. Dandridge requested the colonial secretary allocate a constable to accompany them while they were in the town, warning of 'what outrageous scenes might be expected in the public streets if they wished to go into particular public houses they knew (and they know a great many) and were refused'. Unauthorised photographs were taken later that year when unknown photographers opportunistically came down to Oyster Cove.

Billy was about to ship out on a whaling voyage in November 1866 when a Hobart newspaper reported that 'King William THE LAST OF THE ABORIGINES is about to visit England, and his ambition is to have the honour of an audience of Her Majesty Queen Victoria . . . and seems to think himself every inch a king'. It was nonsense, of course, but the royal appellation took hold. Ever after he was known as King Billy.

In February 1867 Truganini was away on a month-long hunting expedition with Patty Clark and Mannalargenna's daughter Wapperty, while Billy Lanne and Bessy Clark remained at the station. Dandridge was surprised and dismayed when Bessy died on 12 February, as she was the strongest and most likely to survive, with 'no disease about her'. She had been suffering from a bout of dysentery yet seemed to have recovered, when she suddenly stopped eating, drinking or speaking. Mrs Dandridge, who was with her at the end, said Bessy died of inflammation of the bowels. The visiting doctor gave the cause of death as dysentery. Truganini was not there to see for herself, yet she believed that Billy was to blame, telling her settler friend Annie Benbow that Billy had kicked Bessy in the stomach when he was drunk.

Presumably Bessy was buried in the decrepit burial plot above the station, although her body did not lie there for long. In December 1871 Morton Allport sent her complete skeleton to the Royal College of Surgeons in London, along with a male skeleton he had retrieved 'at no small difficulty' from the abandoned burial ground at Flinders Island.

After weeks in the bush in wet weather, Truganini, Wapperty and Patty all succumbed to the annual bout of influenza. Patty was taken ill in the bush and Dandridge had to walk thirty-six miles to fetch her. She was admitted to hospital in April in such a bad way that she was not expected to live. In June, she was joined there by Truganini and Wapperty. Dandridge sent his wife to Hobart to comfort the women in this strange environment and provide clean clothing. He was unable to come himself, he told the colonial secretary, because Billy was still at the station and likely to make trouble.

Patty Clark died on 8 July 1867 and was not returned from the hospital for burial at Oyster Cove. Indeed she received no burial at all. Her skeleton was 'dissected out, not having been buried', according to the description provided by Morton Allport to a British collector. Her skeleton joined the growing collection of remains held by the Hobart museum of the Royal Society. Allport boasted that, unlike other, incomplete skeletons, 'this specimen is perfect'.

Truganini and Wapperty were discharged into the care of Mrs Dandridge, although their recovery was very slow, and Wapperty died at the station on 12 August 1867.

Six months later, in January 1868, Billy Lanne was again living at the station when he and Truganini were required to be in Hobart to be presented to the Duke of Edinburgh at the anniversary regatta celebrating the foundation of the colony. The *Mercury* newspaper described 'King Billy, and the old woman, Truganini' standing on the steps of the pavilion to be presented to His Highness. 'Mrs. Truganini, the wife of King Billy, consented to present the prize,' the paper reported. 'King Billy then called for three cheers for the winners, three cheers for the Prince, and three cheers for the Queen.' Dandridge was with them, keeping an anxious eye on how much of the punch they consumed.

Billy joined the crew of the whaler *Runnymede* at the beginning of March. That was the last Truganini saw of her fourth husband. Twelve months later, the *Runnymede* returned and Billy was discharged with twelve pounds in his pocket. He headed for the familiar haunt of the Dog and Partridge pub in Hobart. He was not well, and complained of stomach pains for several days before he died at the hotel on 3 March 1869.

The very next day, Crowther wrote to the colonial secretary, asking that the body be sent to the hospital morgue and requesting permission to secure the skeleton for the Royal College of Surgeons in London. Almost simultaneously, the Royal Society wrote to secure the skeleton for their own collection. Fearing foul play, the governor issued special instructions for the medical superintendent to protect the body from theft or mutilation. That evening, Crowther arranged for the medical superintendent to take tea with his wife while he and his son stole into the morgue, wearing protective clothing, and removed the skull from the corpse, cunningly substituting into the head another skull taken from a nearby corpse. On discovering the macabre remains of this scientific escapade, the medical superintendent contacted several members of the Royal Society, who came to the hospital and cut off the hands and feet for their collection.

Billy's mangled remains were buried the next day in an impressive ceremony, with a full procession to the graveyard at St David's cemetery in Hobart. That night, the cemetery watch was distracted while three members of the Royal Society dug out the grave, heaved the body into a wheelbarrow and made off with it. Crowther arrived sometime later, to find only the discarded European skull. In the public furore that followed, Crowther claimed that the body was reduced to a skeleton in the back room of the hospital and the bones were secreted away in the Royal Society's collection. He would never acknowledge having stolen the skull. Crowther was suspended as honorary surgeon at the hospital, which must not have greatly troubled him since he became premier of Tasmania less than ten years later.

All this grisly scientific grasping had a very unsettling effect on Truganini, who was aware of the grave robbing at Oyster Cove and was quick to perceive the interest her body would excite. Until then, next to no attention had been paid to her, but almost overnight 'the old woman Truganini' became the subject of sentimental mythologising, cast as an antipodean Pocahontas in newspaper stories, the beautiful but self-denying native princess who had risked her life to save her beloved Mr Robinson. It was awkward that by that time Truganini was both old and ill, with whiskers on her chin. Writer James Bonwick magnificently rose to the occasion in 1870, reminiscing about briefly meeting 'this sylvan goddess' at Oyster Cove in 1858: 'Her coquetry reminded me of the faded loveliness of French courts,' he wrote.

A number of colonial gentlemen claimed a special relationship with Truganini, but only Henry Atkinson had a substantial history with Truganini that gave credence to his recollections of her, published in 1905. Atkinson was the Anglican minister appointed to the Oyster Cove parish between 1869 and 1874, where he got to know Truganini. He bluntly admitted that when he first saw her he thought she looked like an ape, sitting with her hands clasped around her knees, gazing across the channel to her country. As he rode past her she gave him a momentary glance, 'such as an animal in the Zoological Gardens might . . . swift but expressionless and without even the faintest interest or animation'. He thought he had never seen a human so repulsive.

Nevertheless, they became friends. She commandeered the reverend and his boat to take her over to Bruny Island 'scores of times'. In his telling, they were out fishing in his boat or in the bush together 'almost every day'. He never tried to preach to her, recognising that she had no interest whatsoever in Christian belief and that if she had any belief in the supernatural it was in the devil she called Raegewarrah.

Among his down-to-earth reminiscences of hunting and fishing expeditions with Truganini, Atkinson provided a poignant glimpse into her private terror. In March 1869, Atkinson was startled to hear a terrible racket at the station made by Truganini and Mary Ann with their dogs, all howling in unison. Dandridge explained that they had just learnt of Billy's death and this was a mourning ritual where the people would 'kick up a row' for about ten minutes and then never mention the death again. Not so, in this case—Truganini did mention the death again. Days later she asked Atkinson to take her out in his boat to the deepest part of the channel. With tears coursing down her face, she said all the people were dead and people in Hobart had taken their skulls. Now they would want her skull. Suddenly kneeling before him and clasping her arms around his legs, she pleaded, 'Bury me here, it is the deepest place. Promise me. Promise me.'

By 1872, Truganini was the sole resident of Oyster Cove, and the government decided that the station would be sold. She was moved away from her homeland to a house Dandridge had bought in Hobart. Dandridge had stipulated that she be able to continue her regular trips to Bruny Island, but when he died unexpectedly in March 1873 there was no one to take her. Sole responsibility for Truganini passed to his widow.

In these last years of her life, Truganini was a curiosity in Hobart, occasionally glimpsed with Mrs Dandridge taking short walks in the town: a tiny, stout black woman in a dark bombazine dress with a lace collar and wearing a red turban with a pipe tucked into the fold. She received numerous gentleman callers seeking to take her photograph or otherwise exploit her rarity as 'the last Tasmanian'. Prominent members of the Royal Society, including Morton Allport, James Erskine Calder and John Woodcock Graves, visited Truganini in her final days, as did James Gravenor, a man she had not seen for forty-three years. Now a prosperous baker, Gravenor was once a convict assigned to the last mission, who travelled with Truganini and her friends for a few months in 1834. He used this brief connection and deathbed visit to claim a close friendship with Truganini in spurious articles that he later published in the Hobart *Mercury*.

Old and frail, Truganini needed constant medical attention. As her sole carer, Mrs Dandridge had the devil of a job of pushing the necessary pills down her throat with a long pencil. Expecting to die soon, Truganini eagerly anticipated being with her family again. 'Me going back to my people,' she told Mrs Dandridge, saying she was waiting for a message from her father, Manganerer, to know when it was time.

On 4 May 1876, Mrs Dandridge gave Truganini her medicine and checked that she was warm enough, lying on the floor of her room in front of a roaring fire, nestled comfortably into her dogs. A little time later, she heard Truganini suddenly call out, 'Raegewarrah catch me.' By the time Mrs Dandridge reached her, Truganini had lapsed into a coma. Three days later she was pronounced dead.

AFTERWORD

I NEVER SAW Truganini's skeleton on display in the Tasmanian Museum. It was removed from public view the year I was born.

Truganini's body was disinterred from its supposedly secret resting place at the disused Female Factory at the request of the Royal Society. The society had mounted a two-year campaign to get this 'unique' specimen, asserting that it would be 'disgraceful and discreditable to Tasmania were such type of a now extinct race allowed to be cast away'. This line of reasoning held no sway with the colonial secretary until December 1878, when he suddenly relented, no doubt influenced by William Crowther, who became premier of Tasmania that same month.

The explicit instruction given to the Museum of the Royal Society (later the Tasmanian Museum) was that the disinterred body was not to be exposed to public view and that it be 'decently deposited in a secure resting place where it may be accessible by special permission to scientific men for scientific purposes'. After being retrieved from the grave, Truganini's remains were first presented to the public at the Melbourne Centennial Exhibition in 1888, where the Reverend Henry Atkinson came upon her skull on a display table and was mortified to realise what had been done to his old fishing companion.

In 1904, the anthropologist Baldwin Spencer, in his capacity as honorary director of the Museum of Victoria, had Truganini's bones assembled into an articulated skeleton, and in return for this favour got to make a cast of the skeleton—actually several casts—for the museum's own collection. The cast of her skeleton was displayed in the museum in Melbourne until 1969. I remember having seen it—along with Phar Lap—after my family moved to Melbourne. A cast of her skull was traded to the Museum of Natural History in New York in return for the skull of a tyrannosaurus. In the same way, the Tasmanian Museum traded casts of Truganini's death mask for artefacts from museums around the world.

Spencer's arrangement of Truganini's bones was returned to Tasmania to become the centrepiece exhibit in the museum. Contained in one crowded glass cabinet, the skeleton was on public view from 1904 until 1947, when it was removed in response to protests from various respectable citizens, including Atkinson's son, and a rising tide of public distaste.

All that remains of the exhibit is a dingy photograph that shows Truganini's articulated skeleton mounted prominently in the middle of the cabinet, with Benjamin Law's bust of Wooredy on a plinth beside it. Hanging on the solid back wall were Thomas Bock's portraits of Wooredy and of Plorenernoopner (mistakenly believed to be of Truganini), the plaster death mask of Truganini's face, the studio photographs by Charles Woolley taken in 1866, Governor Arthur's picture board, several shell necklaces and a number of woven baskets. Propped against the wall were spears and waddies, and at the base of the skeleton was a scattering of grinding stones.

The purpose of this pitiful display of anthropological trophies was to register the original owners of the land as a long-gone people, as remote from the viewer as Neanderthal Man. The stone utensils, wooden weapons, shell ornaments and grass bags visually reinforced the essential argument for the rapid disappearance of the original owners of the island: these were people utterly unable to adapt. There need be no tortured questions about what debts might be owed them. Future generations could be comfortable in the knowledge that they possessed their property by virtue of natural selection.

For several decades after their removal from display, the bones lay jumbled and neglected in a dusty box thrust into the back of a cupboard in the museum basement. After a lengthy legal battle waged by the Tasmanian Aboriginal Centre, established by descendants of the original people under the chairmanship of the charismatic lawyer Michael Mansell, the trustees of the museum eventually allowed the remains to be cremated on 30 April 1976. Seven days short of the centenary of her death, Truganini's ashes were scattered in the D'Entrecasteaux Channel in accordance with the promise she had extracted from Reverend Atkinson.

On a return visit to Hobart in the mid 1980s, I found that the Tasmanian Museum had a much larger space devoted to the original people, with the same sort of artefacts now reverently displayed. The standout feature was a diorama of a domestic scene of a family in pre-contact times. Rendered in bright technicolour, mother, husband and child were clustered around a cooking fire, as frozen and unresponsive as in death. I gazed at the diorama for a long time before moving on to view the photographs of Truganini and eight companions carefully posed in tableau by Bishop Nixon at Oyster Cove in 1858. The bishop's unwilling subjects were stiff as mannequins in the layers of ill-fitting clothing they had been made to wear. In doleful monochrome, they seemed so desolate I couldn't bear to look at them. The overwhelming mood of the exhibit was elegiac. It was a melancholic requiem for the disappeared that reeked of regret without responsibility.

My guidebook told me the old station at Oyster Cove was now a state reserve near the hamlet of Kettering, on the D'Entrecasteaux Channel, so I made the snap decision to visit. After passing through the village of Snug, the winding Channel Highway dipped down to graze the edge of North West Bay, and here I turned onto Old Station Road. This was the original carriage road, built in the 1820s, that ran over the hills to the old convict station and terminated at the house of Henry Harrison Pybus at Little Oyster Cove. Barely wide enough for one car, the gravel road was cut between the glistening water of the bay and a wall of sandstone, golden and pockmarked like honeycomb. The road meandered along the water's edge towards a picturesque jetty, where four rowboats were winched up under a red-roofed shed. Painted on the side, in bold letters, was the name of my father's brother, Ken Pybus.

Here the road took a sharp right-angled turn away from the water and continued up the hill, past a vertical-board cottage painted in faded turquoise that I recognised as the place where I had spent magical summer holidays in my early childhood. At the brow of the hill I stopped to admire the broad waterway of the D'Entrecasteaux Channel, opened out before me. Wind and currents created swirls of cobalt and cerulean so that the surface of the water looked like the endpapers of an old book. Across the marbled water, North Bruny Island was a closed fist on a long narrow arm, dominated by the defiant fluted cape at its distant southern end. Directly below me was Oyster Cove, where I could see an old colonial homestead at the southern tip. This was the house where my grandfather was born, and inherited by my great-aunts. The landscape spread out before me had been home to my family for generations. My Ithaca. Arriving there was what I was destined for.

Descending from the glorious vista, the road entered a gully of stunted eucalypts and musk trees, and crossed a rickety bridge over a trickle of creek to stop at the old station site. There was not a skerrick of evidence of the old station, just a tangle of bracken and blackberries, and one small area that had been cleared as far as the extensive mudflats exposed by the low tide. Stepping out of the car, I was assailed by the evocative aroma released from the leaves of the musk trees, triggering a memory of myself at this very same spot, running wild with my youngest cousins.

On special Sundays there were family visits to the great-aunts in the homestead next door and we bothersome children were permitted to escape the cloying nostalgia of the dark house to clamber around the water's edge to this abandoned place. We would fossick among ruined foundations for fragments of old china or smashed clay pipes. I never understood whose broken bits we were passing around in our grubby fingers. To be standing in this desolate place where I had carelessly played long ago was a profound shock. Staring out over the mudflats to the D'Entrecasteaux Channel at what had once been my family's land on North Bruny Island, my emotions were in havoc—nothing as intimate and corrosive as guilt, just a powerful sense of complicity in the dispossession, destruction and denial that this dismal place represented.

On leaving the site, I paid close attention to the sign erected by the Tasmanian Aboriginal Centre, who had a land claim over the old convict station. The sign bore the Aboriginal flag, and although it was pockmarked by bullet holes and defaced by spray paint, it was still possible to read the overlaid text, a quotation from Xavier Herbert, author of *Poor Fellow My Country*:

> Until we give back to the black man just a bit of the land that was his and give it back without provisos, without strings to snatch it back, without anything but complete generosity of spirit in concession for the evil we have done him—until we do that, we shall remain what we have always been so far, a people without integrity; not a nation, but a community of thieves.

Turning my car around, I drove back along the old station road, stopping just above the jetty beside the faded turquoise cottage. Stepping out, I opened the gate and walked in. My uncle Ken welcomed me as if I had never been away. Over a cup of tea, he told me that the place was getting too much for him, so I arranged to buy it from him, then and there.

For the past thirty-four years the place I call home has been that cottage on the old station road in the country of the Nuenonne. I lead a charmed life in this paradise of hills and water, and barely a day goes by that I don't reflect on what has been extinguished in order for me to experience such grace.

While my family history provides an unassailable case for my being the beneficiary of stolen land and genocide, the deeper truth is that every Australian who is not a member of the First Nations is a beneficiary of stolen country, brutal dispossession, institutionalised racial discrimination and callous indifference. The expropriation of the territory of a generous people, and the devastating frontier war and dispersal that followed, is Australia's true foundation story, not the voyage of Captain Cook or the arrival of the First Fleet.

The question we must all wrestle with is how the majority immigrant society acknowledges what is owed to the original people, who possessed their territory for more than sixty thousand years, and who have never ceded that sovereignty to the British Crown or the Commonwealth of Australia. The very least we can do is pay attention and give respectful consideration when the original people of this country tell us what is needed.

From all points in the southern sky, leaders of the First Nations of Australia came together in 2017 to produce the Uluru Statement from the Heart. They proposed a *Makarrata*, which is a word in the Yolngu language meaning a coming together after a struggle, facing the facts of wrongs done, and living again in peace. In order to achieve *Makarrata* they asked that a voice for the First Nations be enshrined in the Constitution to 'empower our people and take a rightful place in our own country' and to acknowledge their aspirations for 'a fair and truthful relationship between the people of Australia and a better future for our children based on justice and self-determination'. After two hundred years of hostile occupation, surely *Makarrata* is what we all need, as the Uluru Statement eloquently and emotively claims, 'as a fuller expression of Australia's nationhood'.

The First Nations of this country want their unique relationship acknowledged and respected; they want to hold their heads high in their own country. That is not too much to ask.

TIMELINE

1804

Penal settlement established on Derwent River, later named Hobart

1812

Possible birth of Truganini

1828

April: martial law declared and original people expelled from areas of settlement

1829

March: George Augustus Robinson sent to Bruny Island to hand out food to Nuenonne

April: Robinson finds Truganini at woodcutters' station at Birch's Bay and takes her to Missionary Bay

October: Truganini becomes second wife of Wooredy

1830

January: Truganini, Wooredy, his two sons and Dray leave Bruny Island with Robinson

February: Robinson's mission to clans of west coast departs from Recherche Bay

May: Umarrah and his two companions leave Robinson's mission

June: Peevay joins the mission party on Robbins Island

October: the Black Line begins in Launceston and the mission party goes north-east

November: Mannalargenna and Trowlebunner surrender to Robinson
December: Robinson establishes a holding station on Swan Island

1831

February: Truganini, Wooredy, Dray and Kickerterpoller in Hobart with Robinson
March: Truganini and friends return to Swan Island from Hobart; Maulboyheener and Lacklay arrive; captives move to Gun Carriage Island
June: Robinson's mission to the clans of north coast and interior of the colony begins
August: Umarrah and the 'Stoney Creek band' surrender
December: 'Big River people' surrender

1832

February: mission party visits Flinders Island
March: Umarrah dies in Launceston
April: mission to the clans of the north-west begins
May: Kickerterpoller and Polare die in Emu Bay
July: Wymurric and his people confined on Hunter Island to be sent to Flinders Island
September: Tarkiner attack Robinson at the Arthur River
November: mission to the clans of north-west coast led by Anthony Cottrell begins

1833

January: Cottrell's mission party arrives at Sarah Island in Macquarie Harbour
February: Truganini leads mission to capture some of the Ninine people

April: Robinson arrives at Sarah Island
June: Robinson captures the Ninine and Lowreenne people
July: Robinson captures the Tarkiner people
October: mission party returns to Hobart with Robinson

1834

February: final mission to capture the last of the north-west clans begins

1835

January: Robinson announces Tasmania cleared of the original people
May: Tanleboneyer, Penderoin and Nollahalleker die in Hobart
October: mission party taken to Flinders Island and Mannalargenna dies

1836

March: Truganini, Wooredy and four others leave Flinders Island with George Robinson junior

1837

July: George Robinson junior and mission party return to Flinders Island

1838

July: Robinson appointed Chief Protector of Aborigines for Port Phillip District

1839

February: Robinson takes Truganini, Wooredy and Peevay to Port Phillip

April: Maulboyheener and Lacklay arrive in Port Phillip with their wives

August: Truganini runs away from Robinson's house in Melbourne and is returned

1840

April: all the Van Diemen's Land people run away from Robinson's house

May: Lacklay disappears in Westernport

June: Truganini runs away from Robinson's house and is returned

August: Truganini runs away again and is returned

1841

March: Robinson expedition into the Western District with Peevay begins

May: Truganini and Maulboyheener run away together

September: Truganini, Maulboyheener, Peevay, Maytepueminer and Plorenernoopner move to Westernport

October: two whalers murdered in Lower Westernport

November: Truganini and her four companions arrested in Westernport

December: Truganini, Maytepueminer and Plorenernoopner escape murder charges, but Peevay and Maulboyheener found guilty

1842

January: Peevay and Maulboyheener executed for murder
July: Truganini, Maytepueminer and Plorenernoopner return to Flinders Island with Wooredy, who dies en route

1843

March: Truganini married to Mannapackername
November: Henry Jeanneret dismissed as commandant of Wybalenna
December: Joseph Milligan appointed as commandant of Wybalenna

1845

December: Jeanneret reinstated at Wybalenna

1846

February: Walter George Arthur and others petition Queen Victoria
March: Jeanneret returns as commandant of Wybalenna

1847

May: Jeanneret dismissed as commandant of Wybalenna
June: Milligan reinstated as commandant of Wybalenna
July: Truganini's husband Mannapackername dies
October: forty-six people transferred from Wybalenna to Oyster Cove station

1848

October: Wooredy's son Davey Bruny dies at Oyster Cove

1851

April: Robinson visits Oyster Cove and records thirty people living there

1852

September: Mathinna dies by accidental drowning

1853

December: Milligan reports twenty-seven unidentified deaths at Oyster Cove since 1847

1855

April: Calder and Kirwan visit Oyster Cove and record sixteen people still living there

June: Milligan dismissed as superintendent of Oyster Cove

July: John Dandridge arrives as superintendent of Oyster Cove

1858

October: Tanganutura dies

1861

May: Walter George Arthur dies by drowning

August: Dray dies

1862

June: Henry Harrison Pybus's offer to care for the eight people left at Oyster Cove refused

1864

February: Jack Allen dies

1867

February: Bessy Clark dies
July: Patty Clark dies
August: Wapperty dies

1868

January: Billy Lanne and Truganini presented to Duke of Edinburgh

1869

March: Billy Lanne dies and his body is mutilated

1871

July: Mary Ann Arthur dies

1873

July: Truganini moves to Dandridge house in Hobart

1876

May: Truganini dies in Hobart and is buried in secret

1878

December: Truganini's body exhumed from her grave and given to the Royal Society of Tasmania

BIOGRAPHIES

People of the South-east Nation

MANGANERER

Truganini's father, Manganerer, was the senior man of the Nuenonne, and was born before British settlement. His country encompassed Bruny Island and the mainland coast from Oyster Cove to Recherche Bay, and his Nuenonne clan had close kin connections with the Needwondee and Ninine clans of the south-west, who belonged to the same language group. The scant evidence about Manganerer's first wife (name unknown) suggests that she was from the Ninine, whose territory was on the south-west coast around Port Davey. She was killed sometime before 1820 when a group of sailors made a night attack on the family when they were camped on Partridge Island. Manganerer was known to have had three daughters by his first wife, and his two older daughters, **Lowhenune** and **Magerleede**, were abducted in 1826 by a sealer known as Black Baker, who took them to islands in the Bass Strait. Baker was eventually tried on abduction charges that came to nothing, and the women were never returned. It is not known what happened to them. **Truganini** (see entry) was Manganerer's youngest daughter.

On Manganerer's annual visit to Recherche Bay in the summer of 1829, his second wife (name and clan unknown) was abducted by convicts who had commandeered the government brig *Cyprus*, which they sailed to New Zealand, then to Japan and China. Their young son died soon after his mother's abduction and there is no evidence that his wife survived the voyage across the Tasman.

In October 1829 Manganerer was briefly partnered with Truganini's friend **Pagerly,** whose husband and child had died sometime before April 1829, but he died of venereal disease less than three months later. Pagerly became the wife of **Kickerterpoller** (see entry) and after his death in 1832 she was sent to Flinders Island, where her death, sometime before 1837, was unrecorded.

TRUGANINI (aka Lydgugee, Lalla Rookh)
Born at Recherche Bay in around 1812, Truganini witnessed the murder of her mother when she was still a child. When she was a teenager, her two older sisters were kidnapped by a sealer. There is an account of Truganini also being abducted around this time, although the story comes from a dubious source with no verifiable evidence: it was first reported, a year before her death, by James E. Calder, in his book *Some Account of the Wars, Extirpation, Habits, &c., of the Native Tribes of Tasmania* and was supposedly told to him by the emancipated convict Alexander McKay. In Calder's telling, Truganini was kidnapped and raped by convict woodcutters, and two Nuenonne men who were with her—one of them said to be her 'betrothed'—were thrown from the woodcutters' boat; as they clung to the gunwales their hands were chopped off and they were left to drown in the bloody water. This was just the kind of graphic story that George Augustus Robinson was always eager to hear, and he certainly would have made a record of it if it had been spoken of at the time, or subsequently. Truganini told Robinson about the violence she experienced living with the woodcutters so it is remarkable that she did not mention such a traumatic event. Nor was it brought to the attention of the authorities in 1828, unlike the abduction of her sisters, although it was supposed to have happened around the same time.

Over her life Truganini had four husbands. She was married to her first husband, **Wooredy** (see entry), in October 1829 under pressure from Robinson. She abandoned Wooredy in Port Phillip in 1841 and formed a relationship with **Maulboyheener** (see entry), and in October 1841 they were both implicated in the murder of two whalers in Lower Westernport. Maulboyheener was found guilty and executed in January 1842, while Truganini was acquitted and returned to Flinders Island in July 1842, where she was married to **Mannapackername** (see entry). He died in July 1847, five months before Truganini was transferred to Oyster Cove. Sometime after 1855 she formed a relationship of sorts with **Billy Lanne** (see entry), who died in February 1869.

By 1872 Truganini was the sole resident at Oyster Cove and the superintendent took her to live in Hobart, where she died on 8 May 1876. She was buried in secret in the grounds of the abandoned Female Factory. Two years later, members of the Royal Society of Tasmania exhumed her skeleton, which they kept in the society's collection until 1904, when it was placed on public display. Removed from public view in 1947, her remains were finally released from the museum vaults in 1976 and cremated. Her ashes were scattered on the D'Entrecasteaux Channel.

There is no evidence that Truganini had a child. No contemporary witness ever suggested it. In his reminiscences of 1905, Reverend Atkinson referred to her baby who died on Bruny Island, misunderstanding her reference to swimming with a baby on her back. Most likely this was the baby of one of her kidnapped older sisters—a child who would stand in the same relationship to her as her own—or perhaps her much younger half-brother. She had a close connection to **Pagerly** and **Dray** (see entry), both of whom had babies who died in 1829. Claims by various families in Victoria and New South Wales to be descended from Truganini are not credible, among them that Truganini had a daughter named Louisa who married John Briggs, who was the son of the sealer George Briggs and Mannalargenna's daughter (see entry for Mannalargenna), and who supervised the orphanage at Coranderrk Aboriginal Reserve in Victoria. Louisa Briggs's mother was a mixed-race woman named Polly Munro whose own mother had been a Boonwurrung woman taken from Port Phillip by a sealer.

There are several portraits of Truganini. The best known and most often reproduced is a portrait in watercolour by Thomas Bock, part of a series he did for Robinson in 1835 and now held in the British Museum; various later copies are held in other galleries. Unfortunately, the later copies of the Bock portraits are incorrectly labelled and the much-reproduced portrait said to be Truganini is not of her; it is a portrait of one of her companions, most likely **Plorenernoopner** (see entry). A notation on the back of the original in the British Museum, as well as entries in the catalogue of the collector who purchased the Bock portraits from the Robinson estate, makes it explicit that the portrait of the woman with the shell necklace was Truganini. This portrait is reproduced in the colour picture section of this book. The British Museum also holds a set of five drawings never before identified that are now believed to have been drawn by Thomas Lempriere at Port Arthur in October 1833. His drawing of a woman most likely to be Truganini is reproduced in the colour picture section.

WOOREDY (aka Mutteele, Doctor, Count Alpha)

Born more than a decade before settlement, Wooredy was a warrior and cleverman of the Nuenonne. Stubbornly attached to his traditional ways, he rejected all attempts to make him a Christian and he is a highly significant historical source for information about customs and beliefs of the original people. His first wife (name unknown) died of influenza on Bruny Island in 1829, as did one of his three sons. His surviving sons were **Myunge (aka Davey Bruny)**, born about 1818, and **Droyerloine (aka Peter Bruny)**, born about 1820. The boys left Bruny Island with their father, but Wooredy was separated from his sons for five years and in that time they were renamed Davey and Peter. In 1833 they were admitted to the Orphan School in Hobart. Wooredy was reunited with his sons in October 1835 when they went together to Flinders Island.

Wooredy's sons joined him in Port Phillip in 1838. There they worked for Robinson and members of his family, including Robinson's future son-in-law Dr James Allen. By 1842 Wooredy was showing signs of advanced physical and mental decline and was very ill when he was embarked for Flinders Island in July. He died on the way there on 7 July 1842 and was buried on Green Island.

His younger son, Peter Bruny, continued to work for Robinson at Port Phillip, but often ran off to live with the Boonwurrung. He died on 8 December 1843, aged around twenty-two, and was buried on Robinson's farm on the Merri Creek. Davey Bruny was also a frequent absconder in Port Phillip, joining the Boonwurrung at various times. In 1842 the Native Police eventually tracked him to a pastoral lease at the edge of the Carrum Carrum Swamp. On 23 July 1842 it was arranged for him to go back to Flinders Island, but the ship sailed without him. He must have absconded again, and was brought back by the same Native Police in August 1842.

Davey was sent to Hobart, eventually arriving at the Aboriginal Establishment at Wybalenna on Flinders Island in October 1842. Here he was a leading figure in resistance to authoritarian rule and an agitator for the recognition of native rights. He helped to organise a petition to Queen Victoria that led to the closure of the establishment in 1847. While at Wybalenna, in July 1843, he was pushed into a marriage with **Teddeheburrer (aka Clara)**, the daughter of **Wyne** (see entry), from the Tarkiner clan of the north-west. She died on 7 August 1843, soon after giving birth to a mixed-race child who also died. Davey was then married to **Maytepueminer** (see entry). He and Maytepueminer were relocated to Oyster Cove in October 1847. Davey died in October 1848 at the age of thirty, without children.

People of the South-west Nation

DRAY (aka Sophia)
A woman from the Lowreenne clan from the south-west coast, Dray arrived on Bruny Island in June 1829 accompanied by her Ninine husband and their child for their annual visit. Two months later, three more Ninine family groups arrived, but by September Dray was the sole survivor. In January 1830 she was Robinson's primary guide for his mission to the south-west coast.

Dray abruptly left Robinson in April 1830 and rejoined her people, taking a second husband, **Dewoorady**. They were captured by Robinson in September 1833 and sent to Flinders Island, where Dewoorady died, unrecorded, sometime before March 1839. Dray had a third husband, **Tolelerduric (aka Andrew, Dray's Jerry)**, a Peerapper man, whose death at Flinders Island was also unrecorded. Her fourth husband was known as **Edmund** and they were among the people sent to Oyster Cove in 1847. Edmund's death was recorded on 26 March 1851 and Dray's death on 29 August 1861, when she was said to be not less than seventy-five years old.

PEGERNOBERRIC (aka Bessy Clark)
A Ninine woman, Pegernoberric was taken as a child from Port Davey with her mother, **Tinganoop**, and father, **Cordwanene**, and sent to Flinders Island in June 1833. She was admitted to the Orphan School in Hobart in February 1835 but was taken back

to Flinders Island by Robinson in September that same year. At Wybalenna she did not live with her mother, but she and the other children were housed with the catechist Robert Clark, who changed her name to Bessy Clark. She was transferred to Oyster Cove with her mother in 1847 when she was about twenty-one. She was then the wife of **Thermanope (aka Augustus Clark)**, who was also from the Ninine clan and had been with her at the Orphan School. After he died in 1860, she was courted by an ex-convict carpenter, whose application to marry was approved by the colonial secretary so he could assume economic responsibility for her, but for whatever reason this marriage never took place. Pegernoberric died at Oyster Cove on 12 February 1867, and sometime later her body was secretly removed from the grave. Her complete skeleton was sent to the Royal College of Surgeons in London in December 1871.

TOWTERER (aka Romeo)
The senior man of the Ninine clan from Port Davey, Towterer was captured with his wife **Wongenneep (aka Queen Evaline)** and sent to Flinders Island in June 1833. His daughter, aged about four, was captured separately and sent to Hobart in May 1833. She was admitted to the Orphan School, where she died of measles in June 1835. He and his wife had a second child on Flinders Island, baptised as Mary, whose date of birth is unknown but was possibly 1835. Towterer died at Flinders Island on 30 September 1837 and Wongenneep sometime after March 1839, but her death was not recorded. Before she died, her only surviving daughter was renamed **Mathinna** and sent to live with Governor and Lady Franklin in February 1839. Mathinna's portrait was painted by Thomas Bock in 1842, when she was said to be around seven. The portrait is reproduced in the colour section of this book. The Franklins returned to England in August 1843 and Mathinna was placed in

the Orphan School, briefly returned to Flinders Island, then readmitted to the Orphan School in 1847 until she was ultimately discharged to Oyster Cove in August 1851. She died on 1 September 1852.

People of the Oyster Bay Nation

BULLYER (aka Drummernerlooner, Jumbo, Louisa)
A Parerebeene woman, Bullyer was stolen from Cape Portland by sealer James Munro when she was a child. Bullyer was given up by Munro in 1830 and she acted as a guide on Robinson's missions. In 1831 she became the wife of **Tarnebunner**, who may have been a son of **Mannalargenna** (see entry). He died later that year and she went back to James Munro for a time, returning to Flinders Island at some point. She died there, her death unrecorded.

Her mother, **Poolrerrener (aka Bullroe)**, had been stolen by a sealer named Tomlins around 1814 and taken to Kangaroo Island. She was surrendered to Robinson by another sealer on Hunter Island in August 1832, after which her son **Ned Tomlins** petitioned the governor to allow her to live with him. Robinson advised the petition be denied because Ned Tomlins was 'not a fit person' to have charge of his own mother. She was transferred to Flinders Island, where she died, unrecorded, before September 1835. Ned Tomlins gained a reputation as a highly skilled boatman in the Bass Strait and later as a prominent whaler in Victoria and New Zealand. He died in New Zealand sometime before 1853. He had a son named Edward Tomlins with his Māori wife, Hipora.

KICKERTERPOLLER (aka Tom Birch, Black Tom)
The evidence points to Kickerterpoller having originally been from the Pardarereme clan, whose territory covered the coastal fringe of the lower east. As a child he witnessed sailing ships passing Maria

Island, which must have been the expedition of Nicolas Baudin in 1802. At some point he came into the household of a prominent settler named Thomas Birch and became known as Black Tom. In 1819 he was baptised as Tom Birch by the Hobart Anglican minister Robert Knopwood.

Some historians mistakenly believe that Kickerterpoller was associated with the guerilla fighter known as Musquito and was implicated in the killing of a settler in 1824. However, a man known as 'Black Jack' (who was sometimes called 'Black Tom') was responsible for that murder, and he was executed.

Kickerterpoller ran away from the Birch farm in 1826 and made contact with his clan, looking for a wife. He was said to be leading raids on settlers during the spring of that year and was arrested along with six men, three women and a baby, after an attack by soldiers on a large group of Pardarereme on 9 December 1826, when fourteen others were killed. The group of survivors were taken to the Richmond jail. They were found to have 'no charge against them' and liberated back to their country in early January 1827. Kickerterpoller was nominally released into the charge of Mrs Birch in Hobart before being taken under the wing of the chief constable at Richmond, Gilbert Robertson.

Kickerterpoller lived at Gilbert Robertson's house and became a guide and interpreter for his roving party. Robertson introduced him to the governor as an example of what could be achieved by humane policies of conciliation. He was present at the arrest of **Umarrah** (see entry) and four others on 7 November 1828. Kickerterpoller was transferred from Robertson's roving party to be a guide for Robinson's 'friendly mission' in January 1830. He became Pagerly's third husband and they lived together until his death from dysentery at Emu Bay on 16 May 1832. As he had been baptised, he was given a Christian burial.

MANNALARGENNA

Probably the most powerful leader on the island, Mannalargenna was a great warrior and cleverman, thought to be invincible. There is confusion about his country, as Robinson incorrectly claimed that he was from Ben Lomond, probably conflating him with his close ally **Trowlebunner** (see entry), whose wife was Mannalargenna's sister. What is clear is that Mannalargenna had pre-eminent influence over country from Cape Portland, at the north-eastern tip, to Georges Bay at the mid east coast, and his core clan was likely to have been Trawlwoolway, whose country stretched from Cape Portland to Musselroe Bay. He was sufficiently important to have established an alliance in 1810 with the sealers, led by George Briggs, from Cape Barren Island. The alliance with the sealers was consolidated when Briggs took one of Mannalargenna's daughters as his wife, but by 1816 Briggs had repudiated the alliance.

Mannalargenna's first wife had died before he surrendered to Robinson in November 1830. His second wife, to whom he was devoted, was **Tanleboneyer (aka Sal)**, a Tyreelore from his country who had been stolen by the sealer John Brown. The couple travelled together with Robinson from 1830 to 1835, when Tanleboneyer died in a measles epidemic in Hobart sometime in May. Mannalargenna died on Flinders Island soon after, on 4 December 1835. He had several sons, but only one survived him: **Neenhepeerminer (aka Hector)**, who was captured in January 1831 and died on Flinders Island in October 1837.

Four of Mannalargenna's daughters were taken captive by sealers on the Bass Strait islands. **Woretemoeteyenner (aka Pung, Margaret)**, his eldest daughter, had been the wife of George Briggs, who sold her to 'Long John' Thomas. She was briefly a guide for Robinson and other roving parties but returned to Thomas late in

1831. She was known to have had at least four children, including John Briggs, who moved to Victoria in the 1850s, and **Dalrymple (Dolly) Briggs**, who married an emancipated convict named Thomas Johnson. In 1841 Dalrymple Johnson petitioned to have her mother, now living on Flinders Island, live with her in Latrobe. Woretemoeteyenner died there in 1847. Dalrymple Johnson died on 1 December 1864 and was survived by ten children. Her descendants constitute a significant section of the present-day Tasmanian Aboriginal community.

Wotecowidyer (aka Harriet) was originally stolen by sealer James Thompson, who then gave her to James Everitt. She was taken to Robinson by James Parish in 1830 but was returned to Everitt on her own request in 1831. She was returned to Flinders Island in 1836, transferred to Oyster Cove in 1847 and died there sometime in August or September 1855. Only two of Wotecowidyer's numerous children survived, **Thomas Thompson** and **Mary Ann Thompson**, who lived with their father, the sealer James Thompson. After Thompson died in a boating accident in October 1835, they were sent to the Orphan School in May 1836 and were taken to Flinders Island later that year. Thomas Thompson went with Robinson to Port Phillip, while Mary Ann Thompson went into service with various settlers and was taken to Sydney sometime in 1851. Thomas Thompson stayed in Port Phillip in 1842 and was known to be in Victoria, maybe working the goldfields, in 1851. The eventual fate of the Thompson children remains unknown. Wotecowidyer was transferred to Oyster Cove in 1847, where she died in August 1855.

Wobberety (aka Wapperty) went voluntarily to Flinders Island in August 1844 with her daughter Betsy, whose father was the Māori sealer John Myteye. In 1847 Betsy married the Tahitian sealer John Mirey and lived on nearby Woody Island.

Wobberety was transferred to Oyster Cove, where she died on 12 August 1867.

Teekoolterme was taken first to Kangaroo Island by 'Black Jack' Williams. After he drowned in 1830, she lived with 'Long John' Thomas on Preservation Island. It is not known what happened to her.

MAYTEPUEMINER (aka Matilda, New Maria)
A Leetermairremener woman stolen by sealers from St Patricks Head, Maytepueminer arrived on Flinders Island in June 1836. She was married to **Lacklay** (see entry) but refused to stay with him; however, they were later remarried and she went with him to Port Phillip, where he disappeared in April 1840. Maytepueminer spent some time with four companions looking for him in Lower Westernport where they were implicated in the murder of two whalers in October 1841. Maytepueminer was acquitted of murder and returned to Flinders Island in July 1842, where she was later married to Wooredy's son Davey Bruny. They were among those transferred to Oyster Cove in 1847; she was one of seventeen people whose deaths were not recorded between 1851 and 1855.

TANGANUTURA (aka Tibb, Sarah)
Abducted from Cape Portland by the sealer James Parish when she was an adolescent, Tanganutura was sold to John Smith, who subsequently sold her to the sealer George Robinson. They lived for some years on King Island before moving back to the eastern end of the Bass Strait. She was taken to Swan Island in 1830 and became a guide for Robinson's mission in 1831 before returning to Flinders Island in March 1832. She later married **Nicermenic (aka Eugene)**, a Peerapper man from West Point who was captured at Port Sorrell in September 1831. They were among the people taken

to Oyster Cove, where Nicermenic died on 28 May 1847. Tanganutura died on 3 October 1858. She was known to have had at least four children who survived infancy:

Mary Ann Robinson, whose father was the sealer George Robinson, was born around 1824, and in 1838 she married **Walter George Arthur** (see entry). On his death, she married an emancipated convict, Adam Booker. She died at Oyster Cove on 25 July 1871.

Duke Robinson was born around 1826, and his father was also the sealer George Robinson. N.J.B. Plomley, editor of Robinson's journals, mistakenly conflated him with **Thomas Thompson** (see entry for Mannalargenna), but the records clearly show they were two different children. Duke was sent to the Orphan School from Flinders Island in November 1832 and there apprenticed to the Hobart merchant Thomas Learmonth in February 1840. He appears to have been sent to work for Learmonth's sons in Victoria around 1850 and was known to be in Victoria in 1851. It is not known what happened to him.

Fanny (aka Fanny Cochrane) was born on Flinders Island in December 1834. Her biological father may have been John Smith, the sealer who purchased her mother from James Parish and was for a time coxswain on Gun Carriage and Flinders islands and became a whaler in Port Phillip. She lived in the household of Robert Clark at Wybalenna and was given the surname Cochrane, which was the maiden name of Clark's wife. Fanny was transferred to Oyster Cove, where she lived with her mother until she married a timber splitter named William Smith in October 1854. They lived on land several miles inland from the old station and had eleven children. In 1889 she was given a land grant of 300 acres at Nicholls Rivulet. In 1899 and 1903 she recorded songs on wax cylinders that are the only recordings ever made of the song and speech of the original people of Tasmania. Her descendants constitute a significant section of the present-day Tasmanian Aboriginal community.

Adam was born on Flinders Island on 7 August 1838. His father was Nicermenic. With his parents he was sent to Oyster Cove, and the following year was sent to the Orphan School for four years, being discharged in January 1853. After returning from a whaling voyage, he died at his half-sister Fanny Smith's house on 28 October 1857 with his mother present.

People of the North Midland Nation

MEELERLEETER (aka Leenimeener, Jack Allen, VDL Jack, Paddy)

Originally from the Tyerrerontepanner clan, Meelerleeter was aged about five when he was captured with his mother, **Karnebucher**, by Chief Constable Gilbert Robertson in 1829 and brought to Hobart. They were held in the Richmond jail and among a group of women and children taken to Robinson's house, most of whom were released into the north in March 1830. Reunited with her husband, **Monteener**, Karnebucher and the family tried to seek protection from the Black Line with a settler, who took them to the Campbell Town jail. Karnebucher was removed from that jail by Alexander McKay, and her husband escaped in July 1831, presumably with his son. It is not clear what happened to Monteener after he was recaptured, but Meelerleeter ended up at John Batman's property at Deddington, where he was baptised as **Jack Allen**, the name by which he was usually identified—although Batman often called him Paddy.

In 1836 Batman took him to Port Phillip, and on Batman's death in 1839 Jack Allen became the responsibility of Robinson, who contracted him to work on a station north-west of Melbourne. He ran away in September 1840 after being unfairly accused of killing a horse and was then living among the Boonwurrung on Mornington Peninsula. In 1842 he was working for George Langhorne, who sent him back to Van Diemen's Land in July. Later that year, he was sent to Flinders Island with Davey Bruny, Walter George Arthur and Mary Ann Arthur, and with these same people he was active in opposing the authoritarian rule at Wybalenna, and was one of the authors of the petition that led to the closure of the establishment in 1847. At Wybalenna he was married to **Pieyencomyenna (aka Wild Mary)** and they were among the people sent to Oyster Cove in 1847. After her death, he married a Tyreelore rescued from sealers known as **Emma.** For a short time he worked in the whaling industry, and he died at Oyster Cove on 10 February 1864. He had no children.

RICHARD (aka Cranky Dick)
The original name and clan of the boy whom Robinson called Richard is not known. He was raised by an ex-soldier and local constable named James Brumby on his farm on the Norfolk plains near Longford. One can only imagine the circumstances in which Brumby took possession of the child, and there may be a connection to a massacre said to have taken place close by in December 1825. Richard spoke only English. Plomley identifies the location for this boy as Ben Lomond; however, he has confused Richard with another man also known as Dick.

Richard joined Robinson's mission party in 1832 but was an unsatisfactory guide as he regularly got lost and had little or no interaction with the other guides. He was said to have a 'mental deficiency', perhaps because he was prone to grand mal seizures. Still, Robinson always wanted to have Richard in his mission parties, and often was a messenger because of his fluency in English. He did not take Richard to Port Phillip. Possibly because of his affliction, Richard lived as a single man on Flinders Island and later at Oyster Cove. He died there on 28 October 1848.

UMARRAH (aka Kaneherlargenna)
A renowned leader of the Tyerrerontepanner from the midlands, Umarrah was captured by a roving party led by Chief Constable Gilbert Robertson on 7 November 1828. Also captured were his brother (name unknown), who subsequently escaped, his wife **Laoninlooner**, a man called **Parewareter**, and a boy, **Cowertinner**. Robertson successfully persuaded Governor Arthur that Umarrah should not be executed but treated as a prisoner of war, and he remained confined to Richmond jail, assigned a convict as his servant. He had freedom to visit Robertson's house, where the boy Cowertinner lived. At the end of 1829 Robertson was instructed by the governor to hand over his guides for the friendly mission to the west coast. He agreed to hand over the two men but refused to allow Cowertinner to be taken. Eventually, in March 1831, Robinson gained custody of the boy, who died on Swan Island a month later.

Umarrah went with Robinson on his first mission to the west coast. While he acted as a guide, his wife, Laoninlooner, went to live at Robinson's house, and she was one of six women released back into their country in March 1830. Umarrah absconded in April 1830, with Parewareter and another man, Trepanner. They took the migratory routes from the west coast to the ochre mines of the Surrey Hills, then crossed the central plateau to meet up with Umarrah's brothers and his wife. Umarrah joined a group of remnant clans for a big battle with his traditional enemies, the

Lairmairermener, in 1830, in which his wife was killed, along with at least one of his brothers. Parewareter and Trepanner were probably also killed, as they were not heard of again.

In October 1830, after the battle with the Lairmairermener, Umarrah presented himself in Launceston to be a guide for the Black Line, but soon melted back into the bush to lead a band of displaced people from the north-east and north midlands clans. This group, known to terrified settlers as the Stoney Creek band, conducted raids in the region between the North Esk and Tamar rivers that led to the deaths of several settlers and stockkeepers. Eventually, in August 1831, Umarrah surrendered his band to Robinson and was reintegrated into Robinson's mission with his second wife, **Polare (aka Woolaytopinner)**, a Punnilerpanner woman from Port Sorrell. After contracting dysentery, Umarrah died in Launceston and was buried on 26 March 1832. Polare died at Emu Bay about six weeks later, exact date unknown.

People of the North-east Nation

MAULBOYHEENER (aka Timme, Big Tuery's Jemmy, Robert)
A youth of the Pyemairenerpairnener people of the Pipers River region, Maulboyheener came into Robinson's care in 1829 with his mother, **Luggenemeener (aka Queen Charlotte, Big Tuery)**. She appears to have been an unusually powerful woman of the Plangermairener from Ben Lomond, sister to **Trowlebunner** (see entry), the senior man of the Plangermairener, sometimes mistaken as her husband. Maulboyheener's father was **Woreternaterlargner (aka King George)**, the senior man of the Pyemairenerpairnener and a very important warrior among all the clans of the north-east nation, as was his brother **Moulteherlargener.** This was a notably close family, with strong bonds of affection that were remarked

upon with surprise and admiration by numerous settlers, but which have caused confusion for historians.

When he was about thirteen years old, Maulboyheener was captured by John Batman, who had been tracking and harassing the clan for eighteen months. In a surprise attack on a night camp in May 1828, Batman's roving party had killed most of the men at the camp, but managed to capture Maulboyheener's older brother, **Tillabunner**, who was taken as a guide for a roving party and given the name Mungo. Maulboyheener was taken in a third surprise attack, in September 1829, with his mother, Luggenemeener, and her infant daughter. Also in the group was the son of Moulteherlargener, a boy of two or three named **Rolepana**, who was kept by Batman, baptised with the name **Ben Lomond**.

Maulboyheener, his mother, his sister, another eight captives and several children were sent to Richmond jail and then transferred to Robinson's house in Hobart. Maulboyheener left Hobart with Robinson for the mission to Port Davey in January 1830, but was sent back again in early April to find that his mother had been returned to her country. In May, he went after his mother and was probably the boy arrested with two women in his father's country on 15 May.

In October, when the Black Line was in full swing, Luggenemeener brought her husband Woreternaterlargner, his brother Moulteherlargener and her brother Trowlebunner, as well as seven other men, to Batman's house, where Batman held her eldest son, then known as Mungo or Batman's Jack. He escaped with his family but they were not able to liberate Moulteherlargener's son, known as Ben Lomond. In all, eleven men and two women escaped from Batman's custody and two men were subsequently shot, one of whom was probably Moulteherlargener. The group sought sanctuary with Robinson on 15 November. Maulboyheener was reunited with his family in March 1831 when he was sent from the Launceston jail to join them on Gun Carriage Island. He was reintegrated into Robinson's mission in April. His brother Tillabunner died on Gun Carriage Island on 2 June. His mother, Luggenemeener, died on Flinders Island on 22 March 1837, followed by his sister, known as Eliza Robinson, on 30 June 1838. His father, Woreternaterlargner, died on 1 June 1840.

Maulboyheener was married to a Pallitore woman from the north midlands, whose name was **Semiramis (aka Jenny)**. She died childless just before they were due to leave for Port Phillip on 28 February 1839. He immediately took another wife, a Tyreelore rescued from the sealers known as **Rebecca.** She died childless in Port Phillip on 29 April 1841, and then Maulboyheener took **Truganini** as his wife. By October they were both implicated in the murder of two whalers in Lower Westernport and Maulboyheener was executed with **Peevay** (see entry) at the first public hanging in Melbourne, on 20 January 1842. He was the last of his family.

Maulboyheener had no surviving siblings, although many historians have made the mistaken assumption that **Walter George Arthur** (see entry) was his brother. He was not, although they had very close kin connections, as Walter's father was Maulboyheener's mother's brother. The misidentification follows from the contradictory and unreliable notes on individuals compiled by Plomley, in which he named the father of Walter George Arthur as Rolepa, a man Charles Robinson incorrectly identified as King George; however, King George was the name given to Woreternaterlargner.

PLORENERNOOPNER (aka Woreterpowidyer, Jock, Fanny)
A Pyemairenerpairnener woman, stolen by sealers and liberated in December 1830, Plorenernoopner was the sister of **Woreternaterlargner** and **Moulteherlargener** and therefore close kin

to **Maulboyheener.** Claims that she was sister to **Umarrah** are incorrect, based on Plomley's misidentification of her brother Moulteherlargener as Umarrah. Her first husband was among the Stoney Creek band that surrendered to Robinson in August 1831. He absconded in October but was recaptured and sent to Flinders Island, where he died unrecorded.

Plorenernoopner joined Robinson's mission and married **Peevay** (see entry) and they were together on all subsequent missions. They went to Port Phillip in February 1839 and were together in Lower Westernport in October 1841 when they were implicated in the murder of two whalers. Peevay was executed for murder in January 1842, while Plorenernoopner was acquitted and returned to Flinders Island, where she was married to a Tommigener man from the north-west, **Parloorer (aka Frederick).** They were among those transferred to Oyster Cove, where they died sometime between 1851 and 1855, among seventeen deaths that were not recorded.

People of the Ben Lomond Nation

THOMAS BRUNE

A boy named Thomas Bunce was admitted to the Orphan School in August 1828 on the receipt of a letter from James Grant, a merchant in Hobart, who had been appointed in the previous month to act as agent for James Gilligan, who was leaving the colony. Gilligan was a sheep grazier on the Break of Day Plains on the South Esk River, and several settlers in this area had children of the original owners living with them. There is no evidence that the boy came from Bruny Island; his location with Gilligan suggests he was from one of the 'extinguished' clans of the Ben Lomond nation. Robinson demanded that he be released from the school in 1837 and sent to Wybalenna, where he came to be known as **Thomas Brune.** He was the editor of the newspaper on Flinders Island with **Walter George Arthur** (see entry). He was taken to Port Phillip but ran away from Robinson in April 1840 and never returned. He died on 3 January 1841 after falling from a tree while hunting possum on a pastoral run in Westernport.

TROWLEBUNNER (aka Rolepa, Rolepanner, Achilles)
As the senior man of the Plangermairener, Trowlebunner was a close ally of **Mannalargenna** and together they made a deal with Robinson in November 1830 to allow the clans to stay in their own country, but this was never honoured. Trowlebunner's wife, **Toogernupertooner (aka Maria)**, was the sister of Mannalargenna who had been stolen by sealers, and they were reunited on Swan Island when Robinson rescued her in October 1831. Robinson did not record that the couple had any children, but the evidence strongly suggests that Toogernupertooner was the mother of the boy known as Friday who was found with another boy on the Launceston streets working for a gang of thieves. She died on 30 March 1837—not on 27 October 1838 as Plomley's notes suggest; he has confused her with a Tyerrerontepanner woman also known as Maria, who died on the later date. After her death, Trowlebunner did not take another wife. He died on 4 July 1847.

WALTER GEORGE ARTHUR (aka Friday)
In 1832 a boy known as Friday, aged about eleven, was found with another boy, known as Arthur, on the Launceston streets, working as pickpockets for a gang of thieves. He did not know his original name or language. He was sent from Launceston to Flinders Island, and was transferred to the Orphan School in Hobart in November that year. Arthur died at the Orphan School, and in October 1835

Friday was returned to Flinders Island, where he lived with the catechist Robert Clark and was renamed Walter George Arthur. Robinson had high hopes for this boy, who showed great commitment to the Christian faith. He was made co-editor of the *Flinders Island Chronicle*, but he fell out of favour over his sexual relationship with **Mary Ann Robinson**. They were married in 1838.

It is odd that Robinson never identified Walter George Arthur's parents or recorded his original name and clan association, as he did for almost everyone. As a result, there has been persistent confusion about his birth parents, and who they were may never be known. Later commentators commonly identify him as the son of 'King George'. This misidentification appears to have been made by George Robinson junior, compounded by the catechist Robert Clark, and later by Plomley, who identified his mother as **Luggenemeener**, the wife of **Woreternaterlargner**, known as King George. However, Robinson paid close attention to Luggenemeener and her family and he never mentioned Walter George Arthur in that context. The confusion arises from Robinson's journal account on the day Luggenemeener died (23 March 1837), where he has written, 'Walter was dangerously ill . . . attacked in the same manner as his mother', but this is most likely a reference to **Toogernupertooner**, the wife of **Trowlebunner**. The record of the previous day shows that she was also dangerously ill at that time and died several days later. This would account for Walter's later identification as 'Chieftain of Ben Lomond'. In a letter he wrote to Robinson in February 1847 he enquired about 'the sheep appertaining to my father'. As the sheep in question were granted to Robinson's guides, the context suggests he was referring to his mother's brother **Mannalargenna**, who was also sometimes erroneously known as a chief of Ben Lomond.

In 1839 Robinson took Walter and Mary Ann to Port Phillip to work for his family, until they were returned to Hobart and then to Flinders Island in 1842. Walter was the leader in resistance to authoritarian rule at Wybalenna and promoting recognition of their native rights, including organising a petition to Queen Victoria that led to the closure of Wybalenna in 1847. He and Mary Ann were among the people sent to Oyster Cove, where they were given a lease of 15 acres of land adjacent to the station, which they tried to farm. He also briefly worked in the whaling industry, and drowned when returning to Oyster Cove by boat on 12 May 1861. After Walter's death, Mary Ann married an ex-convict named Adam Booker and continued to live on the land at Oyster Cove until her death on 25 July 1871, when the land reverted to the Crown. She had no children.

People of the North Nation

LACKLAY (aka Probelattener, Little Jemmy, Isaac)
Described as 'a boy', in 1830, Lacklay was of the Punnilerpanner, from the country around Port Sorrell, with close connections to the clans of the north-west. He knew **Peevay** (see entry) and spoke the same language. Before coming into Robinson's charge, he and a boy identified as his older brother, **Merape (aka Proper, Neptune)**, were raiding along the coast in company with **Nicermenic** (see entry for Tanganutura). They had escaped from the assistant government surveyor in September 1830 and were involved in raiding along the north-west coast and robbing sealers' boats at Port Sorrell. Lacklay and Merape were caught by Alexander McKay and sent to Robinson at Port Sorrell on 21 September; the pair ran off with Peevay the next day. Recaptured and again taken to the Launceston jail, Lacklay and Merape escaped, only to be recaptured again.

Lacklay was one of four people sent to Swan Island from the Launceston jail in March 1831. His older brother was probably with him then, as Merape was known to be on Flinders Island in 1832. Lacklay joined Robinson's mission in April 1831 and was with him for all subsequent missions. In 1837 Robinson insisted that he should marry and he chose **Maytepueminer**, recently rescued from the sealers, who was much older and refused to stay with him. They were formally married again in January 1838, and Robinson took them both to Port Phillip in February 1839.

Lacklay left Robinson in April 1840 and was believed to have drowned when a boat belonging to Christopher Berry was reported to have capsized in Westernport Bay sometime in May. However, Berry's boat did not capsize; it sailed to the Bay of Islands in New Zealand. Lacklay may have gone on to have a whole new life in New Zealand, possibly in the whaling industry, where **Ned Tomlins** (see entry for Bullyer) was a prominent figure.

His brother Merape married a young Pennemukeer woman, **Kittewer (aka Amelia)**, and they had at least five children, three of whom survived past infancy: Emily, born March 1838; Moriarty, born June 1840; and Bobby, birth date unknown. This loving family held the survivors' hopes for the future of their people, but Emily and Bobby died, unrecorded, sometime before the transfer to Oyster Cove. Moriarty went with his parents to Oyster Cove and was almost immediately sent away to the Orphan School, where he died on 5 March 1852. He was the last of his family and his clan. His father, Merape, had died at Oyster Cove on 21 March 1851 and his mother, Kittewer, sometime later.

People of the North-west Nation

COONENIA (aka Patty)
There is no record of Coonenia's capture or arrival on Flinders Island. She was a woman from the north-west corner, the wife of **Gonenar (aka Daniel)**, who was among the people taken to Hunter Island in July 1832 and transferred to Flinders Island in November. Plomley's notes suggest that Coonenia may have been taken later than her husband, in December 1834. Gonenar died in June 1837 and Coonenia then married a Punnilerpanner man, **Dowunggi (aka Leonidas, David)**, who died in August 1844. She was one of several single women over forty who were transferred to Oyster Cove in 1847. When she died on 8 July 1867 at the hospital in Hobart, her body was dissected so her skeleton could be removed for the collection of the Royal Society of Tasmania.

PEEVAY (aka Tunnerminerwait, Napoleon, Jack)
An orphaned Parperloihener youth of Robbins Island on the north-west coast, Peevay was about fifteen when he joined Robinson's mission. He had many siblings.

Wymurric, his oldest brother, was recognised as leader by three of the remnant clans of the north-west who sought protection with Robinson in July 1832. He and his family were held on Hunter Island until November, when they were sent for an interview with the governor in Hobart and then taken to Flinders Island, where Wymurric died on 20 February 1833. His wife, **Larratong (aka Queen Andromache)**, died on 8 August 1837. Their son, **Timemendic (aka Adolphus)**, was sent to the Orphan School for a few years, and for a brief spell in 1839 he lived with Governor and Lady Franklin. He was sent to sea on a government vessel, later joining the crew of a ship bound for England. He was never heard of again and was presumed to have died.

Penderoin was also taken to Hobart in November with his wife, **Nollahalleker (aka Kit)**, but they did not go to Flinders Island. Instead they stayed at Robinson's house in Hobart until they were taken as guides on Robinson's last missions to the west and north-west coast in 1833–34. They both appear to have died in Hobart in a measles epidemic sometime in May 1835; their deaths are not recorded.

Pendowtewer (aka Rodney) was introduced to Robinson with his friend **Nicermenic** in 1831 and sent to Launceston, from where he was released back into his own country. In October 1832 he was captured and badly beaten by Alexander McKay, then sent to Flinders Island. His wife was **Loweriddic (aka Deborah)**, and she died on Flinders Island on 3 May 1838. Her skull was removed and sent to Lady Franklin. When Pendowtewer died on 4 August, his skull was also removed and sent to Lady Franklin to make a pair. Their son Robert, aged two, died the following month on 2 September. It is not known what happened to his skull; it may have been the child's skull that Robinson kept in his personal collection.

Pordeboik was Peevay's only known sister, married to a Tarkiner man. She and her family were captured by Robinson in March 1834 and sent to Flinders Island, where they were among the unnamed dead between April 1834 and February 1835.

At some point in 1832, Peevay formed a partnership with **Plorenernoopner.** They went together to Port Phillip in February 1839. Peevay worked for Robinson and his family around Melbourne and accompanied Robinson on a six-month excursion into the Western District between March and August 1841. By October 1841, Peevay and Plorenernoopner were in Lower

Westernport, where they were implicated in the murder of two whalers. Peevay, found guilty, was executed with Maulboyheener at the first public hanging in Melbourne, on 20 January 1842. He was the last of his family.

WYNE

The senior man of the Tarkiner, Wyne was a noted warrior whose territory stretched between the Pieman and Arthur rivers. In September 1832 he orchestrated an attack on Robinson at the Arthur River. His oldest daughter, **Ryenrope (aka Cleopatra)**, was aged about fourteen when she defected to Constable Anthony Cottrell in November 1832. She was sent to Flinders Island, where she died on 31 August 1837 after giving birth to a daughter, who died four months later. Wyne surrendered to Robinson in July 1833 with his wife, **Neerip**, and two younger daughters. He died at the Sarah Island penitentiary on 31 July, and his wife died on 11 August. She had recently given birth to a baby girl, who died the day before her mother.

Wyne's surviving daughters were **Teddeheburrer (aka Clara)**, who was about nine, and **Moihenung**, who was about three. From Sarah Island they were sent to Hobart and then to the Orphan School in 1835 and discharged that same year to Flinders Island, where Moihenung died on 13 October 1837. In childhood Teddeheburrer had been married to a boy from a related clan who was known on Flinders Island as Little Billy, and they were formally married in August 1837. He died on 1 March 1839. It is not known if she had another husband before she was briefly married to **Davey Bruny** in 1843, but she certainly had been sexually abused by unknown men employed at Wybalenna. She died of syphilis on 7 August 1843, a short time after giving birth to a mixed-race child, who also died.

BILLY LANNE (aka King Billy)
The youngest son in a Tarkiner family of two adults and five children that finally surrendered in December 1842, **Billy Lanne** was the sole survivor of the family. In 1847, aged eight, he was transferred to Oyster Cove and was then sent to the Orphan School until April 1853, when he returned to Oyster Cove and lived with **Walter George Arthur** and **Mary Ann** as their 'adopted son'. In June 1859 he was permitted to leave Oyster Cove to join the crew of a whaling ship as a harpooner but he continued to visit the station when he was in port and would share Truganini's two-room hut. As the sole surviving male of the original people of the colony, the settlers called him King Billy. In 1868 he was presented to the Duke of Edinburgh as fellow royalty.

When Billy Lanne died in Hobart on 3 March 1869, his body was mutilated, first by the colonial surgeon, who cut his head from his body to send it to London, then by the medical supervisor and members of the Royal Society of Tasmania, who cut off his hands and feet for their collection. After the mangled remains were buried, members of the Royal Society disinterred the body, removed the flesh from the bones and took the headless skeleton for their collection. The Tasmanian Aboriginal Centre eventually recovered what was believed to be his skull from the University of Edinburgh, although doubt remains that this was his skull. It is not known for certain what happened to the rest of his remains.

People of the Big River Nation

MANNAPACKERNAME (aka Meerkerpakaminer, Big Jemmy, King Alphonso)
Described as a 'big man', Mannapackername was a senior man of the Luggermairrernerpairrer, of the Western Tiers, who was closely allied with the Lairmairermener. His wife **Nurnepattener (aka**

Jemima, Cranky Poll) was reported to have been involved in the killing of two settlers at Port Sorrell in August 1831. They were both captured in December 1831, as was Mannapackername's brother, **Druemerterpunner (aka King Alexander),** whose wife was the sister of **Polare** (see entry for Umarrah). The clan name of his wife was unknown, but at Wybalenna she was called **Caroline,** and their son **Maccamee (aka Washington)** was responsible for killing settlers at Port Sorrell. With twenty-two other Big River people, they were sent to Flinders Island in January 1832. When Mannapackername's wife died on 11 November 1837, Robinson tried to marry him to **Plonermemer (aka Flora),** a Tyreelore woman originally from the Plangermairener clan, who were his traditional enemies. She refused to stay with him. He was married to Truganini in 1842.

Mannapackername was a very significant figure at Wybalenna, as was his brother, both of them appointed to be 'constables' in 1837. The honorific title of King was bestowed on them following the death of **King William (aka Tongelongeter),** who died in June 1837, and **King George (aka Woreternaterlargner),** who died in June 1840. As the dominant men of the community at Wybalenna, King Alphonso and King Alexander were believed to be the most compliant and reliable of the captives, yet they took an active role in the resistance to authoritarian rule and petitioned for the recognition of their rights, which led to the closure of the establishment in 1847. Mannapackername died on 7 July 1847, just months before the transfer to Oyster Cove. About thirty years later, the skeleton of Mannapackername was unearthed from his grave on Flinders Island and added to the collection of the Royal Society of Tasmania.

The rest of the family went to Oyster Cove, where Druemerterpunner and Maccamee both died unrecorded sometime before 1855. Caroline died on 12 July 1860 and her skull was added to the collection of the Royal Society of Tasmania in Hobart.

ROBERT (aka Black Bob)

Taken from his clan when he was an infant, Robert was alienated from his culture and had no language other than English. His adoptive mother, Mrs Busby, said her first husband, Sergeant McCauley, 'found' the child in 1810. The circumstances in which a member of the 73rd Regiment came to find a baby alone in the bush does not bear close scrutiny, especially when the geographic location places him in the territory of the Big River people—an area that became notorious for massacres.

Robinson sent out a circular in May 1829 requiring settlers to hand over any Aboriginal children they had in their employ. Mrs Busby reluctantly complied, feeling 'a parental regard' for the young man and anxiety for his future wellbeing. As Robert spoke fluent English, Robinson believed he would be an excellent role model, and persuaded the governor to make him a grant of 10 acres of land on Bruny Island, plus a cart and bullock so he could become a farmer. The land grant was made, but the farm never materialised.

On 4 January 1830, Robert was 'forlorn and miserable' when he approached Robinson in Hobart, offering his services for the mission to the west coast. Robert proved to be an expert hunter with a gun, but had poor bush skills and was rarely included among Robinson's guides. He was never accepted by the other men on Robinson's missions, who were all traditional enemies of the Big River people. He got lost on more than one occasion, and in October 1830 he was arrested and taken to the Launceston jail. At Robinson's request, Robert was sent to Gun Carriage Island on 1 January 1831 and was subsequently reintegrated into Robinson's mission team. He died from influenza in Launceston on 23 March 1832 and was given a Christian burial.

NAMING

It is not possible to know the true names of any of the original people in this book or how to write them. The original people of Tasmania had two or more clan names, as well as the various names that colonists bestowed on them. Robinson's journals detail interaction with people from many clans who spoke at least eight different languages from five distinct language groups. He wrote their names as he heard them and then spelt these names in all kinds of different ways. Other curious colonists heard the names differently. The French explorers heard something else entirely.

The woman Robinson first named as Trugernanna he also named Lydgugee, and he would persistently slip between these two names, sometimes in the same sentence. After 1835, he added the name Lalla Rookh to the mix, often abbreviated to Lalla. Other colonists referred to her as Truganinni or Truganini and that is the name by which she has become widely known, so it is the name I use.

These complications hold for all the other original people in this book. For consistency, I have chosen one version of the name that Robinson heard, using one of the various ways of spelling that is most familiar to me. For several people who were baptised with Christian names—by which they were consistently known in colonial records—I have used those names rather than their original clan names.

What is true of the names of the people is equally true of the names for the supernatural. The malevolent spirit that loomed so powerfully in the lives of the people, that Robinson called Raegewropper, has been named many different ways in various settler narratives and secondary sources. I have settled on Raegewarrah, as it most satisfies my sense of how this word might have sounded.

SOURCES

THE NARRATIVE IN this book has been derived from contemporaneous eyewitness accounts, documented at the time in diary entries and journals, personal letters or official correspondence, newspapers or court reports. Books published in the final years of Truganini's life by authors who had some personal interaction with her, such as James Bonwick and James Erskine Calder, have been discounted as untrustworthy as they are so coloured by mawkish inventions that fed into the mythologising of 'the Last Tasmanian'.

MANUSCRIPT SOURCES

Papers of George Augustus Robinson, Mitchell Library, State Library of NSW

George Arthur Papers, Mitchell Library, State Library of NSW

Joseph Orton Journal, Mitchell Library, State Library of NSW

Colonial Secretary's Correspondence (VDL), Archive Office of Tasmania

Morton Allport Papers, Allport Library and Museum of Fine Arts, State Library of Tasmania

Inward Correspondence, Superintendent Port Phillip District, Victorian Public Record Office

Samuel Rawson's Diaries and Papers, 1831–1857, National Library of Australia

Original Correspondence, Secretary of State Colonial Office, CO 280, National Archives of the United Kingdom

EDITED SOURCES

Clark, Ian D., *The Journals of George Augustus Robinson, Chief Protector of the Port Phillip Protectorate*, vols 1–3, Heritage Matters, Melbourne, 1998

Dredge, J., 'The hanging of two Aboriginals 1842', reprinted in *La Trobe Library Journal*, no. 7, 1971

Plomley, N.J.B., *The Friendly Mission: The Tasmanian journals and papers of George Augustus Robinson 1829–1834*, Quintus Publishing, Hobart, 2008

Plomley, N.J.B., *Weep in Silence: A history of the Flinders Island Aboriginal Settlement*, Blubber Head Press, Hobart, 1987

Stephens, Marguerita, *The Journal of William Thomas, Assistant Protector of the Aborigines of Port Phillip and Guardian of the Aborigines of Victoria, 1839–1867*, vol. 1, Victorian Aboriginal Corporation for Languages, Melbourne, 2014

NEWSPAPERS

Austral-Asiatic Review

Colonial Advocate

Hobart Mercury

Hobart Town Courier

Hobart Town Gazette

Launceston Advertiser

Launceston Independent

Port Phillip Gazette

Port Phillip Herald

Port Phillip Patriot and Melbourne Advertiser

True Colonist

WEBSITES

Colonial Frontier Massacres in Central and Eastern Australia, 1788–1930, <https://c21ch.newcastle.edu.au/colonialmassacres/map.php>

Records generated from researching and cataloguing Ernest Westlake's papers in the Pitt Rivers Museum and the Oxford University Museum of Natural History, <www.westlakehistory.info/WESS01.htm>

The Resident Judge of Port Phillip, <https://residentjudge.com/>

ACKNOWLEDGEMENTS

I ACKNOWLEDGE THE First Nations of Australia, pay my respects to Elders past and present and thank them for their custodianship of this land.

This book would not have been possible without the extraordinary work of the late N.J.B. Plomley in transcribing Robinson's Tasmanian journals, as well as his many letters and reports. However critical I may be of Plomley's errors and cultural bias, his achievement in making Robinson's horrible handwriting legible is nothing short of monumental. I am also very grateful to Ian Clark for transcribing Robinson's Victorian journals. These are remarkable sources, really without parallel in Australian colonial history. Rebe Taylor's exemplary work in digitising the papers of Ernest Westlake has been another invaluable contribution. Equally, I applaud the National Library of Australia and the fantastic resource Trove, for digitising Australian colonial newspapers and giving free access.

I cannot overstate my debt to the pioneering work of Lyndall Ryan, to whom this book is dedicated, and Henry Reynolds. I happily acknowledge that I stand on the shoulders of these two important historians and I greatly value their friendship, counsel and encouragement. I am also very grateful to Gaye Sculthorpe, curator and head of the Oceania section of the British Museum, for her encouragement, for sharing with me her research into her ancestor Tanganutura, and for helping me to correctly identify images of Truganini and her companions.

Undertaking research in Victoria was made possible by invaluable financial support from the Peter Blazey Fellowship awarded by Melbourne University and I am very grateful to Clive and Penny Blazey and Tim Herbert for their generosity. Likewise, I am grateful for the Neilma Sidney Literary Travel Fund awarded by The Myer Foundation and Writers Victoria, which enabled me to conduct research in London.

Thanks to Adam Low, Bruce Ormiston and their dog Eden for providing a warm and welcoming place to stay in London; and to Carol Pybus, James Boyce, Rebe Taylor, Hamish Maxwell-Stewart, David Hansen, Brad Manera, Gareth Knapman, Ian Robinson and Bob Graham for spirited discussion and valuable insights. Above all, a heartfelt thanks to Lucy Frost for all she has done to assist me in this difficult project, especially driving along many a rough dirt road in godforsaken corners of the Tasmanian bush.

I am indebted to Julianne Schultz and the team at *Griffith Review* for publishing the novella that was the germ of this book in *The Novella Project V* in 2017, which gave me the courage to proceed, as well as my agent Virginia Lloyd for believing in the project. Lastly, a huge thanks to Liz Dombrovskis for allowing me to use Peter Dombrovskis' photograph on the front cover, and to Elizabeth Weiss, Angela Handley and the team at Allen & Unwin, for turning my words into a wonderful book.